Telling Tales

T0316050

Young writers have historically played a pivotal role in shaping autobiographical genres, and this continues into the graphic and digital texts which increasingly characterise contemporary life writing. This volume offers a selection of case studies which illuminate some of the core themes considered in recent autobiographical writings of childhood, including: cultural and identity representations and tensions, coming into knowledge and education, sexuality, prejudice, war, and trauma. The book also reveals preoccupations with the cultural forms of autobiographical writings that childhood and youth take, engaging in discussions of archives, graphic texts, digital forms, testimony, didacticism in autobiography and the anthologising of life writing. This collection will open up broader conversations about the scope of life writing about childhood and youth and the importance of life writing genres in prompting dialogues about literary cultures and coming of age.

This book was originally published as a special issue of *Prose Studies*.

Kylie Cardell is a Lecturer in the School of Humanities at Flinders University, Adelaide, Australia. She is the author of *Dear World: Contemporary Uses of the Diary* (2014).

Kate Douglas is an Associate Professor in the School of Humanities at Flinders University, Adelaide, Australia. She is the author of *Contesting Childhood: Autobiography, Trauma and Memory* (2010), and the co-editor (with Gillian Whitlock) of *Trauma Texts* (2009).

Telling Tales

Autobiographies of Childhood
and Youth

Edited by
Kylie Cardell and Kate Douglas

Routledge
Taylor & Francis Group

LONDON AND NEW YORK

First published 2015 by Routledge

2 Park Square, Milton Park, Abingdon, Oxon OX14 4RN
711 Third Avenue, New York, NY 10017, USA

Routledge is an imprint of the Taylor & Francis Group, an informa business

First issued in paperback 2017

Copyright © 2015 Taylor & Francis

All rights reserved. No part of this book may be reprinted or reproduced or
utilised in any form or by any electronic, mechanical, or other means, now
known or hereafter invented, including photocopying and recording, or in
any information storage or retrieval system, without permission in writing
from the publishers.

Notice:
Product or corporate names may be trademarks or registered trademarks,
and are used only for identification and explanation without intent to infringe.

British Library Cataloguing in Publication Data
A catalogue record for this book is available from the British Library

ISBN 13: 978-1-138-77498-8 (hbk)
ISBN 13: 978-1-138-05902-3 (pbk)

Typeset in Perpetua
by RefineCatch Limited, Bungay, Suffolk

Publisher's Note
The publisher accepts responsibility for any inconsistencies that may have
arisen during the conversion of this book from journal articles to book chapters,
namely the possible inclusion of journal terminology.

Disclaimer
Every effort has been made to contact copyright holders for their permission to
reprint material in this book. The publishers would be grateful to hear from any
copyright holder who is not here acknowledged and will undertake to rectify
any errors or omissions in future editions of this book.

Contents

Permissions

The images in Chapter 3, 'Trauma and Young Adult Literature: Representing Adolescence and Knowledge in David Small's *Stiches: A Memoir*', are reproduced by kind permission of W.W. Norton & Company, Inc., with credit to *Stiches: A Memoir* by David Small. Copyright ©2009 by David Small.

Citation Information

The chapters in this book were originally published in *Prose Studies*, volume 35, issue 1 (April 2013). When citing this material, please use the original page numbering for each article, as follows:

Chapter 1
Telling Tales: Autobiographies of Childhood and Youth
Kylie Cardell and Kate Douglas
Prose Studies, volume 35, issue 1 (April 2013) pp. 1–6

Chapter 2
Childhood and Ethnic Visibility in Gene Yang's American Born Chinese
Rocío G. Davis
Prose Studies, volume 35, issue 1 (April 2013) pp. 7–15

Chapter 3
Trauma and Young Adult Literature: Representing Adolescence and Knowledge in David Small's Stitches:
A Memoir
Leigh Gilmore and Elizabeth Marshall
Prose Studies, volume 35, issue 1 (April 2013) pp. 16–38

Chapter 4
"Indecent Exposure? Margaux Fragoso and the Limits of Abuse Memoir"
Kylie Cardell and Kate Douglas
Prose Studies, volume 35, issue 1 (April 2013) pp. 39–53

Chapter 5
Potential*: Ariel Schrag Contests (Hetero-)Normative Girlhood*
Emma Maguire
Prose Studies, volume 35, issue 1 (April 2013) pp. 54–66

Chapter 6
Alice Pung's Growing up Asian in Australia*: The Cultural Work of Anthologized Asian-Australian Narratives of Childhood*
Pamela Graham
Prose Studies, volume 35, issue 1 (April 2013) pp. 67–83

Please direct any queries you may have about the citations to
clsuk.permissions@cengage.com

Notes on Contributors

Tully Barnett completed a Ph.D. on representations of Information Technology in contemporary literary fiction at Flinders University, Adelaide, Australia, where she is a project manager for the Australasian Consortium of Humanities Research Centres, AustLit: the Resource for Australian Literature, and Building Reading Resilience: Developing a Skills-Based Approach to Literary Studies.

Kylie Cardell is a Lecturer in the School of Humanities at Flinders University, Adelaide, Australia. She is the author of *Dear World: Contemporary Uses of the Diary* (2014).

Rocío G. Davis is Professor of English at City University of Hong Kong. She has published *Relative Histories: Mediating History in Asian American Family Memoirs* (2011) and *Begin Here: Reading Asian North American Autobiographies of Childhood* (2007).

Kate Douglas is an Associate Professor in the School of Humanities at Flinders University, Adelaide, Australia. She is the author of *Contesting Childhood: Autobiography, Trauma, and Memory* (2010), and the co-editor (with Gillian Whitlock) of *Trauma Texts* (2009).

Leigh Gilmore is the author of *The Limits of Autobiography: Trauma and Testimony* and *Autobiographics: A Feminist Theory of Women's Autobiography*, as well as co-editor of *Autobiography and Postmodernism*. She has been Professor of English at Ohio State University, Columbus, USA and Visiting Professor in the departments of Rhetoric and Women's Studies at the University of California, Berkeley, USA. She was the first holder of the Dorothy Cruickshank Backstrand Chair at Scripps College, Claremont, California, USA.

Pamela Graham is a Ph.D. candidate in the Department of English, Creative Writing and Australian Studies at Flinders University, Adelaide, Australia. She is a member of the Flinders Life Narrative Research Group and her research interests include the political and social utility of contemporary life narratives, memory studies, and public history.

Leena Kurvet-Käosaar is Associate Professor of Literary Theory at the University of Tartu, Estonia and a Senior Researcher of the Archives of Cultural History of the Estonian Literary Museum. Her research interests include life writing studies, trauma, feminist theories of affectivity and corporeality, Baltic women's representations of the experience of the repressions of the Soviet regime and the study of women's experience of modernity.

Claire Lynch is a Senior Lecturer in English at Brunel University, London, UK, where she works on the Burnett Archive. Her research focuses on the ways people recall and reimagine their lives in writing. Her publications include *Irish Autobiography* (2009) and several articles linking life writing to class, gender, and new media.

Emma Maguire is a Ph.D. candidate at Flinders University and Monash University, both Australia. Her research interests include the autobiographical practices of girls and young women, DIY textual cultures, and comics/graphic narrative. She is a member of the Flinders Life Narrative Research Group.

Elizabeth Marshall is the co-editor of *Rethinking Popular Culture and Media*. She is an Associate Professor in the Faculty of Education at Simon Fraser University, Burnaby, BC, Canada, where she teaches children's and young adult literature. Her research on the representation of childhood and adolescence in memoir has been published in *College English*, *The Lion and the Unicorn*, *The Alan Review*, *Gender and Education*, and *Feminist Studies* (with Leigh Gilmore).

Anna Poletti is a Lecturer in Literary Studies at Monash University, Clayton, Victoria, Australia. Her research interests are autobiography beyond the book, the autobiographical practices of young people, feminist and queer studies. With Julie Rak, she is the editor of the collection *Identity Technologies* (2014).

Kylie Cardell and Kate Douglas

TELLING TALES: AUTOBIOGRAPHIES OF CHILDHOOD AND YOUTH

Introduction

Life writing has become an important umbrella term for considering the array of methods and texts which enable life storytelling. Written modes of biography and autobiography have rich traditions dating back for hundreds of years and crossing the globe. Oral and visual traditions go back much further – providing links, for example, to indigenous stories and histories predating the written word. Life stories have long offered a backbone to history, particularly in linking communities and in forging and recording experiences and identities. When we think of life writing, we perhaps conventionally think of mainstream publications. But life writing goes well beyond this: life narrative is a useful term for thinking about the ways in which the spoken words – songs and performances, for instance, contribute to a history of life writing. And of course, there is a growing awareness of the role that new and digital media play in life storytelling.

One of the central foci of life writing texts, particularly in recent decades, is childhood. This is unsurprising: everyone begins life as a child and whatever the age of the author, childhood has been, at least in part, experienced in the past. The presence (or indeed absence) of childhood in autobiographical writings reveals something of the cultural position of the child within society and culture of the time. Valerie Sanders explains how childhood was given little attention in European life writing until the eighteenth century (203–4). In the early nineteenth century, the Romantic poets wrote about childhood as a way to reflect on human development. By the twentieth century, the *Bildungsroman* – works focused on the growth of the individual – had become a prominent theme in fiction, non-fiction, and crossover forms. Of course, in the *Bildungsroman*, childhood is retrospective, although the narrative may proceed from the child's point of view, as in Jeanette Winterson's *Oranges are Not the Only Fruit*, and even in nonfiction, such as Frank McCourt's *Angela's Ashes*. Here, the narrator has the benefit of hindsight, and the ability to structure and shape a narrative to either explain or contest their current experience. The child, along with his or her experiences, functions to explain the adult self that the subject becomes, and the adult controls the way that representation is told.

The earlier modes of life writing about childhood are highly influential in the literature that has followed. However, in the late twentieth and early twenty-first centuries, the representation of childhood in life writing has assumed a crucial place rather than an inevitable place. That is, childhood has become of interest in itself: no longer simply a piece of the puzzle in an illumination of the adult self. This shift mirrors broader changes in the cultural symbolism of the child and childhood and in cultural representations of childhood. In the early twenty-first century, a global community is interested in lives of children and youth; their rights and their citizenship have become a preoccupation. Childhood has come to be recognized as a diverse experience, located in cultural and temporal spaces, and the universal child figure of classical art is revealed as a myth. Life stories about childhood are cultural and collective rather than simply individual and the broad social and political issues of race, culture, class, gender, and sexuality all impact upon the experiences and representations of childhood and youth.

The "autobiography of childhood" (a term employed by Kate Douglas to examine different forms of life writing in which childhood is the central representation and theme) emerged strongly (particularly in the USA and the UK) in the 1990s and 2000s as a response to particular Western cultural moments. Authors such as Mary Karr, James McBride, and Frank McCourt "burst onto the American literary scene…paving the way for a plethora of similarly styled texts to follow. These autobiographies were distinctive for their depiction of challenging, often traumatic childhoods – characterized by abuse, poverty, discrimination, and identity struggles" (1). Such texts – often bestselling and critically acclaimed – were also highly influential in terms of paving the way for different considerations of childhood. The autobiography of childhood as a form endured into the 2000s, spawning a range of new subforms: such as memoirs of childhood illness and disability, graphic memoirs of childhood, and stories of youthful addiction and/or sexuality. In 2013, life writing about childhood is a literary trend that shows no sign of abating.

Historically, life writing about childhood has been dominated by adult writers retrospectively reimagining their childhood self. But as new cultural terms have emerged to consider and define childhood (child, tween, teenager, youth, and generation) – and young people's relationship with culture has reorientated, there has been a greater cultural awareness of the ways in which young people author their own lives (both in the present and the past). For example, although writing a century apart, World War I poet Wilfred Owen and "Baghdad Blogger" Salam Pax each write about their first-hand experience of warfare, drawing our attention to the significant contribution young writers have made to life writing about war. Young life writers emerge across a range of autobiographical genres – from poetry and art, self-publishing (for instance, zines), through published forms, and (perhaps most notably) into the digital realm (see Buckingham and Willett; Poletti; Spencer). Scholars have noted the rising preoccupation with the so-called digital generation, in which young people not only consume but have begun to produce digital media (Buckingham and Willett). Young writers as cultural makers have employed life narrative forms for self-determination – to write themselves into culture, to make art, to build communities, and to control the public representations of childhood and youth.

In the Australian winter of 2012, supported by generous assistance from the Flinders Institute for Research in the Humanities, we invited a small group of life narrative scholars with a particular interest in childhood studies to a mini-symposium at

Flinders University in South Australia. In the presentations and workshopping that followed, clear synergies began to emerge: many of us were interested in new and marginal forms (the graphic, the "non-book," and the performance), were inspired to explore controversial subjects (sexual abuse, trauma, racism, and sexuality), and were attentive to the diverse and significant ways in which narrative about and of childhood garner attention in the twenty-first century literary marketplaces.

Emerging from that symposium, this special issue of *Prose Studies* responds to the growing significance of young people in both the production and consumption of autobiographical narrative. Indeed, though it is often to the consternation of cultural commentators, young people are speaking about and revealing their lives in increasing numbers. While social networking sites such as Facebook, Twitter, instagram or YouTube are some of the most visible locations in which young people formulate representations of their own lives, the production of literary memoir and other traditional published forms by young authors is also on the rise. Some forms, like the graphic (comics) memoir, have been particularly resonant with young authors, a product both of comics lingering status as a "childish" form and its subversive and disruptive appeal. Rocío G. Davis is among several contributors in this issue to consider graphic narrative, an emerging literary form that has been taken up very energetically by young life writers in particular. In "Childhood and Ethnic Visibility in Gene Yang's *American Born Chinese*," Davis explores how Asian-American memoirist Gene Luen Yang uses the medium of comics to make literally visible the cultural stereotypes and racism that have characterized images and representations of Asians in American mainstream media. Written for a young adult audience, the comic narrates through its teenage protagonist the experience of being simultaneously "visible" – in the prevalent pop cultural stereotypes and iconography of the "Oriental" – and "invisible" when individual histories and experience are collapsed into broad categories of "Asian." Tracing how Yang deploys conventional narrative arcs such as the *Bildungsroman*, as well as traditional Chinese mythology, Davis energetically argues that Yang's protagonist shows how childhood is universal in its *diversity*, a representation that equally powerfully relates to (and unsettles) stereotypes of ethnicity.

The graphic memoir is also a focus for Leigh Gilmore and Beth Marshall in "Trauma and Young Adult Literature: Representing Adolescence and Knowledge in David Small's *Stitches: A Memoir*"; they are equally interested in the disruptive and political power of the form. A controversial National Book Award finalist in the young people's literature category, Small's memoir, *Stitches*, became the latest example in "an ongoing debate about the limits of knowledge, agency, and youth that plays out in conflicts over genres, audiences, markets and texts". Like Davis, Gilmore and Marshall point to the significance of form in both the memoir's circulation and its success – the graphic narrative has a special role to play in representing young lives and in speaking to young readers. However, while *Stitches* represents the successful deployment of a genre associated with childhood and childishness, the content of the memoir as a trauma narrative emphasizes that cultural boundaries around appropriate representation and young lives, especially in contexts where the readers are also young, remain strong and are anxiously monitored. Moreover, as a narrative that resists "ameliorative or neoliberal agendas" by sidelining the convention of an "uplifting" arc, displacing the dominance of "strategic trauma" in representations of childhood, the controversy around *Stitches* shows how powerful idealizations of childhood are to the national political imaginary. In their incisive exploration of this memoir and of its reception, Gilmore and Marshall argue that this is a memoir that literally, as well as figuratively, makes visible the fractured landscape of diverse "childhoods" and so ultimately contests the fantasy that fuels neoliberal and conservative agendas.

In "Indecent Exposure? Margaux Fragoso and the Limits of Abuse Memoir," Kylie Cardell and Kate Douglas consider another contemporary memoir of childhood that has encountered a particularly strong, and frequently hostile, reception. Deemed "the year's most controversial memoir" in several culturally prestigious venues, Fragoso's memoir of the author's childhood sexual relationship with a 57-year-old man, a relationship she by turns paints as exploitative, manipulative, and loving, produced a flurry of cultural commentary on "appropriateness": critics questioned Fragoso's subjective point of view, her representation of her experience, the literariness of her style, and repetitively asked why a reader should "bother" given the traumatic and unsettling material narrated. In tracing the debate that emerged around this text, Cardell and Douglas reveal the ways in which depictions of childhood sexual abuse in particular can provoke strong and conservative public discourse, particularly, as in the case of Fragoso, where the representation deviates from (and so makes visible) culturally decreed "scripts" for appropriate representation around young lives and experience.

In "*Potential*: Ariel Schrag Contests (Hetero-)Normative Girlhood," Emma Maguire continues this issue's interest in graphic forms, as well as in marginalized experiences, by exploring the work of teenage author Ariel Schrag. Schrag, who began self-publishing her comics recounting high school life while herself still a student, documents her high school experiences and her identity as a lesbian girl. Emphasizing the significance of Schrag's narrative for its explorations and contestation of what "girlhood" is and should be, Maguire convincingly argues that Schrag uses both visual form and narrative exploration, and particularly, the cultural tropes of teenage experience (prom virginity and rebellion) as a way of making visible the oppressions, limitations, and subjugations of teenage girlhood.

Also considering identities that have been marginalized or heavily stereotyped in mainstream discourse, in "Alice Pung's *Growing up Asian in Australia*: The Cultural Work of Anthologized Asian-Australian Narratives of Childhood," Pamela Graham performs a fascinating analysis of a popular anthology of Asian Australian life narrative in which contributors have frequently focused on representations of their childhood experience. Noting that the work seeks to be both a popular publication and an accurate representation of frequently difficult or marginal childhood experiences, where discrimination, racism, and isolation are common features, Graham explores how the anthology form in particular might unsettle hegemonic notions of an "Australian" childhood and create space for the articulation of more diverse experiences and identities.

The potential of childhood as a highly strategic site in the representation or consolidation of adult identity is also explored by Tully Barnett in "'Reading Saved Me': Writing Autobiographically About Transformative Reading Experiences in Childhood." Identifying a sub-genre, namely, memoirists of childhood who are also cultural gatekeepers, Barnett explores how adult memoirists employ nostalgic, sentimental frames and deploy *Bildungsroman*-esque structures in ways that are strategically aligned to both their adult achievements and their sense of a need to protect and advocate for book culture, the book object, and literature in general. As implicit members of a "literary elite," writers, academics, and other literary/cultural gatekeepers have a particular investment in mythologizing a bookish childhood and Barnett's argument that this has consequences for contemporary understandings of literary culture, and the book itself, as well as for a particular branch of memoir culture, is a stimulating new insight.

Also offering new and innovative approaches, Anna Poletti and Claire Lynch separately consider ideas of a childhood archive and this is a catalyst for an analysis of the treasured detritus, ephemeral documentation, and diverse artifacts of childhood "play." In a fascinating essay that reflects on the author's own artifacts of childhood in the form of life writing produced in (and for) the author's childhood educational setting, Lynch offers ways in which to understand the life writing produced by very young children, an interpretation that must also reflect and mediate with the structures (social/educational/familial) of that child's life. In an essay that delightfully moves between innovative analysis and the author's own childhood archive of lists, drawings and "about me," Lynch explores how the often neglected or passed over archive of childhood can in fact reveal how deeply the social works in the formation of the individual, something the autobiography "proper" can often, consciously or not, elide or gloss.

In "Autobiography and Play: 'A Conversation With My 12 Year Old Self,'" Poletti explores an archive of a different kind, one that remediates or is prompted by new technology. An analysis of a YouTube video that "went viral," Poletti's essay illuminates how the child self and the adult self are linked in a mutual continuum of self-creation. Encountering the child self through play (in this case, a VHS video made by the author as a child becomes the subject of adult reminiscence and a staged retrospective dialog, posted on YouTube) prompts the adult to reflect on or reassess their current identity. In a reading that engages extensively with Winnicottian psychology and theories of subject formation, Poletti innovatively explores how "playing" can be both performative and constitutive acts in the representation of identity, for the contemporary autobiographical subject, and for their past and future readers.

Concluding this issue, Leena Kurvet-Käosaar offers a moving analysis of the childhood autobiography of the well-known Estonian children's author Leelo Tungal. In "'Who knows, will I ever see you again,' said the one-eyed duck': Reflections on a Soviet Childhood in Leelo Tungal's Life Writing," Kurvet-Käosaar considers how Tungal's representations of her childhood reflect and also subtly dismantle the oppressive ideologies of Soviet era Estonia, and especially the mythology of the "happy childhood."

The inclusion of this paper on Tungal as well as the papers on Yang and Pung is significant as a reminder that life writing about childhood and youth circulates across the globe. Although this collection of papers focuses predominantly on US examples, this simply reflects the relative visibility of these texts – and the significance of the USA as a site for the emergence (and indeed negotiation) of life stories about childhood and youth. We hope that this special issue of *Prose Studies* opens up broader conversations about the scope of life writing about childhood and youth and the importance of life writing genres in prompting dialogue about literary cultures and coming of age.

Acknowledgments

The authors would like to thank Clare Simmons from *Prose Studies* for her support of this special issue. And they would also like to thank the Flinders Institute for Research in the Humanities and its director Associate Professor Karen Vered for supporting this event. Thanks to Professor Julie Rak for taking up the role of respondent for the symposium and for her ever insightful, generous, and invaluable comments for the revision of the papers. Finally, thanks to all who took part in this Life Narrative Research Group symposium and for their creativity, intellect, and collegiality that made all of this possible.

References

Buckingham, David and Rebekah, Willett, eds. *Digital Generations: Children, Young People, and New Media*. Mahwah, NJ: Lawrence Erlbaum Associates, 2006.

Douglas, Kate. *Contesting Childhood: Autobiography, Trauma and Memory*. New Brunswick: Rutgers, 2010.

Poletti, Anna. *Intimate Ephemera: Reading Young Lives in Australian Zine Culture*. Melbourne, UP: Carlton Vic Australia, 2008.

Sanders, Valerie. "Childhood and Life Writing." In *Encyclopedia of Life Writing*, edited by Margaretta Jolly. London: Dearborn, 2001, 69–70.

Spencer, Amy. *DIY: The Rise of Lo-Fi Culture*. London: Marion Boyars, 2005.

Rocío G. Davis

CHILDHOOD AND ETHNIC VISIBILITY IN GENE YANG'S *AMERICAN BORN CHINESE*

Gene Luen Yang's American Born Chinese *(2006) raises questions of Asian American visibility and invisibility through the juxtaposition of legend,* Bildungsroman, *and sitcom. Using the graphic form, a medium that foregrounds the image and, consequently, the visible more directly, Yang engages with the ways persons of Asian descent in the USA have been simultaneously rendered invisible by racism or made visible in stereotypically damaging forms (based on the model minority stereotype, for example, or through the commodification of particular images of Asians in films and other popular media). This essay explores the ways Yang approaches the history and forms of Chinese American visibility through multilayered storytelling and the graphic form.*

Gene Luen Yang's semi-autobiographical graphic narrative for young adults, *American Born Chinese* (2006), raises questions of Asian American visibility and invisibility through the juxtaposition of legend, *Bildungsroman*, and sitcom. Using the graphic form, a medium that foregrounds the image and, consequently, the visible more directly, Yang engages with the ways in which persons of Asian descent in the USA have been simultaneously rendered invisible by racism or made visible in stereotypically damaging forms (based on the model minority stereotype, for example, or through the commodification of particular images of Asians in films and other popular media). For Asian American men, subjected to a discourse of feminization, issues of visibility have been particularly complicated. Yang's book is composed of three parallel narratives that merge at the end: first, he retells the story of Monkey King, based on the legendary character of the 16th century novel *Journey to the West*; in the second thread, Jin Wang, a Chinese American boy, struggles to fit in; and finally, Danny is a blonde teenager mortified by yearly visits from his Chinese cousin Chin-Kee, the embodiment of the Chinese stereotype. All three threads approach the issue of race and visibility in different ways, connecting with Asian American historical discourse and contemporary cultural representations. In this essay, I will explore the ways Yang deals with the history and forms of Chinese American visibility through multilayered storytelling and the graphic form.

Eleanor Ty, in her study, *The Politics of the Visible*, offers a cogent discussion on Asian American visibility and invisibility, stating that,

in one way or another, Asian Americans deal daily with what Shirley Geok-lin Lim calls "birthmarks," the visible hieroglyphs imprinted on their eyes, black hair, noses, faces, and bodies, the resonance of another tongue, the haunting taste of another culture, as well as the perception, real or imagined, of being from another place. These hieroglyphs mark them indelibly as other, as Oriental, as exotic, subservient, mysterious, deviant, or threatening (3–4).

Other critics have also examined the forms of Asian American visual presence or absence in American social and political life and in cultural representations from different perspectives. Timothy Fong's sociological approach, for example, explains that Asian Americans are visible only in such stereotypes as "perpetual foreigners," "overachievers," or the "model minority," yet rendered invisible "due to widespread ignorance of their distinct histories and contemporary experiences" (2). Traise Yamamoto similarly notes that Asian Americans are "invisibilized" as "model minorities" or "honorary whites," or usually just considered Asian nationals (64). In particular, she points out that Asian American women are simply regarded as part of an indistinguishable "pool of Asian women" whose (assumed or enforced) foreignness and physical exoticism promise a range of delights, evidenced by a series of names typically attributed to them: Lotus Blossom, China Doll, Madame Butterfly, Geisha Girl, Suzy Wong, Dragon Lady, among others (65). Jessica Hagedorn, in her introduction to the fiction anthology *Charlie Chan is Dead*, lists some of the stereotypes of the "Oriental": "The slit-eyed, bucktoothed Jap... The inscrutable, wily Chinese detective... The childlike, indolent Filipino houseboy... the sexless, hairless Asian male. The servile, oversexed Asian female..." (xxii). The dangerous symmetry that exists, then, between forms of visibility and invisibility becomes a crucial factor in Asian American *graphic* self-representation. Yang's engagement with this issue not only presents a way of thinking about visibility and identity in the context of transformation but also, I argue, becomes a culturally audacious way of appropriating and subverting stereotypes. In particular, I will focus on the way Yang engages stereotypical forms of Asian American visibility from the perspective of a memoir of childhood.

Race and racism are as much about visual meaning-making as they are about textual storytelling, and as such are powerfully suited to a narration that relies on both elements. In the context of a graphic narrative, Scott McCloud explains that "Cartooning isn't just a way of *drawing*, it's a way of *seeing*. The ability of cartoons to focus our attention on an idea is, I think, an important part of their special power, both in comics and in drawing generally" (31). Memoirs about childhood similarly focus our attention on specific forms of understanding the world, the writers' individual itinerary of selfhood which, when lived in the context of ethnic visibility, can be both visually and textually realized in complex ways. *American Born Chinese* might thus be said to draw on and articulate its author's personal childhood experiences, marked by mythic stories heard in childhood, through the lens of the history of visual representations of Asian Americans, with its attendant implications for masculinity and agency.

Yang's blending of the legend of Monkey King with the American stereotype of Chinese men as part of his protagonist's itinerary of cultural and personal knowledge reproduces the strategy that other autobiographers, such as Maxine Hong Kingston, enact as they explore possible meanings of Chineseness in the shifting American context. Patricia Chu explains that Asian American writers now reject the "dual personality" model in favor of representations that are "organically connected but requiring different rhetorical gestures. To be Asian *American*, one claims Americanness but reshapes conventional narratives of American subject formation; given national narratives that position Asian Americans as ethnic, racialized outsiders in America, Asian American authors respond by imaginatively inhabiting and transforming such stories" (6). Thus, "Asian American subjectivities in these texts are characterized by the emergence of a critical ethnic intelligence that deploys and interrogates traditional narratives of Americanization" (Chu 6–7). All the central characters in *American Born Chinese* have to deal with particular forms of visibility: Monkey, in the first chapter, is barred from a dinner party in heaven (to which he had not been invited) because he is not wearing shoes; Jin is cast as a foreigner with a difficult name and unacceptable customs on his first day at his new school at a predominantly white area of the city and assumed to be linked to the only other Asian person in the class, Suzy Nakamura; Wei-Chen, a recent immigrant made even more "visible" by his accented English, is initially shunned by Jin. In the text, Monkey King, Wei-Chen, and Chin-Kee serve as signposts to possible forms of identification with Chinese heritage for Jin. The forms of the three stories – the first is a legend, the second a *Bildungsroman*, the third a "sit-com on paper" (Yang, "Why Comics?") – also reproduce the narrative paradigms available to the protagonist and allow Yang to articulate not only the images that dominated his childhood but also the way he imaginatively appropriated them.

References to the Monkey King appear in several notable Asian diasporic novels, including Timothy Mo's *The Monkey King* (1978), Maxine Hong Kingston's *Tripmaster Monkey* (1989), and Patricia Chao's *Monkey King* (1997), generally to represent forms of immigrant adaptation. By presenting the Monkey King's story first, Yang uses it as the frame through which to read the rest of the book, which illustrates themes of transformation, ethnic self-acceptance, and empowerment. As Binbin Fu explains,

> The legendary trickster figure has been repeatedly re-imagined by Chinese American writers as a source of cultural strength, a symbol of subversion and resistance, and a metaphor for cross-cultural and interracial negotiation. Yang's new rendition, by transforming the proverbial monkey's tale into one of self-search and self-acceptance, provides an illuminating parallel to Jin Wang's/Danny's coming-of-age narrative (275).

Interestingly, the waiting line for the party hosted by the gods recalls an immigration line, which Yang draws as a row of diverse characters, faces marked by eager anticipation, who have to pass the guards' interrogation and judgment before they are let in. Pulled aside and told he cannot enter because he has no shoes, Monkey returns home humiliated and learns the 12 disciplines of Kung Fu to prove to the deities that he is a god. Yang's subsequent renditions of Monkey show him larger than life, ready to take his revenge on those who refused to recognize his rank. His obsessive training in the martial arts become his means of transforming himself out of himself – making himself bigger, stronger, and otherwise unlike a monkey. The creator Tze-Yo-Tzuh punishes him for his pride and stubbornness by trapping him under a mountain for 500 years. He breaks out of this prison when he accepts his condition as a monkey. The lesson is that until Monkey is able and willing to accept himself, rather than strive to remake himself to suit the requirements of other people or places he would like to be in, he can be neither truly strong nor authentic. This lesson connects with Jin Wang's struggle to resist the implications of his Chineseness, as he tells the herbalist's wife, he wants to be a "transformer" when he grows up. She tells him, "It's easy to become anything you wish. . . so long as you're willing to forfeit your soul" (29). For a while, he does become someone else: Danny, a white boy haunted by the (literal) specter of the Asian stereotype.

Jin Wang's story – he is the only son of upwardly mobile immigrants who remind him that he must be proud of his heritage – reproduces the pattern evidenced in many other Asian American autobiographies of childhood, particularly those written for younger audiences. Thus, though Yang's child characters' existence and experience as cultural beings must be negotiated critically by readers, the author develops meaning in the text by also deploying the traditions and experience of collective children's culture that each of them experiences individually (Carpenter 56). This allows him to address children generally, admitting reflections on multiple claims on identity that many young Americans encounter. Meaning then develops from the text's involvement with the nature of childhood itself, more than merely with the experience of ethnicity. By requiring his protagonist to make decisions regarding ethnic and cultural affiliation, Yang shows how children develop as individuals and within interpersonal relationships, underscoring the diversity of childhood and contradicting any tendency to essentialize the "Asian" or "American" subject. Jin, then, has to patiently correct his teacher who carelessly introduces him to his new class as "Jing Jang" and says he came all the way from China, rather than San Francisco (30) and negotiate (not very successfully) the school's playground dynamics. A series of events, including his excitement about a crush on a classmate, forces Jin to believe that being Chinese complicates his relationship with his peers. Only by concealing his ethnicity, he thinks, can he assimilate and belong.

Because of his youthful rejection of his heritage, Yang chooses to actually embody the reality of Jin's Chineseness. Interestingly, this move recalls Laurence Yep's description in his autobiography, *The Lost Garden*, of the presence of his grandmother in his life. His grandmother, Yep says, "represented a 'Chineseness' in my life that was as unmovable and unwanted as a mountain in your living room. Or rather it was like finding strange, new pieces to a puzzle that made the picture itself take a new, unwanted shape" (46). Importantly, she initiates his process of reciprocal appreciation of ethnicity: "I knew she accepted her strange, American-born grandson – far better than I accepted my China-born grandmother. In many ways, she came to embody what I came to consider my 'Chineseness' – that foreign, unassimilable, independent core" (2). Having to negotiate the reminder of one's difference becomes, for many Asian American children, a strategy for self-acceptance. For Jin, apart from his introduction to his new class, this means realizing that his only friend at the school is a recent immigrant from Taiwan, Wei-Chen. Interestingly, Wei-Chen does not seem to have the issues Jin does with ethnicity. He actually appears more able to adapt to the circumstances: two weeks after Jin snaps at him – "Stop acting like such an F.O.B.!" (89) – he begins dating Suzy Nakamura. Jin, who is warned off Amelia, the white girl he has a crush on, by another boy who tells him that "I want to make sure she makes good choices, you know? [. . .] start paying attention to who she hangs out with" (179), blames ethnic visibility for his failure to be considered an acceptable boyfriend for the (white) girl of his choice. Jin/Danny's ethnic reminder takes the form of yearly visits from a "Chinese cousin" whose main purpose appears to be to unsettle his fragile position in a mainstream world of his own imagination.

The section entitled "Everyone Ruvs Chin-Kee" thus becomes Yang's way of dealing with several key paradigms: first, with the kind of Asian/American visibility acceptable by the mainstream and that Asian Americans have to deal with; second, the kind of racism Chinese American children and teens might experience; third and most crucially, a racism toward Asians that they might somehow internalize and project. Yang's overdrawn depiction of Chin-Kee, though logically problematic for many readers and critics, was deliberate. As Min Song explains,

> Chin-Kee is exactly what his name calls forth. He is a grotesque stereotype of the Chinese as racially alien, a stereotype first cast in the nineteenth century as Western imperial countries chipped away at China's sovereignty and Chinese workers began to populate California and the rest of the American West in visibly large numbers (78–80).

Yang's drawing of the short, yellow-skinned, buck-toothed, grinning asexual man with a queue clearly recalls the image originally established in newspapers, popular entertainment, and film in the late 19th and early 20th centuries, notably through depictions such as Mickey Rooney's 1958 I.Y. Yunioshi in the film version of Truman Capote's *Breakfast at Tiffany's* or the representations of Charlie Chan in over 40 movies from the 1930s to 1940s (all played by Caucasian actors). The "visual vocabulary" developed by these caricatures makes Chin-Kee a complex and troubling figure in *American Born Chinese* (Song 80). Crucially, Yang reminds us that these images, imprinted in the minds of mainstream Americans, are equally constitutive of the vision of Chineseness that Asian American children receive, consume, and project. His engagement with his childhood, thus, negotiates the insidious effects of internalized racism against his own ethnic group, a visual category that Jin seeks to transform himself out of.

Chin-Kee embodies several visible stereotypes of Chinese, both positive and negative: first, the "Heathen Chinee" – slit-eyed, bucktoothed, speaking pidgin English (note the phonetic pronunciation of his name) – that originated from 19th century American cartoons and early 20th century films. He is represented generally as an entertaining but essentially harmless figure, yet one best avoided. In the context of representations of Asian American masculinity, Donald Goellnicht explains that

> the restrictive and exclusionary laws instituted by the dominant white culture against the Chinese has emasculated these immigrant men, forcing them into "feminine" subject positions of powerlessness and silence, into "bachelor" Chinatowns devoid of women and into "feminized" jobs that could not be filled by women (192).

Chin-Kee both replicates and invalidates these images. His exuberant arrival – "Harro Amellica!" (48) – and his ostensibly childish excitement at all around him make him appear harmless at first. But exclamations such as "Such pletty Amellican girl wiff bountiful Amellican bosom! Must bind feet and bear Chin-Kee's children!" (50) or "Now Chin-Kee go to Riblaly to find Amellican girl to bind feet and bear Chin-Kee's children" (120) take readers back to a time when people were alerted to the fact that the seemingly benign Asian presence (Charlie Chan) actually concealed sinister intentions (Fu Manchu). Indeed, at one point Chin-Kee is depicted in the stereotypical Fu Manchu manner, hunched over, drumming his claw-like fingers, buck teeth prominent, and drooling, as he says: "Chin-Kee have such lorrikingly good time! [at the American school]!" (120), just before announcing he will head to the library to find an American girl to bear his children.

Foregrounding the idea of menacing Asian men conquering innocent American women reactivates old prejudices, albeit humorously. Chin-Kee's alienating representation includes Yang's foregrounding of the stereotypical idea that Chinese enjoy unacceptable and disgusting (for Americans) food and behavior: at lunch, Chin-Kee asks "Would cousin Da-nee care to tly Chin-Kee's Clispy Flied Cat Gizzards Wiff Noodle?" (114). Furthermore, to get even with a boy who had been bullying Danny, Chin-Kee informs him that: "Me Chinese, me play joke! Me go pee-pee in his Coke!" (118). These contrasting images accentuate the unassailable difference and unknowability of the Chinese in popular imagery, projecting them as suspicious, the ultimate aliens.

Second, Chin-Kee reproduces the visible stereotype of the Asian as a "model minority" student. When he accompanies Danny to school, he responds to all the questions asked in every class and is actually put forward by the teacher as an example to other students: "You know, people—it would behoove you all to be a little more like Chin-Kee" (111). Nonetheless, what might be considered a "positive" stereotype (in the form of academic excellence and admiration by faculty) is viewed by Danny as excessive visibility and, as the day at school progresses, the boy is increasingly mortified by his cousin's behavior. Furthermore, the teenager believes that Chin-Kee's overtures toward Melanie the night before has ruined his chances with her, leading him to insist: "I'm not like him, Melanie. [. . .] I'm nothing like him! In fact, I don't even know how we're related!" (123). Melanie's explanation that her decision to remain just friends with Danny has nothing to do with his cousin reveals to readers Danny's obsession with the role of Chin-Kee in his life. The boy's persistence in detaching himself from Chin-Kee and all he represents is partly an attempt at individuality and partly a refusal to accept the reality of ethnicity in his life.

The style of Yang's drawings also focuses particular attention on the figure of Chin-Kee. In general, the characters in *American Born Chinese* are drawn and colored in a way reminiscent of the kinds of comics and cartoons that Yang would have read as a child growing up in San Francisco. The style is similar to that of 1960s Archie comics and 1980s Hanna-Barbera cartoons such as *Scooby-Doo*, with realistic individuals, sharp outlines, and solid colors. The depiction of Chin-Kee, however, offers a visible contrast to this comics style: his body is shorter, rounder, and somehow disproportionately larger than the other figures. His Chinese-style tunic, cap and queue also mark him as an alien presence in Danny's home and the school, where the students wear contemporary clothes. Yang makes it clear that this character does not "fit" in Danny's world – the visual markers of difference on the page mirror the teenager's perception of Chin-Kee's difference and undesirability. By drawing Chin-Kee as a perceptible contrast to the characters whose shapes and coloring recall popular American comic books and cartoons about white teenagers, Yang makes a persuasive point about the problematic of ethnic visibility in a *Bildungsroman*. Also, framing sections that feature Chin-Kee with the words "ha ha ha ha" and "clap clap clap clap," which replicate the canned laughter and applause of television sit-coms, emphasizes the element of viewership. The reader, then, is cast as a viewer watching a TV show, heightening the sense of participating in an act of popular comic entertainment. Indeed, Chin-Kee appears to play for laughs, his postures, side comments, and general bearing evidencing not only his awareness of being watched, but also his obvious enjoyment of his *performance* as a Chinese stereotype.

Significantly, Yang references a specific performance of ethnic visibility in the full-page illustration of Chin-Kee dancing on top of a library table, as he sings "She bang! She bang! Yeah baby! She move! She move! I go crazy!" (203). This portrait showcases a disturbing side to the contemporary, as opposed to historical, Asian American stereotype as it reproduces the image of the Hong Kong-born Berkeley engineering student William Hung's infamous 2004 *American Idol* performance of the popular Ricky Martin song. The YouTube video of Hung's off-key and clumsy performance went viral (it was one of the first YouTube videos to be classified as having gone "viral") and his celebrity status grew, with the creation of fan clubs, the production of three studio albums, and numerous talk show guest appearances. It also led to several serious critical discussions about Chinese American stereotypes and visibility in the 21st century. As Guillermo, writing for the *San Francisco Chronicle*, commented several months after the performance: "Here was an accented Asian American with bad hair, bad teeth, bad moves and a bad accent. And even though he can't sing, America still loved him." Troubled by the kind of attention this singularly untalented young man was receiving, Guillermo asks, "is there any other reason to extend the joke on America except that it plays to a racist image of the ineffectual Asian-American male?" Disturbingly, then, Yang draws on a real-life performer who appears to embody the earlier stereotypes, exposing the forms of visibility that Chinese Americans have sought to disavow. Indeed, James Hou wryly observes that "As Asian Americans, we look through this racial lens, and we see this guy who embodies all the stereotypes we're trying to escape from" (quoted in Guillermo). Katherine Meizel's reading of the events links Hung to the discourses of ethnic visibility in the USA. Though she does not think his failure at the audition stemmed from racism, she suggests: "racial and related sexual discourses have played an important role both in the show's mocking portrayal of him and in his ultimate popularity" (93). Crucially, Yutian Wong notes that Hung's

> public persona as a nerdy, unattractive, tone-deaf, and uncoordinated engineering student at UC Berkeley registers identically with Hollywood stereotypes of Asian men (such as the infamous Long Duk Dong in *Sixteen Candles*). But, in the case of William Hung, his public persona is not an act (231).

This point reminds us of the pervasiveness and endurance of ethnic stereotypes: William Hung arguably became popular not only because he looked and acted in a way that *reminded* the public of the media images of Asian men, but because he *embodied* it. Every TV appearance served to reinforce the vision of Asians that Asian Americans had struggled to invalidate. The fact that the loveable and harmless Hung was very popular among Asian Americans as well complicates this issue. But in Ng's view, Hung's performance covers for many Asian American insecurities: "For Asian Americans, Hung represents everything we don't want to be seen as (foreign, nerdish, a joke), and thus his oddball fame reinforces our own happily assimilated identities." Weaving stereotypical images from the media and their embodiment in a topical phenomenon (*American Born Chinese* was published in 2006, the height of Hung's popularity), Yang does not spare his protagonist the consequences of distressing ethnic visibility. Indeed, though one might rather easily challenge or dismiss stereotypical media images of Asians, Yang's incorporation of a clear reference to William Hung forces the reader to negotiate *reality* as much as possible. Dealing with stereotypes thus becomes a more urgent imperative.

So, in *American Born Chinese*, Yang uses the comic form to draw (or draw out) his Asian American character's most secret fear: the classification into a stereotype. Indeed, Yang seems to argue, this is how children in the USA — even Asian American children — receive and, therefore, perceive Chineseness. Jin becomes a victim of the pervasiveness of racial stereotypes: he suffers the consequences of their existence at the same time that he accepts them. Yang knowingly exaggerates the stereotype to force the character to reconsider the origins and nature of his perceptions about his heritage. Immersed within the paradigms of American culture, Jin/Danny strives to separate himself from all that Chin-Kee represents. Ironically, only when he accepts what Chin-Kee was created to remind him of can he successfully transcend (by symbolically beheading) the stereotype and accept himself. So Jin deals with his Chinese visibility by imagining himself invisible — blending into the scenery as Danny, a "typical" American (read: white), so to speak. Chin-Kee, by deliberately and shamelessly playing to all kinds of Asian stereotypes — lusting after white women, wanting to bind their feet, eating horrible food, knowing all the answers to the questions — forces him to face his own fears. In the conclusion to *American Born Chinese,* we realize that Chin-Kee is merely the disguise that Monkey King took on to teach Jin/Danny the lesson he himself had learned: "how *good* it is to be a *monkey*" (223). Appearing as the embodiment of the stereotype that the boy abhors, he serves as Jin/Danny's "*conscience* [. . .] a *signpost* to your *soul*" (221).

Yang's incorporation of an "alien" character — and Chin-Kee's portrayal classifies him an "alien" — connects with Chinese American children's author Laurence Yep's idea that writing about aliens reflects his process of self-awareness: "In writing about alienated people and aliens in my science fiction, I was writing about myself as a Chinese American" (104). But Yang uses this figure to acknowledge, appropriate, and overcome the Asian American child's fear of stereotypical visibility. The psychological implications of Yang's metacritical use of the stereotype of Chineseness resound as a vital part of Asian Americans' process of individuality and self-acceptance. Yang's characters' journeys, ultimately, involve facing stereotypes, conquering them, and understanding the multiple cultural forces that intervene in one's self-understanding and self-representation.

References

Carpenter, Carole H. "Enlisting Children's Literature in the Goals of Multiculturalism." *Mosaic* 29.3 (1996): 53–73.

Chao, Patricia. *Monkey King*. New York: Harper Collins, 1997.

Chu, Patricia P. *Assimilating Asians: Gendered Strategies of Authorship in Asian America*. Durham, London: Duke University Press, 2000.

Fong, Timothy P. *The Contemporary Asian American Experience: Beyond the Model Minority*. Upper Saddle River, NJ: Prentice-Hall, Inc., 1998.

Fu, Binbin. "Review of American Born Chinese." *MELUS* 32.3 (2007): 274–6.

Goellnicht, Donald C. "Tang Ao in America: Male Subject Positions in *China Men*." In *Reading the Literatures of Asian America*, edited by Shirley Geok-lin Lim and Amy Ling. Philadelphia, PA: Temple University Press, 1992, 191–211.

Guillermo, Emil. "William Hung: Racism or Magic?" *San Francisco Chronicle*, April 6, 2004. 28 Oct. 2012. <http://www.sfgate.com/politics/article/William-Hung-Racism-Or-Magic-2798362.php>

Hagedorn, Jessica. *Charlie Chan is Dead: An Anthology of Contemporary Asian American Fiction*. New York: Penguin Books, 1993.

Kingston, Maxine Hong. *Tripmaster Monkey: His Fake Book*. New York: Vintage Books, 1989.

McCloud, Scott. *Understanding Comics: The Invisible Art*. New York: HarperPerennial, 1994.

Meizel, Katherine L. *Idolized: Music, Media, and Identity in American Idol*. Bloomington, IN: Indiana University Press, 2011.

Mo, Timothy. *The Monkey King*. London: Faber & Faber, 1978.

Ng, David. "Hung Out to Dry." *The Village Voice* March 30, 2004. 28 Oct. 2012. <http://www.villagevoice.com/2004-03-30/news/hung-out-to-dry/1/> (2004).

Song, Min Hyoung. "'How Good It Is to Be a Monkey': Comics, Racial Formation, and *American Born Chinese*." *Mosaic* 43.1 (2010): 73–92.

Ty, Eleanor. *The Politics of the Visible in Asian North American Narratives*. Toronto: University of Toronto Press, 2004.

Wong, Yutian. *Choreographing Asian America*. Middletown, CT: Wesleyan University Press, 2010.

Yamamoto, Traise. *Masking Selves, Making Subjects: Japanese American Women, Identity, and the Body*. Berkeley, CA: University of California Press, 1999.

Yang, Gene Luen. *American Born Chinese*. New York, London: First Second, 2006.

———. "Why Comics?" Lectured delivered as part of the Graphic Novel Speaker Series at the University of Pennsylvania, December 10, 2008. 28 Oct. 2012. <http://www.youtube.com/watch?v=xYA3HNbc7Rs>

Yep, Laurence. *The Lost Garden*. New York: Simon and Schuster, 1991.

Leigh Gilmore and Elizabeth Marshall

TRAUMA AND YOUNG ADULT LITERATURE: REPRESENTING ADOLESCENCE AND KNOWLEDGE IN DAVID SMALL'S *STITCHES: A MEMOIR*

This essay focuses on the graphic memoir Stitches, *written by award winning children's picture book author and illustrator, David Small. Unlike Small's other projects aimed at school-aged children, including* So You Want to be the President? *and* Imogene's Antlers, Stitches *is a graphic trauma narrative intended for an older audience. Through a visual language of gray shadows and bold, off-center outlines, Small's comics chronicle his traumatic coming-of-age, including psychological abuse within his family, and radiation-induced cancer. When* Stitches *was nominated for a National Book Award in the young people's literature category rather than in the adult category, its placement exposed assumptions about the line between young adult (YA) and adult literature. Drawing on theories of trauma and self-representation, we consider how the placement of* Stitches *within the YA category and the ensuing controversy calls into crisis how youth is framed, by and for whom, and with what limitations. Graphic storytelling allows Small to engage with traumatic material visually and in turn to expose conventional ideas about youthful knowledge, agency, and witness.*

"I'm not really ironic about anything in this book; it's pretty sincere, without, I hope, ever falling into sentimentality, which I despise" (Small qtd. in Allen, no page).

Introduction

In 2009, David Small, celebrated children's picture book author and illustrator, published a graphic memoir, *Stitches*, that became a *New York Times* bestseller, won an Alex award for books written by adults with special appeal to teen readers, and secured a place in the young adult (YA) literary market. Small's memoir chronicles a traumatic coming-of-age in the USA in the 1950s, in which his benign sinus problem and "frequent bouts with this and that" (20) were treated routinely with high-dose X-rays by his radiologist father. As a result of this misguided therapy, 14-year-old Small developed a cancerous tumor on his vocal cord. He was never told about his diagnosis or its implications. Instead, he underwent an operation for what he understood to be a "growth" and woke up with a surgical scar, unable to talk as a result of the removal of one of his vocal cords and the tumor.

Stitches was a controversial National Book Award finalist in the young people's literature category. The placement of Small's graphic memoir in this category rather than in the adult category sparked disagreements around the book's appropriateness for a YA audience (Hogan; Springen; Weldon). When W. W. Norton (also the publisher of graphic novelists R. Crumb and Will Eisner) nominated *Stitches* in the young people's literature category rather than nonfiction adult, it entered an ongoing debate about the limits of knowledge, agency, and youth that plays out in conflicts over genres, audiences, markets, and texts. Although the conventional association of comics with adolescence helps to explain why Small's book was considered "YA," *Stitches* was only the second comics work to be nominated for the National Book Award after Gene Luen Yang's 2006 novel *American Born Chinese*, also nominated in the young people's category. Yet even if *Stitches'* status as a graphic narrative, as well as Small's established reputation, prompted its placement in young people's literature, its status as a nonfictional trauma narrative caused many to challenge the decision.

Children's merchandise manager at Bookazine Heather Doss, for one, told *Publisher's Weekly*, "I would not hand it to anyone under the age of 16" (Springen, no page). While YA literature characteristically covers disturbing topics related to coming-of-age, which Doss readily acknowledges, *Stitches'* status as nonfiction, and thereby Small's claim to represent his actual experience, rendered this graphic memoir unacceptable: "[T]he fact that this is nonfiction brings it to another level. You're stretching the boundaries to give it a YA award" (Springen, no page). Norton executive editor Robert Weil, on the other hand, defended the book's placement based on market research about who was reading *Stitches*: "It has been a crossover book. We found a great appeal to kids between 12 and 18. Many of the comments we've gotten are from teens. It is a growing-up story, but the issues addressed in the book are ones that a lot of teens face" (Springen, no page). Clearly, *Stitches* reveals fault lines within the category of YA literature, including the correlation of genre with tolerances around the representation of trauma for young readers.[1]

The controversy around *Stitches* is hardly unprecedented. It can be meaningfully contextualized within a specific history of longstanding and ongoing debates among authors, literary publics, and publishers about youth and definitions of YA literature (Hunt; Talley; Trites). Indeed, such episodes routinely erupt around the definition of youth and this subject's interpellation into the social. In terms of memoir, battles about where to draw the line between youth and adulthood, and among reading publics, can be read as a struggle to frame knowledge about youth, trauma, and truth telling. As Hillary Chute observes, "[G]raphic narratives . . . are not only about events, but also, explicitly, about *how* we frame them" (2). The positioning of *Stitches* within the YA category as a memoir calls into crisis *how* youth is framed, by and for whom, and with what limitations around youthful knowledge, agency, and witness.

Small's graphic memoir prompts us to consider how and when representations of trauma become too much for the YA category, given that traumatic events, including war, sexual and physical abuse, and illness have been experienced by the memoirist during adolescence. The main objection to trauma narratives, like *Stitches*, we argue, lies less in their subject matter than in their refusal to represent trauma in the service of ameliorative or neoliberal agendas. In what follows, we analyze the representation of adolescence within Small's graphic memoir to mark out the tolerances (and intolerances) around the representation of youth, trauma, and truth telling that inform the marketing of YA literature. We include an analysis of Jeanette Walls' memoir, *The Glass Castle*, as an example of what we call a *strategically grim* representation of trauma in contrast to how David Small draws abuse within his family.

Crossovers, adolescence, and the Alex award

Stitches enters a literary marketplace in which books are invariably placed into categories as part of a marketing strategy. Currently, children's/YA literature is a highly lucrative market, and strategic placement of texts within it represents one way that book publishers and marketing teams drive sales. Book reviews and literary prizes, as well as targeted advertising in social media and print, become part of marketing campaigns to promote books, to be sure, but they also develop national and international markets for YA literature as a category. Consider *Harry Potter* in this context.[2] Of all the transformations J.K. Rowling's series wrought upon the cultural landscape, one that was little noted by non-specialists was the *New York Times Book Review*'s creation in July 2000 of a Children's Literature Bestseller List shortly before the release of the fourth *Harry Potter* book (Corliss). With the three previous books in the series crowding out other authors on the bestseller list and thereby restricting the list's promotional utility, *Harry Potter* was used to create an additional index of bestselling children's literature. The *Book Review*'s original hardcover and paperback fiction and nonfiction lists have also calved off Advice and How-To lists which offer a representational map of value: not only by tracking weeks on the list or numbers sold, but by building additional categories, naming market segments, targeting readers, and increasing sales.

At issue for us is less whether Harry Potter is "really" a children's book or work of adult fiction. We are concerned here with how a book is positioned to expand readership and sales by crossing over the boundaries of age and genre. While crossover books are obviously attractive to publishers and booksellers, any particular book's placements at the limits of market segments can also crystallize cultural conflicts. Histories of reading point to the instability of categories, including the adolescent reader of YA fiction, and to the cultural negotiations waged through categories. Coming-of-age texts like *Stitches* traverse the provisional boundary between memoir (written by and marketed to adults) and YA literature (written by adults and marketed to youth). In its transit from one readership/market to another, a crossover text tries to gain readers, but it may also raise questions about the division between "adult" and "children's" books and disturbing the authorities and interests that cluster there.[3]

Unlike *Harry Potter*, which was marketed initially as children's literature and reached an enormous audience without challenging that classification, the publishers of *Stitches* claimed they had always intended to market Small's memoir as a crossover title. In an interview, Norton's assistant directory of publicity Erin Sinesky Lovett stated that "because Small had never written for an adult readership before, the graphic novel could be seen as a 'transitional' work, building from his distinguished background as a children's book writer and illustrator" (Hogan).[4] It seems that for Lovett, "YA" functions as a mapping device, a guide to help readers find a familiar author who is doing something different. Yet a crossover book risks alienating its base readership in its search for additional readers, a risk of which Small was aware. In an interview with *Publisher's Weekly*, Small says he knew kids would see his book: "There were things I refrained from talking about, knowing that the book might fall into the hands of kids" (Springen, no page). For example, he did not talk about masturbation: "I'm not saying that I'm a fuddy-duddy, but I think it was unnecessary in this case to be that candid about my entire adolescent life. It had nothing to do with the arc of the story I was telling" (Springen, no page). Small nods here to the conventional policing of age-appropriate representations of youthful sexuality for young readers, but he also offers charged and disturbing representations of adult sexuality as perceived by his younger self, including the discovery of his mother's closeted lesbianism (272) and his grandmother's gleeful naked dance outside the house she has just set on fire after locking her husband in the basement (277).

Small recognizes that his success as an author and illustrator of children's books explains *Stitches'* placement on book lists for YAs, but he also calls attention to the fungibility of genre within YA literature. In an interview, he states

> I do not believe that it [the memoir] was miscategorized. I think it was categorized exactly where it should be. I didn't think of categories when I was writing the book. I knew that I was stepping out of the children's world, but I never thought that I was stepping completely into the adult world, because the book is about a teenager, for example. It really – the principal ages are six and 14 – of the main character. And when the controversy started, I began having second thoughts and wondering, hmm, did I put some things in there that, you know, teenagers couldn't handle? I didn't think so. I mean, they see so much now, and things are talked about so openly in young adult literature. (qtd. in Allen, no page)

Memoir enables Small to represent his younger self in a way that is consistent with how he has come to understand it. Traumatic material is presented for younger audiences for whom the child narrator is resonant, but Small is not writing from a child's perspective. As the depiction of his work with a life-saving therapist makes clear, he is representing a past not repeating it. *Stitches'* appearance on the American Library Association Alex book award list for 2010 follows the ALA's tradition of recommending memoirs to young readers.[5] The Alex award list is generated annually by an adult committee of the American Library Association and suggests titles that were originally published for adults, but that the committee recommends to a YA audience. To be included on the ALA Alex award list, "titles are selected for their demonstrated or probable appeal to the personal reading tastes of young adults" (ALA website). The memoirs that consistently appear on the Alex list take numerous forms, including the adventure tale, the hard luck story of survival and overcoming, the rise or redemption narrative, narratives of "foreign" childhoods, and medical/illness stories. Memoirs by first-time authors, as-told-to or otherwise co-written texts, and texts by established writers all appear. There is not only considerable diversity in the levels of literary skill, but also in the claims to transparency the texts make. *Stitches* is just one example of YA's assimilation of memoir and its emphasis on coming-of-age and trauma to build out its list. YA literature, then, can be theorized as less a static genre than as a set of heterogeneous texts, as well as "a marketplace phenomenon of the twentieth century" (Trites 7).

Graphic memoir

In the late 20th and early 21st centuries, nonfiction became an increasingly popular genre. During the same time frame, numerous social movements propelled previously marginalized and disenfranchised persons into political and literary representation. Many women, people of color, gays and lesbians, immigrants, and the disabled wrote memoirs and participated in documenting how the personal was political. One theme that emerged from personal histories in this time period was trauma.[6] Authors skilfully documented the embeddedness of personal struggle and suffering within larger cultural formations. David Small's representation of adolescence fits within the larger context of memoir and graphic narrative in particular, as well as his use of the child/adolescent to represent trauma. The inclusion of Small's book in the YA category is due in part to his use of comics. Small's memoir can be considered alongside other graphic memoirs like Lynda Barry's *One Hundred Demons* and Marjane Satrapi's *Persepolis*, two other Alex award winners. As Chute observes, graphic narratives "reject the categories of nonfiction and fiction altogether in their self-representational storylines" (3). YA literature's inclusivity extends formally to comics and the current explosion of graphic novels and memoirs, particularly those with a coming-of-age theme.

Comics themselves have a contentious relation to the category of youth. During Small's 1950s childhood, comics become the subject of the US Senate's attempt to censor reading material for youth consumption because of the graphic (sexual and violent) content. The controversy around *Stitches* as a National Book Award finalist echoes earlier panics around youth and comics, including Dr Fredric Wertham's *Seduction of the Innocent*, a book that was central to the Senate Subcommittee Hearings that began April 21, 1954 into the comic book industry and juvenile delinquency. The result was the formation of the Comics Magazines Association of America (CMAA) and the Comic Codes Authority (CCA) Stamp, a code that aimed to censor violence, sex, and other graphic material from comics.[7] Thus, Small's decision to use graphic narrative to tell his story belongs to a larger politics about adolescence in the USA.

Small participates in a politics of youth by revising the assumed association of comics with innocent adolescent subjects to include a child's first-hand knowledge of psychological abuse. The "seduction of the innocent" in his memoir is turned on its head as he disrupts the innocence/knowledge binary. Although *Stitches* slips into the YA category because it uses the childlike form of comic, it offers up violent material that occurs not in the world of superheroes but in the white middle class American family. Small's memoir suggests that cultural panics around youth and reading/viewing material are a decoy that ignores the range of traumatic knowledge/experience that youth can experience (rather than just read about). In this way, a newly expanded sense of YA's audience beyond youth, and the prevalence of representations of trauma in memoir and autobiography, dovetail with the historical antecedents of the YA market.

From its inception, the genre of YA literature has included both fictional and autobiographical texts. Its founding texts straddle this divide in the form of autobiographical fiction and include *The Outsiders* (Hinton) and *The Bell Jar* (Plath).

Some of YA's most representative texts belong to the multiform discourse of life writing. *The Diary of Anne Frank* (Frank), *I Know Why the Caged Bird Sings* (Angelou), and *Night* (Wiesel), as well as texts that draw a portion of their authority for readers from their autobiographical elements, including the anonymous diary *Go Ask Alice* (Anonymous), the autobiographical novel *Bastard out of Carolina* (Allison), and even the novel, *To Kill A Mockingbird* (Lee) represent a range of life narratives fully at home as YA. That these texts are also crossover narratives suggests how dynamic and durable tolerances, anxieties, and fantasies are about "the adolescent" as a category.

A focus on memoir allows us to expose some of these dynamics and reveals, further, how YA, as a category, is simultaneously the object of representation and a subject produced and remembered by many adults who "know better." In one of the best known cases in this context, therapist and Mormon youth counsellor Beatrice Sparks published *Go Ask Alice* (1971) as the anonymous diary of one of her teenage patients. The diary was exposed as a fabrication, a cautionary tale about drug use Sparks wrote herself and attributed to a teenage girl. Whether the adults who "know better" are librarians, book editors, members of book prize committees, sales and marketing teams at publishing houses, booksellers, parents, adult readers, or authors, they all claim an authority over adolescent knowledge superior to the knowledge of actual adolescents. In the current debate, the question of how (or whether) traumatic material ought to emerge in YA literature is enjoined by adults on behalf of a readership assumed to need protection, but whose presence is mediated through adult memory, and whose capacity to exert meaningful agency over the representation of adolescence is highly unstable.[8] Thus, the underrepresentation of actual youth in YA literature serves to leave youth as the object of representation strategically undefined. The specularity of youth is further intensified by the memoirist himself or herself, whose representation of a young self strengthens the construction of youth in YA literature as that which is remembered and contested by adults and in which youth participate as readers whose access to these texts is highly mediated.

Small's representation of the adolescent in *Stitches* is highly constructed and exposes how this specter of youth functions as a politicized figure created primarily by adults. In her theory of infantile citizenship, Lauren Berlant claims that abstractions like the nation and citizenship are translated into deeply held feelings and internalized as identity through the interrelation of representation and affect in reading practices. A key example is her notion of infantile citizenship in which the "fetal/infantile person is a *stand-in* for a complicated and contradictory set of anxieties and desires about national identity" (6). Especially relevant here is Berlant's claim that a figure of the person (in her reading, the infantile person; in ours, the adolescent person) remains open and available as more than a mere reflection of a past phase, or spur to reminiscence, and rather becomes a way to embody desires and anxieties that are themselves contradictory and fully political. The motive energies are sentimental because they are not only nostalgic but also aspirational. One identifies with the infantile or adolescent person not to make an argument about the past, but to enter the suspended temporality of belonging that is always being negotiated through reading popular literature. Berlant argues that powerful national fantasies flow through the figure of the child and help to create infantile citizenship as a belief that the state is invested in the overall good of ordinary persons.

The elastic category of YA literature suggests a readership with multiple, interrelated, and sometimes conflictual views about youth, through which different realities and fantasies are negotiated. The notion that a memoir like *Stitches* is not appropriate for a YA audience is less a challenge to the facticity of the account than a declaration of preference for the preservation and renewal of uplift and other positive feelings in which youth can be associated with the ameliorating fantasies of the nation (e.g., filled with good-enough families, adequately supported by discrete but offstage institutions, offered opportunity, and so on). Yet, for what public is this fantasy meaningful and consoling? For what public is it compulsory?

Berlant's observations about reading and the literary marketplace as a site of citizenship formation help us to frame further questions in our analysis about how dissonant and traumatic materials are purged, and through what representational strategies. Although we have identified the strategies about crossover marketing and the production of "adolescence" by a variety of interests and entities, we have not yet elaborated any specific political program they possess beyond increasing sales. In what follows, we provide further analysis of the interests such strategies promote.

Strategically grim

The age/genre fault lines of YA literature/memoir and adolescent/adult readers acquire densities of meaning as other issues and investments cluster along them. We have identified how adolescence is produced on and at these fractures and limits. Here, too, emerge representations of trauma that we argue are "strategically grim." These representations of trauma are employed as part of a narrative of the young protagonist's redemption or maturation (Gilmore, "Neoconfessional"). In contrast, as is the case with *Stitches*, we find representations of trauma rooted in circumstances the young person survives, but which resist incorporation in an uplifting storyline. Although narratives for teen readers often depict danger and crisis, we characterize them as strategically grim if crises resolve as a young protagonist steers out of harm's way. That is, resolution occurs as a matter of narrative convention, affirms the cultural construction of growing up as an individual, if perilous, passage, and refrains from a critique of the formations that permit violence. At the heart of strategically grim narratives of trauma for YA audiences rests a bargain to represent trauma as consistent with closure and not as the grounds for critique of middle class family norms.

A recent Alex award winner and memoir, *The Glass Castle* by Jeanette Walls, faithfully executes on just such a bargain and provides a counterexample to *Stitches*. Her memoir begins in a limo as Walls, a successful writer, glides home through the streets of Manhattan to the Park Avenue apartment she shares with her handsome husband. This opening evokes "Cinderella," fast-forwarded 10 years into her happily ever after. The surface of this sleek image is disrupted by the sight of a homeless woman picking through a dumpster. Walls recognizes the woman, but withdraws behind the limo's darkened windows, hoping she has not been seen: the woman is her mother. From this pretext, Walls describes a childhood of poverty and transience, including precarious high school years in Appalachia in which her family lived in a shack without plumbing and Walls had to scavenge food from the garbage at school. Yet, Walls paints her parents as dreamers and artists, iconoclasts who opt for poverty and homelessness, whose choices should, indeed, make everyone realize that people can choose to be homeless. With this revelation, which scales up from family history and amounts to an argument about social policy, Walls asserts that she turned out just fine, with an inspirational story to share about pulling herself up by her bootstraps. Walls reabsorbs the bleak material about childhood poverty and casts it as charmed by centering the story on her father's plan to build a glass castle, further echoing fairy tale imagery and its underlying popular messages about rescue. Based on the success of her memoir, Walls has launched a career as a motivational speaker, in which the author, protagonist, and inspirational persona blot out any critical or political perspective on adolescence and poverty.

Reviews of *The Glass Castle* focus on themes of resilience and forgiveness in this strategically grim coming-of-age text. As Jessica Hockett observes, "Unlike many memoirists, [Walls] chooses not to weave commentary, reflection, or psychoanalysis into her account, instead relating each episode from the vantage point she experienced it. This technique allows Walls to avoid judging how her parents chose to live or dwelling on their negligence" (269). Walls makes a pact with readers not to dwell on what she cannot reconcile about poverty or negligent parents, but to present herself as intact from the beginning through a narrative voice that does not change. Her bargain is to depict trauma, but not to be damaged by it, to hold it outside her narrative voice, which defies any meaningful engagement with its effects. YA texts like Walls' certainly include bleak themes, but strategically so. They feature adolescents who come of age in hard circumstances, but find redemption in adulthood. When the adolescent narrator or protagonist ends up wiser for the hardship, difficulty is incorporated into a meaningful lesson. In other words, as Hockett concludes, it becomes pedagogical: "As a case study in resilience, Jeanette Walls' memoir highlights effective coping strategies for and protective factors that may contribute to overcoming adversity" (270). One hears the full absorption in Walls of the lawyerly language David Small was coached to use, given his very different representation of his parents: "In public interviews my editor has advised me, regarding my parents, to use the phrase, 'They did the best they knew how'" (Small qtd. in Tindell, no page).

Strategically grim narratives are neoliberal when they present overcoming individual challenges (rather politicizing them or opposing structural inequalities and power dynamics) as a way of belonging to the nation. Memoirs that shuttle between the categories of adult and YA such as *The Glass Castle* are unremarkable when they incorporate the adolescent citizen into current normative politics. In Walls' memoir, sentimentality and citizenship fuse as the adolescent saves herself and achieves personal and professional success. Choosing not to incorporate dissonant material conserves the pleasure of normal: the normative relationships and intimacies of legally sanctioned, heterosexual, middle-class, white families. When this "make lemonade" project is not followed, it risks the hegemony of national belonging and the notion that life is good. When *Stitches* refuses to be "strategically grim," it challenges readers to engage with the complex specificities of danger and harm, as well as the choices Small makes visually and verbally about how to frame them in relation to the canon of children's literature, for an audience that includes younger readers.

Stitches

Stitches is a memoir of psychological abuse that centers on Small coming-to-know that he has throat cancer. The title captures the literal wound to Small's throat that is sutured shut; it also references his family "ties that bind" and how Small comes to know psychological abuse and to name through visual testimony that which was unspeakable in his childhood and adolescence. Using black and white ink washes that resemble X-rays, Small frames trauma visually and verbally through the figure of the child/adolescent, which allows him to simultaneously narrate and witness the trauma of his youth through image and text.

 Stitches opens with a black page on which the words "I was six" are handwritten in white. The next page, also in black, reads "Detroit." The handwritten text provides an intimacy and authenticity that generic fonts do not (Chute). The opposite page features an almost entirely black illustration of a factory emitting smoke. The visual images bring the reader from macro-Detroit to the micro-world of Small's living room where he lies drawing on the floor. In this movement, the reader takes on the role of the child witness and enters Small's home as an innocent observer with little context for the experiences that will unfold. How Small frames this trauma story and the child/adolescent central to its telling for the reader is crucial in representing the entangling of unknowing with secrecy, abuse, and lies.

 Small organizes *Stitches* into five parts. In the first part, he is 6 years old. The four subsequent parts chronicle his illness from diagnosis and surgery through discovery and recovery at 11, 14, and 15 years of age. In the final part, an adult Small returns to his 6-year-old self in a dream sequence. However, Small's use of comics disrupts this explicit chronology through his representation of memory's characteristic layering of time and space, and complicates a simple narrative thrust. The main character in *Stitches* is a male child while the story of that child's coming-of-age is narrated and illustrated by an adult David Small. Although she has not written about Small, Chute's comment on the figure of the child is relevant here: "[T]his emphasis on the child affords a conspicuous, self-reflexive methodology of representation. It is a way to visually present a tension between the narrative 'I' who draws the stories and the 'I' who is the child subject of them" (5). In Small's self-representational project, the 6-year-old child (dressed in a striped t-shirt and shorts), the adolescent, and the adult are represented simultaneously on different textual and visual levels and at different moments in time and space within single frames. Comics allows the viewer to experience the past through images at the same time she experiences the perspective of an adult Small, who narrates his childhood memories (Figure 1).

 In this panel, an adult Small narrates for the reader/viewer: "Dad, home from work, went down to the basement and thumped a punching bag. That was his language" (17). The upper left of the image shows Small's father from behind and the sound of the punching bag "Pocketa, pocketa, pocketa. . ." On the upper right in the shadows of the staircase sits a 6-year-old Small observing his father. In the lower left of the panel Small's brother beats on a drum set and on the right side, Small becomes literally small as he shrinks into a corner clutching his teddy bear.

 Small frames his boyhood in a slightly out-of-focus visual language of gray shadowed forms that are only partly contained by outlines. No stable borders surround

DAD, HOME FROM WORK, WENT DOWN TO THE BASEMENT AND THUMPED A PUNCHING BAG. THAT WAS HIS LANGUAGE.

POCKETA POCKETA POCKETA POCKETA POCKETA

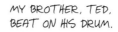

MY BROTHER, TED, BEAT ON HIS DRUM.

BUM BUM BUM

Used with permission by Simon and Schuster.

17

FIGURE 1

the images of father and brother. Throughout the memoir bordered boxes give way to borderless panels and full bleeds when Small dreams, imagines, or hallucinates. The borderless images in this panel suggest that this is Small's memory and capture the instability of Small's 6-year-old world in which violent noises ("pocketa pocketa," "bum bum bum") replace speech. Small positions himself as observer in these images and a metaphorical punching bag within his family. Small uses the "idiom of witness" that

Chute describes as "a manner of testifying that sets a visual language in motion with and against the verbal in order to embody individual and collective experience, to put contingent selves and histories into form" (3). Small crafts a mediated image through which he represents the psychological landscape in which he grew up, the repressed rage that defined his family, as well as the inability to escape the home in which he is confined.

Because Small grows up in a house in which the language of the family consists of the slamming shut of cupboard doors, the thump of a punching bag, and the beat of a drum, and in which his mother's rage erupts throughout the text as sound effects, he adapts: "And I, too, had learned a way of expressing myself wordlessly... getting sick that was my language" (18–19) (Figure 2).

Of the use of images in the book to represent his family's language, Small writes

I know now that the graphic form was the only way my memoir could have been told. First of all, drawing is my most fluent means of expression. Secondly, it's a story about being voiceless. It demanded a visual treatment because it involved so much of that guessing game we played in our family, of trying to figure out why someone was mad at us – someone who refused to communicate by any other means than slamming things around. If told in words – even if I could have – the story would have lost that visceral impact. (Small qtd. in Amazon.com, no page)

Small's visual language suggests an almost ectoplasmic field of frightening personalities thrown into sharp relief when they threaten young David. The adults that surround him are a study in repressed rage, either cold and inaccessible (father) or seething with latent violence (mother/grandmother).

Instead of using the iconic symbolism of comics, Small's style renders the characters in his story as recognizable people with identifiable characteristics. To this end, Small includes a photo of himself at age 6 at the end of the book (329) wearing the same t-shirt he has on in the comic; he also includes pictures of his father and his mother as a young woman before Small was born. The decision to include photos of his family underscores the memoir as an act of truth telling. This verisimilitude also fails to protect his mother and father: it refuses to let them off the hook as people "who did the best they knew how," or to depict them as stock characters in a larger coming-of-age storyline. Here, we see Small refuse the bargain of strategically grim narratives marketed to young readers in which bad adults are tolerated because they are not real. The marketing of Small's memoir as a crossover text with appeal to adolescents raises eyebrows because he fails to follow a formula in which a legally sanctioned, heterosexual, middle-class, white family is upheld as desirable. Indeed, Small refuses the fantasy of belonging that Berlant specifies; there is no nostalgia for the past or sentimentality about adolescence. Instead, Small's representation of the child/adolescent highlights alternative desires and intimacies.[9] More specifically, through memoir, an adult Small uses the figure of the unknowing and vulnerable child to represent his youthful self. Small marks this tension between himself as child and adult by his use of the character of Alice from *Alice's Adventures in Wonderland*. David Small watched the 1951 Disney version of *Alice in Wonderland* (Tindell), and adapted the images both from the film and from John Tenniel's 1865 illustrations of Lewis Carroll's text for his visual representation of childhood/adolescence. Small writes, "I had fallen

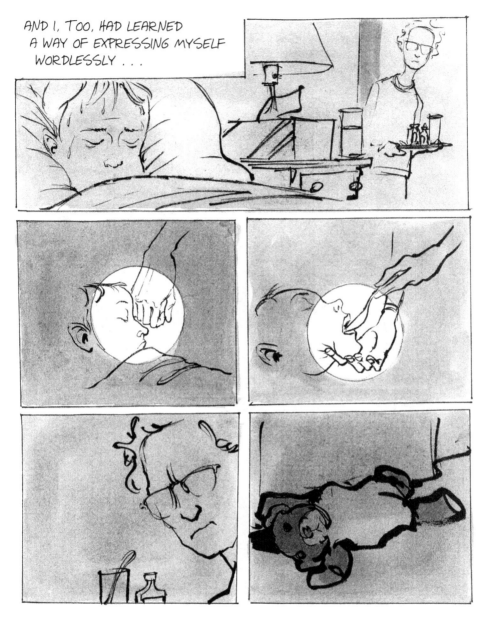

AND I, TOO, HAD LEARNED
A WAY OF EXPRESSING MYSELF
WORDLESSLY . . .

Used with permission by Simon and Schuster.

18

FIGURE 2

in love with Alice. I thought it must be her hair that gave Alice the magic ability to travel to a land of talking animals, singing flowers and dancing teapots. I wanted to go there immediately" (56). In the image, we see Small's back, his hand on the doorknob, ready to go outside. In a series of panels, the viewer sees a 6-year-old Small with a yellow blanket wrapped around his head, pretending to be Alice (Figure 3).

I HAD FALLEN IN LOVE WITH ALICE.

ESPECIALLY WITH

HER LONG

BLONDE

HAIR.

I THOUGHT IT MUST BE HER HAIR THAT GAVE ALICE THE MAGIC ABILITY TO TRAVEL TO A LAND OF TALKING ANIMALS, SINGING FLOWERS AND DANCING TEAPOTS.

I WANTED TO GO THERE IMMEDIATELY.

Used with permission by Simon and Schuster.

56

FIGURE 3

Small ties Alice's descent into the "curiouser and curiouser" to his own childhood epistemology. "At six I knew that x-rays were pictures of the secret places inside us. I imagined myself going down into those shadowy places and finding–what? I don't know. A better world, I suppose" (Small qtd. in Amazon, no page). Like Alice, a child who understands that something is wrong, but is made to feel like she is crazy, Small inhabits an absurd adult world. Unlike Alice, Small experienced himself as a reliable child witness to disturbing events with limited knowledge or agency (Gilmore "Witnessing"). In contrast to the fictional knowing child created by the adult Charles Dodgson/Lewis Carroll, David Small shares knowledge experienced by the adult writer/illustrator with readers that his/her younger self did not have access to. This is crucial for the establishment of a reliable child witness.

Stitches is less a traditional coming-of-age narrative than it is a graphically oriented coming-to-know story in which traumatic material serves as Small's curriculum. As Chute points out, graphic narratives offer a unique form for telling about trauma and childhood:

> Images in comics appear in fragments, just as they do in actual recollection; this fragmentation, in particular, is a prominent feature of traumatic memory. The art of crafting words and pictures together into a narrative punctuated by pause or absence, as in comics, also mimics the procedure of memory. (4)

The visual images within the book, many of them unaccompanied by captions, create a form to express and refute the impossibility of fully articulating the traumatic material Small experienced as a child and adolescent. Small makes visible the psychologically abusive family lessons his grandmother insisted that her "durn grandson...needed to learn" (105) (Figure 4). Through visual images Small "voices" the emotional experience that he could not speak in childhood because of family dynamics or in adolescence because of a surgical procedure; they speak for the young Small and make claims about his own experience that are belatedly articulated. In relation to psychoanalytic claims about traumatic events (Caruth), such material is incomprehensible and cannot be transferred as concrete knowledge. Yet in a generative shift that takes us away from more familiar strategically grim narratives, Small recasts "[t]ime as space" (Chute 7) such that the "time" of adolescence is theorized as a space rather than a linear becoming or outgrowing. Small challenges the traditional plot of the *Bildungsroman* in which the inexperienced boy ventures out into the world, finds himself at odds with larger social institutions, and later accommodates to them. Instead, Small remains at home for most of the narrative, and what he "comes to know" is a family pedagogy that he refuses to assimilate and ultimately rejects.

That Small represents adolescence as a space of trauma rather than as a site of learning all the right lessons for successful adulthood enables him to rewrite his relationship to knowledge and re-imagine his growing body as the site of trauma. It is Small himself who learns he has had cancer and was expected to die from it by discovering a letter in his mother's desk he was not supposed to see. In an interview, Small states

> And of course, what I discovered on my own was that, you know, that I'd had cancer, but then I found out later that it was my dad who had given it to me in his practice as a radiologist, and that was just sort of the tip of the iceberg in terms of – mixed metaphors – family skeletons, you know. It was the least of the ones that came tumbling out of the closet one after another at that point (qtd. in Allen, no page).

Used with permission by Simon and Schuster. 106

FIGURE 4

Small exposes how the strategically grim format common in YA literature fails in the face of traumatic memory in his use of comics to make that trauma visible. The lessons Small learns wound rather than provide a prompt for redemption, they mark body and mind in ways that make understanding traumatic events an ongoing process of "unknowing." Thus, the marketing of Stitches strikes all the wrong chords with booksellers, reviewers, and others interested in the idea of YA literature as a form of moral uplift. However, actual readers, like the "real" adolescent David Small, have lived experiences that refuse to assimilate the knowledge and political implications adults try to market through strategically grim narratives.

Small asserts agency around knowledge in counterpoint to the normative lessons his family tries to teach him. In a scene in which Small knows something is growing in his throat and his parents know he should have had an operation years ago, his parents call him in for a lecture about his posture (150-1). His mother is also concerned with her adolescent son's reading material and that he might be learning about sex. In a series of speech bubbles, she says: "And that is not all!" "What about the literature he's been reading? Talk about that." "All those books in his room..." "All that SMUT!" (153). On the next two pages, the reader views the mother enter Small's bedroom where she makes a pile of books including Nabokov's *Lolita*, places them in a box, throws them in a trash can, and lights it on fire (154-6).

Small's representation of his mother's censorship through visual images makes a commentary on how parental guidance – proper posture and appropriate reading material – are useless knowledge for an adolescent with cancer. Here, the putatively salacious nature of *Lolita* pales in comparison to the kinds of protections his family offers him against knowledge of a terminal illness. The mother's burning of *Lolita* as a book with inappropriate material for an 11-year-old foreshadows the controversy that will occur over *Stitches*. That books with unconventional knowledge about sexuality, relationships, and kinship consistently cross the market segments of adult and YA literature and pass between adult and adolescent readerships specifies how the specter of the adolescent, a liminal cultural construction, allows adult writers to tackle uncomfortable knowledge that destabilizes the adult/child binary.

In *Lolita* the role of knowledgeable adult and innocent minor is transposed; likewise, in *Stitches*, adults act like children and the adolescent must learn to parent himself. For instance, Small finally has two operations when he is 14 (3.5 years after the initial diagnosis). He has no knowledge of what happened to him and Small captures his adolescent self uncovering literally and metaphorically what has been done to him. "Then as I slowly regained strength, one evening I decided to change the bandage on my neck by myself...and I saw for the first time what they had done" (189) (Figures 5 and 6).

Small comes to know the horror of the surgery. The image of the wound captures the barbarism of the surgery. In this image, Small speaks to the wound/self, saying "surely this is not me," and the wound responds, "No friend it surely is" (191). Through the representation of his adolescent self, Small's visceral coming-to-know does not map onto traditional ideas of coming-of-age primarily defined as learning about sex. In a twist on the coming-of-age story, Small learns about sexuality after an alternative coming-of-age in which his throat is cut and sutured and his family betrays him.

Small's memoir does not end in adulthood, but with a dream the adult Small has of himself as a 6 years old. He plays with a toy car in his house. It flies out a window. A full-page panel shows a 6-year-old Small trapped within the house, within a family history (Figure 7).

"There was only one thing to do: To get that car moving again, I had to leave the safety of my house. I had to go outside" (321). When he does go outside, he finds his mother sweeping a path from his house to another one. "Suddenly I realized the building was the one where grandma had been locked away. The old central state asylum. The figure was my mother, sweeping the path, clearing the way for me to

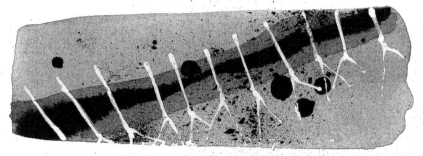

A CRUSTED BLACK TRACK OF STITCHES; MY
SMOOTH YOUNG THROAT SLASHED AND LACED
BACK UP LIKE A BLOODY BOOT.

"SURELY THIS IS NOT ME."   "NO, FRIEND. IT SURELY IS."

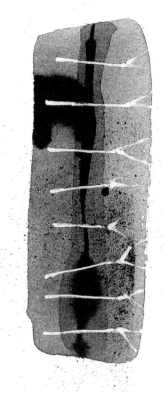 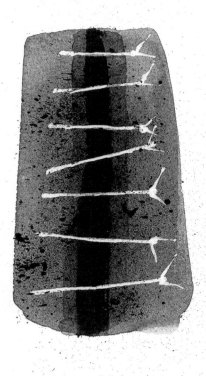

Used with permission by Simon and Schuster.

191

FIGURE 5

follow" (324). The last page of the memoir show the handwritten words "I didn't," this time in black ink on a white background. An inverted X-ray or a transposed image reflects back a pattern broken.

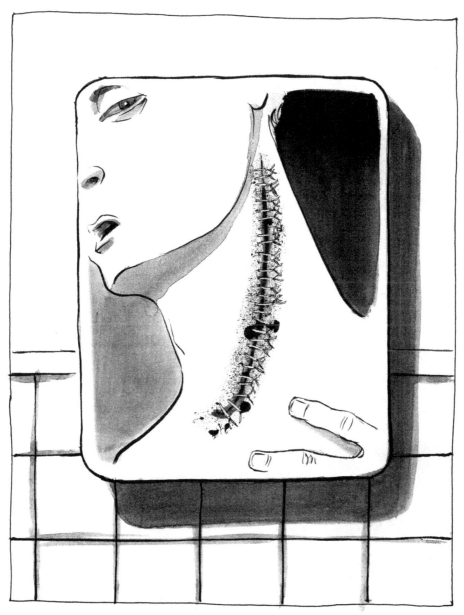

Used with permission by Simon and Schuster.

190

FIGURE 6

A strategically grim memoir would end with the author in adulthood, a successful artist possessing knowledge to pass on. Rather than tell the reader that the adults in his life "did the best they knew how," Small shows the ways in which redemption and traumatic memory are at odds. He does not tell the story from any other perspective than his own, nor does he include a fictionalized version of his

320   Used with permission by Simon and Schuster.

FIGURE 7

parents' point of view. He acquires the knowledge that he grew up with people who were incapable of providing him with what he needed and, in fact, almost killed him. When *Stitches* refuses to be "strategically grim," it challenges readers to engage with specificities of danger and harm in young people's lives, with the adults we can become in response to trauma, and with the benefit of such knowledge for younger readers.

Conclusion

It is important to analyze how memoir is taken up in the YA genre/market because it represents a site where knowledge about youth clashes with social norms about what youth can and should read. And it offers a discourse in which adolescents are represented by the adults they have become, a crossover reflected in the diverse readership of Small's memoir. The adult memoirist who writes about his or her own youth is a distinctive figure in the debate about who can speak to, about, and for youth. We have indicated two different ways in which this figure can enter the debate: either through the strategic use of grim material in the service of the redemption plot or through the representation of the past that incorporates traumatic material, and politicizes this representation or permits social critique through it. Here, we would argue that *Stitches* is controversial less because of its traumatic details than that the lessons Small learns are ultimately inadequate for his young self. The traumatic coming-of-age he describes contains no moral uplift or principle through which stability can be reasserted. Instead, he points to the ongoing work of representing his experience and perspective in the visual and verbal idiom of witness. *Stitches* ultimately asks a different question: not "whether or not this or any book is appropriate for young readers," but rather "how might youthful trauma be represented such that representation becomes an act of witness and for whom?"

Acknowledgements

This research was supported by the Social Sciences and Humanities Research Council. The authors gratefully acknowledge that the images from *Stitches* are used with the permission of David Small and W.W. Norton.

Notes

1. Hereafter, we use young adult and YA interchangeably.
2. See Falconer for an analysis of children's novels, including the *Harry Potter* series, as global crossover texts. Beckett provides an overview of crossover texts and the relationship among readership, authors, and the children's literature industry.
3. Susanna Kaysen's *Girl, Interrupted* provides another example of a coming-of-age memoir that crossed the marketing categories of adult/young adult and raised questions about appropriate readership, see Marshall "Borderline" for a more detailed analysis.
4. Small's picture book for young readers, *Imogene's Antlers*, about a young girl who wakes up with antlers on her head works through similar material about a child's body being radically altered and parents who are ill equipped to deal with this change, is a precursor to *Stitches*.

5. Our decision to choose *Stitches* as a case study is the result of an analysis of the representation of adolescence and trauma in the 17th memoirs that received an Alex award from 1998 to 2011.
6. For a critical analysis of the memoir boom and trauma, see Gilmore *Limits* (1–15).
7. For an in-depth discussion of Wertham, the subcommittee hearings, and the CMAA, see Wright.
8. For a recent example, see Gurdon and Alexie's response to her article.
9. The reaction to Small's representation of adolescence and family is similar to Kathryn Harrison's use of adolescence in her controversial memoir *The Kiss*, see Marshall "Disenchantment."

References

American Library Association. <http://www.ala.org/yalsa/bfya/policies>. 30 Jan 2013

Alexie, Sherman. "Sherman Alexie Defends Young Adult Novels With Dark Themes." *Indian Country*, Today Media Network, LLC, 11 Jun. 2011. <http://www. indiancountrytodaymedianetwork.com/2011/06/11/sherman-alexie-defends-young-adult-novels-with-dark-themes-37820>. 15 July 2012

Alice in Wonderland. Clyde Geronimi, Hamilton Luske, and Wilfred Jackson. Walt Disney Company, 1951

Allen, Austin. "A Graphic Memoir of Psychological Abuse." *Bigthink*, Bigthink, 18 Nov. 2009. < http://www.bigthink.com/ideas/17399>. 26 Oct 2012

Allison, Dorothy. *Bastard Out of Carolina*. New York: Dutton, 1992.

Angelou, Maya. *I Know Why the Caged Bird Sings*. New York: Random House, 1969.

Anonymous. *Go Ask Alice*. Englewood Cliffs, NJ: Prentice-Hall, 1971.

Barry, Lynda. *One Hundred Demons*. Seattle: Sasquatch Books, 2002.

Beckett, Sandra L. *Crossover Fiction: Global and Historical Perspectives*. New York: Routledge, 2009.

Berlant, Lauren. *The Queen of America Goes to Washington City: Essays on Sex and Citizenship*. Durham: Duke University Press, 1997.

Caruth, Cathy. *Unclaimed Experience: Trauma, Narrative, and History*. Baltimore: Johns Hopkins University Press, 1996.

Chute, Hillary. *Graphic Women: Live Narrative & Contemporary Comics*. New York: Columbia University Press, 2010.

Corliss, Richard. "Why 'Harry Potter' did a Harry Houdini." *Time.com*, Time, 21 Jul. 2000. <http://www.time.com/time/nation/article/0,8599,50554,00.html>. 24 Oct 2012.

Falconer, Rachel. *The Crossover Novel: Contemporary Children's Fiction and Its Adult Readers*. New York: Routledge, 2009.

Frank, Anne. *The Diary of a Young Girl/Anne Frank*. New York: Globe Book, Co., 1988.

Gilmore, Leigh. "American Neoconfessional: Memoir, Self-Help, and Redemption on Oprah's Couch." *Biography: An Interdisciplinary Quarterly* 33.4 (2010): 657–79.

———. *The Limits of Autobiography: Trauma and Testimony*. Ithaca, NY: Cornell University Press, 2001.

———. "Witnessing *Persepolis*: Comics, Trauma, and Childhood Testimony." In *Graphic Subjects: Critical Essays on Autobiography and Graphic Novels*, edited by Michael A. Chaney. Madison, WI: The University of Wisconsin Press, 2011, 157–63.

Gurdon, Meghan Cox. "Darkness Too Visible." *The Wall Street Journal*. Dow Jones & Company, 04 June 2011. <http://www.online.wsj.com/article/SB100014240527 02303657404576357622592697038.html>. 15 July 2012.

Hinton, S. E. *The Outsiders*. New York: Viking Press, 1967.

Hockett, Jessica. "Rev. of *The Glass Castle: A Memoir* by, Jeannette Walls." *Gifted Child Quarterly* 52.3 (2008): 269–70.

Hogan, Ron, David Small's *Stitches*: YA? Really? OK! *Galleycat*. WebMediaBrands, 14 Oct. 2009. <http://www.mediabistro.com/galleycat/david-smalls-stitches-ya-really-ok_b10257>. 20 Oct 2012

Hunt, Caroline. "Young Adult Literature Evades the Theorists." *Children's Literature Association Quarterly* 21 (1996): 4–11.

Lee, Harper. *To Kill a Mockingbird*. Philadelphia: Lippincott, 1960.

Marshall, Elizabeth. "Borderline Girlhoods: Mental Illness, Adolescence, and Femininity in *Girl, Interrupted*." *Lion and The Unicorn* 30.1 (2006): 117–33.

———. "The Daughter's Disenchantment: Incest As Pedagogy in Fairy Tales and Kathryn Harrison's *The Kiss*." *College English* 66.4 (2004): 395–418.

Nabokov, Vladimir. *Lolita*. Paris: Olympia Press, 1955.

Plath, Sylvia. *The Bell Jar*. London: Faber and Faber, 1966.

Satrapi, Marjane. *Persepolis*. New York: Pantheon, 2003.

Small, David. *Imogene's Antlers*. New York: Crown Publisher's Inc., 1985.

———. "Interview." *Amazon.com*, Amazon.com, n.d. <http://www.amazon.com/Stitches-A-Memoir-David-Small/dp/0393068579>. 5 Nov 2012.

———. *Stitches: A Memoir*. New York: W.W. Norton, 2009.

Springen, Karen. "YA or Not YA?: 'Stitches' Gets NBA Nomination." *Publishersweekly.com*, PWxyz, 15 Oct. 2009. <http://www.publishersweekly.com/pw/by-topic/childrens/childrens-book-news/article/15228-ya-or-not-ya–stitches-gets-nba-nomination-.html>. 26 Jul 2012

St. George, Judith. *So You Want To Be The President?* edited by Illus David Small. New York: Philomel Books, 2000.

Talley, Lee A. "Young Adult." In *Keywords for Children's Literature*, edited by Philip Nel and Lissa Paul. New York: New York University Press, 2011, 228–32.

Tindell, Julia. "A Conversation with Illustrator David Small." *World Literature Today*, The University of Oklahoma, March 2012. <http://www.worldliteraturetoday.com/2012/march/conversation-illustrator-david-small-julia-tindell>. 25 Oct 2012

Trites, Roberta Seelinger. *Disturbing the Universe: Power and Repression in Adolescent Literature*. Iowa City: University of Iowa Press, 2000.

Walls, Jeannette. *The Glass Castle*. New York: Scribner, 2005.

Wiesel, Elie. *Night*. Trans. by Stella Rodway New York: Hill and Wang, 1960.

Weldon, Glen. "The Curious Case of David Small's *Stitches*." *Monkey See: Pop-Culture News and Analysis from NPR*, National Public Radio, 21 Oct. 2009. <http://www.npr.org/blogs/monkeysee/2009/10/the_curious_case_of_david_smal_1.html>. 20 Oct 2012

Wertham, Fredric. *Seduction of the Innocent*. New York: Rinehart, 1954.

Wright, Bradford W. *Comic Book Nation: The Transformation of Youth Culture in America*. Baltimore: Johns Hopkins University Press, 2001.

Yang, Gene Luen. *American Born Chinese*. NY: First Second, 2006.

Kylie Cardell and Kate Douglas

"INDECENT EXPOSURE? MARGAUX FRAGOSO AND THE LIMITS OF ABUSE MEMOIR"

In 2011, North American creative writing graduate Margaux Fragoso published her first book, a memoir titled Tiger, Tiger. *Detailing the author's childhood sexual "relationship" with a 57-year-old man, the memoir was highly controversial. In critical receptions of the memoir, three themes recurred: a sense that it exceeds the limits of appropriate representation, unease with Fragoso bringing child abuse into a stylized literary space, and the question "why do we need to read this story" — a view that it is potentially damaging for readers to consume such narratives. In this paper, we explore the reception of* Tiger, Tiger *and we argue the text reveals how memoir remains lodged in an uneasy relationship to ideals of public good (dictated by critics and reviewers) versus the needs and ethics of individual representation.*

The representation of "difficult" childhoods has been a staple of American memoir in the 1990s and 2000s — Mary Karr, Frank McCourt, and Dave Pelzer are just a few of the bestselling authors who have gained fame and notoriety publishing accounts of childhood abuse or neglect (Douglas; Gilmore, *Limits*). More specifically, memoirs of youthful sexuality and sexual abuse, such as Kathryn Harrison's *The Kiss* and Augusten Burroughs's *Running with Scissors* have emerged to provide insights and make cultural interventions.

As texts that deal with particularly difficult and unsettling personal experiences, some of these memoirs focus on the individual as the site of trauma and the personal struggle toward healing, other memoirs engage in political and social debates on topics of public importance — for instance, around gender or class. A memoir's focus — whether (inwards) on personal pain or (outward) on broader social inequality — has become a particular point of scrutiny when it comes to critiquing memoir's cultural value. Now that memoir has become so well established, these texts confront different discourses and sets of expectations regarding what memoirs are "for." Memoirs that represent childhood sexuality and sexual trauma in particular seem to feed anxiety about what constitutes an acceptable, public, or literary representation of taboo topics, and they draw attention to the complex cultural investments in memoir, which manifest in its reception contexts.

In this paper, we analyse the reception of *Tiger, Tiger*, a controversial 2011 memoir by the U.S. author Margaux Fragoso, to consider what this reveals about memoir's relationship to public discourse on childhood sexual abuse. In doing so, we engage with a dominant though subjective question that has defined critical and other responses to this text: as a representation of childhood sexual trauma, what insights or perspectives does Fragoso's memoir bring to public discussion of childhood sexual abuse? Critics of the work point directly to this question and many critical responses to the book have been vehemently negative.[1] Fragoso's memoir, an account of the author's childhood sexual "relationship" with a 57-year-old man, like other similar memoirs before it, is treated with suspicion by critics who seem increasingly wary that the post-"memoir boom" memoir trades in trauma – sensationally exploiting its subject for material or personal gain. In a review of the book, Diski, herself the author of a memoir of childhood domestic violence, frames just such an approach:

> Is the book, which is called a memoir, "true"? Is it excessively explicit and prurient? Is it, as many have suggested, Lolita's version of *Lolita*? Is it therapy for the writer? Is it reasonable to publish such an account on the grounds that it will educate the public about the complex relationship between paedophiles and their victims? Or is it published, as the publicity suggests, for "talk-about-ability," and therefore about making Penguin's accountants happy? (no page)

Three themes recur in the reception of this memoir: a sense that it exceeds the limits of appropriate representation, unease with Fragoso bringing child abuse into a stylized literary space, and the question "why do we need to read this story?" – the view that it is potentially damaging for readers to consume such narratives. These critical responses are anticipated within *Tiger, Tiger* – which attempts to find an appropriate language and style, an aesthetic or poetics, for representing childhood experience, and reflects an awareness of the cultural field within which this text emerges. In this article, we explore how the complex and often aggressively negative reception surrounding *Tiger, Tiger* seems to reveal the uncertain position of memoir as it straddles literary/artistic and (often) psychological or sociological discourses.[2] We argue that memoir does not have to contain overt political or sociological references to be politically conscious or powerful (although this is perhaps what critics have come to expect from memoirs). Instead of reading Fragoso's stylized representation of abuse as distasteful and exploitative, we suggest a different reading: that this is a strategic means for Fragoso to bring abuse into the public domain, to confront her experiences and to challenge and implicate readers into understanding.

"What is the point of reading this memoir?"[3] Child abuse and memoir in the 2000s

In March 2011, the UK's *Guardian/Observer* ran a feature titled "*Tiger, Tiger*: What is the point of reading this memoir of abuse?" The memoir in question belonged to first-time author Fragoso, a recent creative writing Ph.D. graduate. In this feature, a writer, a psychologist, and a survivor each give their "verdict" on "the most controversial book of the year." How does she represent her childhood sexual abuse? Does this representation "fit" within established paradigms for representing abuse, or does Fragoso push the limits of representation toward something taboo?[4] The assumption underlying this and many other reviews of *Tiger, Tiger* is that when it comes to representing child abuse, lines of acceptable representation have been drawn and are conventionally agreed upon. This is a reasonable assumption: one only has to look at the outpouring of child abuse memoirs, particularly over the past 20 years to see these conventions at work. There are well-worn narrative templates, most of which present particular recovery arcs, for example, memoirs that reflect therapeutic discourse (the writing cure) or memoirs in the form of *Bildungsroman* in which education or cultural pursuits save the author. These conventions respond to broader historical and cultural norms for considering and representing child sexual abuse (for example, what is circulated via medical, legal and therapeutic discourses, and within news media and in film and television). But of course, these conventions have not dulled the presence of texts that have tested the moral boundaries of acceptable representation in relation to child sexual abuse. Fictional films such as *The Woodsman* (2004) and *Little Children* (2006) offer complex and thus controversial representations of pedophiles.

However, memoir circulates within a different economy to fiction, and "truth" is the key compact between reader and writer in the genre. To put it simply, readers have expectations of memoir that they do not necessarily have for fiction. Memoirs of child abuse are offered as "truth" and this adds another layer of confrontation: we imagine that the events represented actually did happen and the author of the text offers testimony to their suffering and survival. But when it comes to writing about personal trauma, there are many different modes of representation. For example, Couser observes the prevalence and potency of what he calls the "comic plot," in which the "defining element [. . .] is that it ends well for the protagonist" (44). Memoirs of survival, in which the writer who endures to produce the narrative account becomes part of the arc, fits the rhetoric of the happy ending that Couser observes in memoir: "we all like to think we are better – or better off-than we once were. We dislike telling stories that turn out badly for us. It may be 'human' to do so" (45). Similarly, identifying what she calls the "American neoconfessional," Gilmore observes a shift to,

> stories of personal trauma with happy endings [that] direct the sympathy that autobiography can mobilize away from nonnormative life narrative and toward life writing that allows readers to experience compassion for similar others. (660–1)

As Gilmore observes, the rise of popular memoir has brought with it a celebration of particular types of narratives: neoliberal redemption narratives which focus on the individual recovery at the expense of more complex representations of survivors and perpetrators, located within complex historical conditions. This is not to say that these more complex narratives do not circulate, but they are often overshadowed by the mass circulation of similarly styled redemption and recovery narratives. The dominance of certain scripts for representing traumatic experience in particular means that authors who offer controversial representations may be accused of also crossing out of the frame of life narrative as a whole. Gilmore says:

> Free to compel certain kinds of storylines, to lionize and demand writers who succeed in varying degrees to produce normative stories, and to curtail discussion about the more volatile elements of confessional speech, audiences consume life

story with an emerging set of conventions about veracity, authenticity, and autobiographical narrative. (660)

This context is important when reading a memoir like Fragoso's, which emerges from, and responds to these anxieties and insistencies. Moreover, *Tiger, Tiger*, an examination of damaging boundary-crossing, in itself contests and challenges the dominant script, offering an uncomfortable point of view and eliciting critical consternation: even though there are memoirs which offer graphic representations of child abuse, there are many fewer memoirs which spend time representing abusers or considering their point of view (Douglas 146–9). This is a primary complaint about Fragoso's memoir: Fragoso gives too much "air time" to her abuser. But there are other complaints too and these criticisms of *Tiger, Tiger* reveal that there are conventions for and limits of representing and defining child sexual abuse in contemporary memoir. They provide a window into memoir's discursive functions: what good can memoir do/what good is it expected to do (according to cultural critics) and what harm can it do (when it comes to representing child sexual abuse?). The investment in memoir's representations also reveals something of memoir's perceived agency – as culturally influential and engaged in broader constructions of meaning. A tension here, then, is how we define and measure what sorts of representations within memoir are considered politically significant or as doing important cultural work.

"[This] is not a straightforward misery memoir…"[5] Fragoso's *Tiger, Tiger*

Tiger, Tiger, published by Penguin and "blurbed" by Alice Sebold, has since been sold to over 20 countries and was described as 2011s "most hyped memoir" (Cooke, James, Anon no page).[6] Yang calls the memoir a "publisher's dream" because it is a memoir of extremity (no page). This memoir follows a significant recent tradition of memoirs about child abuse, where it seems as though each one "ups the ante" on what had been published previously.[7] Yang describes *Tiger, Tiger* as the "*ne plus ultra* of the genre – the thing that is more like the thing that it is than any other thing can ever hope to be" (no page). But Fragoso's is not a simple confession and recovery narrative. For example, Fragoso is careful to explain and implicate her family's class and cultural background in her trauma. The memoir details her childhood poverty, her witnessing of domestic violence, her mother's mental illness and neglectful parenting, and her father's similarly self-absorbed unavailability, before showing her childhood sexual exploitation. It is a highly confronting memoir, containing many graphic descriptions of pedophilia and detailing the young Margaux's complex emotional responses to this abuse.

Tiger, Tiger is Fragoso's account of her sexual relationship with a middle-aged man, Peter Curran. Beginning when Fragoso was 7 years old, the relationship lasted 15 years, until Curran's suicide at age 66. This event prompted Fragoso to write her memoir:

Hoping to make sense of what happened, I began drafting my life story. And even during times when I hadn't worked on it, when it sat on a shelf in my closet, I felt its presence in the despair that comes precisely at two in the afternoon, which was the time Peter would pick me up and take me for rides; in the despair again at five p.m., when I would read to him, head on his chest; at seven p.m., when he would hold me; in the despair again at nine p.m., when we would go for our night ride, starting at Boulevard East in Weehawken, to River Road, down to the Royal Cliffs Diner, where I would buy a cup of coffee with precisely seven sugars and lots of cream, and a bread pudding with whipped cream and raisins, or rice pudding if he wanted a change. (3)

The most striking and frequently commented on aspect of the memoir is that Fragoso represents her youthful self in love with Curran. Though also describing herself as being under Curran's manipulative spell, the text leads the reader to understand Curran's complex controlling abuse of Fragoso through its unrelenting, up-close-and-personal narrativization of his actions from the child Margaux's point of view. It is a shocking and very disturbing relationship, and a difficult representation to read.[8] Yet the experience Fragoso represents reflects experiences in the real world – and they are not limited to Fragoso. As Lovrod contends, narratives of child abuse are confronting because they disrupt conventional cultural images of what childhood is and should be: "The appearance of survivor narratives [. . .] of an experience that has long been both denied by and sanctioned within Western culture, necessarily fractures received constructions of childhood" (23). *Tiger, Tiger* is an uncomfortable read but it is not a romanticized representation of pedophilia; such a reading of the text is extremely limited and imagines child abuse to be a homogenous experience. However, Fragoso's does not fit the expected template: it is a complex narrative construction precisely because it attempts to show the child's limited, naive interpretation of the relationship with her abuser.

Fragoso introduces the complexities of childhood sexuality and disempowerment from the outset in the book's paratextual matter. In the author's biographical note, on the inside cover, Fragoso juxtaposes her childhood self with the adult author self in writing:

Margaux Fragoso grew up in Union City, New Jersey. At seven years old, she loved the red gumballs that came from gumball machines but left the blues and greens; later, she loved Madonna and still later Nirvana. She still loves dogs and Kurt Cobain, Margaux is happily married with one child and is currently writing full-time. *Tiger, Tiger* is being published in twenty-two countries.[9]

Author biographies conform to particular templates (most likely dictated by editors and publishers) but there is something destabilizing about Fragoso's here. Fragoso moves away from standard statements about family background and educational history to mention, instead, something of the simple minutiae of her childhood. In doing so, Fragoso reminds us that her childhood was not conventional, and in writing about gumballs, dogs, and her favorite singers, Fragoso recasts her childhood in light of fonder memories. But there is also a discomforting infantilization of the adult self in these statements which flags to the reader the ongoing legacies of Fragoso's lost childhood. At the end of the bio we learn that Fragoso has survived her childhood, is married, and has a child and a successful book.[10] Although this is comforting (and perhaps functions to authorize Fragoso as a survivor and thus it is worth reading her story), it is awkwardly placed alongside the earlier, fraught symbolism.

Tiger, Tiger has been widely reviewed by major news and cultural publications. To say that this memoir received a mixed reception is an understatement. This is perhaps not surprising in light of the fact that this is a book about a vulnerable, neglected child who is abused by a pedophile. Such texts almost always elicit impassioned responses from adults wanting to affirm culture's strong position on child abuse, and in recognition of adults' role in protecting children. But further, these passionate responses to the memoir are written by the gatekeepers of literature, offer (at times) judgement, social commentary, personal reflection, and aesthetic review of the memoir. As previously suggested, three themes recur in these reviews. The first of these themes is that Fragoso is "A survivor [who] tests the boundaries of just how far a memoir of child abuse can go" (Yang no page). Critics have branded Fragoso's memoir as one that transgresses the limits of acceptable representation. This is a common criticism of memoir; the thresholds for what should be represented in memoir respond to cultural norms regarding what it is possible to say at different historical moments. When it comes to narratives of trauma, as Gilmore writes, "the choreography of scandal is by now familiar": a "chorus" of critics "bemoaning how narcissistic memoirists are destroying culture" ("American Neoconfessional" 657).

But as Haaken argues, society has always been resistant to acknowledging the "extent and scope of child abuse" (*Pillar of Salt* 4) and this resistance is central to understanding the reception of Fragoso's memoir. Fragoso's is an assertive representation – its complexities defy the idea of simple heroes and villains – and *Tiger, Tiger* demands an acknowledgement of the sorts of difficult experiences Fragoso represents. In doing so, Fragoso becomes part of a wider feminist project for making sexual abuse more visible within culture.[11] For Kitzinger, the articulation of child sexual abuse is a "complex process" of recognition, naming, and articulation which shifts with changing cultural contexts (86). She considers the role that feminist memoir has played in bringing the testimony of survivors into the public domain. But, as Kitzinger argues, there's a downside to visibility. For example, child sexual abuse narratives can be used in within cultural texts to "titillate and fascinate" (87). Circulating and receiving these narratives is a complex act. As we have suggested with Fragoso, representations of child sexual abuse within culture do not manifest in simple "good/bad" paradigms, they cannot always fit redemptive neoliberal arcs. These are products of the specific culture and experience from which they derive and must be inevitably interpreted within subjective, complex frameworks.

In light of this, the sustained criticism of Fragoso's memoir seems overly crude. Yang, in the *New York Magazine*, describes the memoir as "perhaps the most indecent thing published in any major book of the last decade" (no page). The memoir contains "every last detail" of Fragoso's childhood abuse by a pedophile Peter Curran, "it delivers a stomach-churning kind of paedophile porn" (Bradbury no page), it is "cringe-makingly titillating" (Bradbury no page), "eroticizes paedophilia" (Kois no page), and is "disturbing and vulgar" (Liem no page). According the Rachel Cooke's in the *Guardian / Observer* article, Fragoso is

> determined to spare us absolutely nothing [. . .] a sign of her bravery? I'm not sure. It felt as blank as pornography to me – and the more it went on, the more convinced I was that only a voyeur or a pervert could admire it. (Cooke, James, and Anon, no page)

And the anonymous survivor who forms the *Guardian / Observer* reviewing triad with Cooke and James writes:

Who is it written for? It is truly a horrible read [...] the sensationalism will undoubtedly sell many copies.

The real question is whether this book is necessary [...] the cynic in me can't help but feel it was, in part, published to capitalise on the inevitable controversy, thereby continuing the cycle of exploitation. (no page)

The idea of a memoir "without limits" is fascinating because memoir, by its form, has to impose boundaries – it has to give a story shape. So, the issue then is moral boundaries – the judgment being that Fragoso, in exploring the consequences of broken taboo in her own life, has somehow also ventured into the taboo in her choices in writing *Tiger, Tiger*. This, in turn, raises questions: Who are the gatekeepers of what it is morally acceptable to write about in life narrative? And what is it about Fragoso's memoir that renders her description of her child abuse so unpalatable? In the reviews above, it seems that the "problem" relates more to the way that the subject is presented than the subject itself. How do we distinguish between a text that is radical and confrontational in its representations and a memoir that exploits its subject? Art and culture have traditionally been mandated to unsettle the reader or audience – so, context is important here. Does Fragoso's position, in a popular, or perhaps middlebrow, literary form such as memoir render her more vulnerable to accusations of sensationalism and exploitation than being applauded for her artistic, cultural agitation? The boundaries and thus the rules are different for memoir in comparison with "high art." Significantly, Fragoso does not conform to the reserved, circumspect, confession, and redemption script that reviewers have come to expect from memoir.[12] Straying from the script incurs penalties. Gilmore reminds us that the "American neoconfessional" template has become so pervasive for memoir that it "makes it increasingly difficult for [...] counter-confessional and redemption-wary discourse of self-representation to gain traction, as critical energies are recruited to the task of judgment" (658). It is difficult for Fragoso's memoir, or other similar popular/middlebrow memoirs, to engage in cultural work, to test an appropriate literary aesthetic for representing trauma, when critics are part of the project of "curtail[ing] discussion about the more volatile elements of confessional speech" (Gilmore, "American Neoconfessional" 660).[13]

The second theme to (perhaps paradoxically) emerge in criticism of *Tiger, Tiger* is the notion that representations of trauma cannot or should not be "literary." Yang describes Fragoso's memoir as "an unstable mixture of bildungsroman, dirty realism, and child pornography" (no page). Fragoso's is a literary presentation of child abuse which is highly aestheticized and largely ambiguous. Yang refers to her "pitiless precision" (no page), Bradbury writes: "Fragoso's book is not a straightforward misery memoir, in the sense of being a simply written account of abuse, but an intensely artful literary creation we are told she worked on while she was a creative writing student" (no page). Diski too pronounces judgement based on the memoir's literary-or-not status: "Having a story to tell isn't really enough to justify a book beyond a tabloid existence. And this story is especially dependent on the manner in which it is told" (no page).

It is interesting to consider why critics are so surprised or offended by Fragoso's literary choices in the rendering of her experience. One of the complex tensions at play here is between the articulation of trauma and assumptions about art. Writers have long been searching for appropriate language and style to represent and understand abuse. As Lovrod writes, a survivor narrative:

> inscribes the experience of a particular child's body in relation to adult bodies, to language, literature, and culture. The body of each child has been isolated as the site of an abuse of cultural power. The production of a record of the event situates its reader as a medium through which culture is forced to confront its own complicity. While any such reading is necessarily conflicted and difficult, none is more so than for the survivor who reads or translates a personally damaging and culturally denied event into language. The writer as reader of her or his own experience seeks to build a bridge between what Virginia Woolf describes as the violent shocks for which there have been no words and the reader of the survivor narrative so that the process of mediation between abuse and culture may proceed toward validation of the experience and transformation of the culture. (23)

Fragoso has justified her style by suggesting that she attempts to portray the "fantastic type of reality" that comes with being trapped by a pedophile. But for Bradbury there is an uneasy "fit" between the poetics of writing and the experiences Fragoso narratives: "While it details the sexual acts themselves – and no one would suggest they should be edited out of a work of this kind – these moments are overpowered by the weight of the poetic language they are forced to bear" (no page). Bradbury here suggests that Fragoso might have positioned her work as fiction (that her style is more appropriate to fiction). Diski, commenting unfavorably on Fragoso's stylistic technique in the memoir, states: "It's not surprising that people who expect a memoir to tell them documentary fact, or people who require some kind of truth in novels, have problems with the book" (no page). Such responses are telling in that they suggest a critical consensus, around this text at least, that suggest memoir is not conventionally literary (which of course it is), and that elements of style can only "burden" memoir.

Fragoso's narrative and poetic choices come under heavy scrutiny in a representation that challenges (and makes visible) current assumptions about how survivors of childhood abuse should speak. For example, there is an incident in *Tiger, Tiger* where Curran persuades the 8-year-old Margaux to fellate him. During the act, Margaux thinks of a fairytale, which becomes an allegory for what is happening to her.[14] The narrative then follows Margaux's stream-of-consciousness through her memory of the tale as the child tries to distract herself from the action in the present (95). Through this and in many other scenes, the reader is reminded that Curran is a highly dangerous, highly manipulative character who wears Margaux down into submission. Margaux constantly asserts her "maturity" but, the narrative retrospectively rebuts this claim. It is a cleverly structured, provocative narration; the child subject appears in-the-moment, her story is from her state of vulnerability, positioning the reader as the child's confidant and protector. For the reader, it is a particularly uncomfortable and destabilizing position, that of belated witness, and a position from which nothing can be done to protect the young Margaux.[15]

In light of this, the third theme emerging from criticism of *Tiger, Tiger* is perhaps predictable: the notion that, as Yang posits, "Many readers will find too much to bear" (no page). For example, Yang writes,

A scene in which an 8-year-old Fragoso begs to be spared the oral-genital contact that Curran is urging upon her is perhaps the most indecent thing published in any major book of the last decade. It is executed with remorseless candor that cannot fail to sear itself into the memory of whoever reads it. . .Many who have been thus seared will regret having witnessed what no person should have to see. Others will delight in her audacity for a range of savory and unsavoury motives. (no page)

Tiger, Tiger is criticized because it brings far too much confrontational material into the public domain: Bradbury writes that Fragoso "seems to delight in thrilling the reader" and adds, "The deliberately provocative cover line – 'We were friends, soul mates and lovers. I was seven. He was 51' – is set against an alluring, slightly wistful author photograph. And this effect continues within the pages" (Cooke, James, and Anon, no page).

If you want to know more about Margaux and Peter's 15-year relationship – conducted in full view of a number of perfectly sentient adults, it ended only when Peter killed himself by jumping off a cliff – then you should head out to your local bookstore and reserve a copy of *Tiger, Tiger* [. . .] this is a book, its publisher insists, which 'has to be talked about.' But first, have a think, How *much* more do you want to know? Or, to put it another way, how much more can you take? (no page)

In his contribution, Oliver James writes: "Fragoso offers us an undigested fact. In being so frank, perhaps she feels relief. But she simply transfers the damaged feeling from herself to the reader" (Cooke, James and Anon, no page).

In these reviews there is an assumption that there is a singular reading position from which to access this text; the reader will necessarily be emotionally damaged from reading *Tiger, Tiger*. Another way to look at this is that the memoir is highly confrontational, asking the reader to face up to a serious social problem. *Tiger, Tiger* opens up the possibility of better knowing a pedophile as much as it offers contact with a survivor and this is an uncomfortable proposition. For example, Fragoso asks the reader to witness Peter Curran, and while he is clearly represented as a manipulative sexual predator, he is not a one-dimensional character. Fragoso details his manipulations and also his complexities (he was abused as a child, for example). Fragoso gives Curran a personal history, a relationship and work history. Fragoso could have offered a much less complete representation of Cullen, and she could have glossed over her own strong, fraught and desperate affections toward him. In a post-"memoir boom" era, it might be argued that Fragoso is simply pushing the envelope: she knows what has gone before and she is in the memoir game to sensationally trade on her past. But the memoir does not read this way because Fragoso is careful to open up histories and contexts for the characters and events. As Harrison writes:

To bear witness to a numbingly long series of violations of a child by a man who has honed his wickedness for decades is not more pleasant than it sounds. As a society we are energetically opposed to sexual abuse; as individuals most of us shy away from investigating [. . .] we defend cowardice by calling it discretion [. . .] Maybe a book like *Tiger, Tiger* can help us be a little braver. ("The Man who Molested Me" no page)

Harrison's proposition that *Tiger, Tiger* offers a mandate to the reader is significant. It acknowledges that society more broadly is keen (rightly) to condemn pedophilia, but less willing to "investigate," or look closely at what happens in such circumstances. Harrison asks "us" (the reader) to be "braver" and to consider how the act of reading a book like *Tiger, Tiger* might be a catalyst for not only bearing witness to such narratives and experiences more generally but also for identifying how such manipulation unfolds in the community: "because we glance away from crimes – abominations – prevented only by vigilance, the most disheartening aspect of this story is sickeningly familiar" ("The Man Who Molested Me" no page).

Fragoso's memoir reflects an attempt to understand and share a story that often, dangerously, remains untold. The memoir is a deeply self-conscious one and Fragoso (particularly in the memoir's prologue) posits that her account should and will encourage an understanding of how she came to be abused by Peter Curran:

> In one of his suicide notes to me, Peter suggested that I write a memoir about our lives together, which was ironic. Our world had been permitted only by secrecy surrounding it; had you taken away our lies and codes and looks and symbols and haunts, you would have taken everything; and had you done that when I was twenty or fifteen or twelve, I might have killed myself and *you* wouldn't get to look into this tiny island that existed only through its lies and codes and looks and symbols and haunts. All these secret things together built a supreme master key (4). (emphasis added)

Two observations are particularly significant here: first the way in which Fragoso addresses the reader and thus implicates him/her in the events and their interpretation and second the symbolism of the key. Here, Fragoso asserts directly, the role of memoir. Memoir, retrospectively told, employing literary tools such as powerful language, symbolism, and address, for instance, has the power to demystify and promote understanding of child abuse and pedophilia.

Tiger, Tiger is an uncomfortable text precisely because it chooses to render its pedophile character as human and multi-dimensional while it also attempts to shed light on his motivations and the predicament of the child caught within. Fragoso writes,

> spending time with a pedophile can be like a drug high [...] it's as if the pedophile lives in a fantastic type of reality, and that fantasticness infects everything. Kind of like they're children themselves, only full of knowledge that children don't have. Their imaginations are stronger than kids' and they can build realities that small kids would never be able to dream up. They can make the child's world... ecstatic somehow. And when it's over, for people who've been through this, it's like coming off heroin and, for years, they can't stop chasing the ghost of how it felt [...] like the earth is scorched and the grass won't grow back. (5)

Fragoso thus explains her childhood attraction to Curran in light of his child-like qualities, "he had so much energy and brightness that he didn't seem old. He didn't even seem adult in the sense of that natural separateness adults have from children" (17). As Fragoso maps Curran's obsession, the reader is left to feel increasingly uncomfortable perhaps because, as readers we may not want to understand why pedophiles act the way that they do or why their victims might respond in such a way as Fragoso does. *Tiger, Tiger* confronts the reader with Curran's gradual manipulation and grooming of the child Margaux over many years. In presenting her "love" for Curran, Fragoso represents how the successful manipulation childhood naïveté works. For example, at eight and sensing a rival for her affections, Fragoso constructs her childhood imaginings, "It was *me* who had the potential to be his wife and the mother of his children, because I was already mature for my age" (72). And again, the reader is placed in a position of knowledge and in turn, discomfort.

Conclusion

One of the primary ways that we come to understand memoir – what it is and what its cultural functions are – is via reception contexts. Professional critics and scholars, in their writings about memoirs, shape the meaning of these memoirs for readers; they also set limits for representation, something made explicit in the reception of trauma memoir in particular. Thus, a significant responsibility comes with this critical engagement. In this paper we have explored some of the critical responses to Fragoso's childhood trauma memoir, *Tiger, Tiger*, and in doing so have suggested the implications of these readings and considered the ways that this (and perhaps also memoirs like it) test the limits of trauma representation. We have challenged these critics and highlighted the limits of the tropes through which this memoir is read. For example, critics of Fragoso are concerned about her memoir's damaging effects on readers, and are also reporting unease with memoir giving trauma an aesthetic. They are anxious about "purity and danger" (Gilmore, *Limits* 2), setting themselves the task of policing where memoir seems to veer too close to the techniques of fiction, citing a moral gatekeeping function as authority for their judgement and the rationale for silencing nonnormative stories of abuse and suffering. These critics see *Tiger, Tiger* as a memoir characterized by sensationalism and provocation, a text that readers might need to be protected from, that "lowers" the tone of literary memoir even as they struggle to identify how the literary functions in this context. "*Lolita* it isn't" says Diski:

> With all its explicit sex, melodramatic conversations and dogged chronological detail, *Tiger, Tiger*, is as dreary a read as soft porn. It will titillate paedophiles and fantasists, but for most people reading it will have the dismal, lowering effect of either reality TV or a very bad novel. (no page)

Moreover, and as a literary text, *Tiger, Tiger* does not offer the kinds of redemptive or confessional arcs that it seems critics want and this means that conservative commentators are disorientated by what is the *good* here. That is, it is not enough that the trauma survivor find words to articulate their experience, they must do so in a way that satisfies the dominant cultural scripts of the time. In the turn to validate only those narratives that "allows readers to experience compassion for similar others" (Gilmore, "American Neoconfessional" 661), memoirs that offer more complex, more ambivalent examples of individual experience, risk being silenced. The specificity and potential of memoir as a vehicle for exploring complex individual histories gives way to consolatory universals – "Is it a good book?" asks Diski, responding to her own question: "It isn't a good book if it doesn't convince, but that would be a test of good fiction and good non-fiction" (no page). When the primary criteria for a memoir is whether or not a reader should subject themselves to the narrative, it is clear that a significant shift has occurred and that the "good of memoir" is no longer simply lodged in its accessibility to diverse voices but has been commodified such that its good must benefit the reader as consumer. Fragoso's explication of her circumstances is refracted through its potential as a "good read," with critics dictating that trauma must be told simply, unpoetically, and with a clear moral arc. Gilmore writes:

> I urge a pause in the American neoconfessional moment to consider whether certain critical responses are more likely to preserve or restrict the cultural space of self-representation before self-help absorbs memoir [...] I want to encourage a broadening of the ethical frame to include ambivalent pleasures and mixed motives, to engage life writing judged polluted by lies, contaminated by exhibitionism, dominated by unsavory characters [...] and to do so in a way that interrupts the reproduction and redemption by returning to the histories that exceed this market. (674)

In this article, we have tried to show an important link between Fragoso's provocations, her literary aesthetic, and the memoir's cultural-political agency. *Tiger, Tiger* establishes a relationship to other public discourses on childhood sexual abuse by offering a more complex rendering of the child and perpetrator and it shows how memoir (and indeed other creative, cultural forms) has the potential to reveal that the experience of trauma is not uniform and is not defined by neoliberal recovery narratives and simple representations of heroes and villains. Fragoso challenges the reader to witness her particular and specific account; her subjective experience is framed through the stylized language of her memoir. Thus memoir can show a diversity of experiences and negotiate and shape these experiences as it brings them into the public domain, though not without challenge.

Acknowledgements

Many thanks to Tully Barnett, Rocio Davis, Leigh Gilmore, Pamela Graham, Leena Kurvet-Kaossar, Claire Lynch, Emma Maguire, Anna Poletti, and Julie Rak for their insightful feedback on this work-in-progress.

Notes

1. We examined many reviews of *Tiger, Tiger* available on the web. Although, some reviews praised the memoir (for example, Hampson; Harrison; Jackson; Kois; Liem; and Tkacik), an equal number or more expressed strongly negative responses to the text (Bradbury; Bywater; Cooke, James, and Anon; Diski; Mackenzie, Young – to name a few examples).
2. Of course it is important to note that reviews influence the content of other reviews. It is perhaps difficult, once a dominant view has emerged, for reviewers to "go against

the grain" of dominant views (unless you are a memoirist/author like Kathryn Harrison or Jenny Diski, who is not bound by the same conventions).

3. Cooke, James and Anon no page.

4. The evaluative tone of the article, encapsulated in its titular question, frames the act of reading as one fraught with potential trauma and pain and the review article presents itself as a kind of intervention, a justification or warning for the confronting material in the memoir. Such a response raises difficult questions around what we might think as an ethics of memoir, and especially in relation to thinking about whom (and what) is memoir for. Indeed, the assumption underlying this and many other reviews of *Tiger, Tiger* is that memoir is for its readers: this is a discernible shift from how critics have theorized life writing in the past, and particularly in relation to testimonial or other kinds of narratives involving the disclosure of private individual trauma or pain, where responsibility and listening on behalf of the reader, positioned as a belated witness, have been considered of paramount importance. A shift to readers of memoir (and to the affect of their reading experience) is congruent to a contemporary context where life narrative has powerful cultural capital as a marketable commodity.

5. Bradbury no page.

6. The choice of "blurbers" is always significant as a hint to the reader that this new memoir may be like the blurber's. In this instance, the choice of Sebold is highly significant. Sebold is best known for her prize-winning, critically acclaimed bestseller *The Lovely Bones* (2002) but also for her memoir *Lucky* (1999). In both texts, Sebold represents sexual abuse.

7. See Douglas 110–3.

8. For example, Fragoso describes it as a "relationship", in her prologue:

> I started writing this book in the summer after the death of Peter Curran, whom I met when I was seven and had a relationship with for fifteen years, right up until he committed suicide at the age of sixty-six. (3)

9. Penguin paperback edition, 2011.

10. As Douglas has argued elsewhere, such statements function as plot spoilers in memoir (70).

11. For example, Kitzinger writes of how the media has "encouraged the formation and expression of private identities around previously fragmented and silenced experience. It helped sexual abuse, particularly incest, to enter public discourse." (86)

12. Douglas talks about this elsewhere,

> We readers might be forgiven for believing that these narratives of resilience and forgiveness are more broadly representative of the ways in which people remember and write about their traumatic childhoods, rather than considering these autobiographies as idealized templates that prescribe the ways in which traumatic childhood can be recalled and written about. (74)

13. It is also important to note that book reviewing is a discourse and reviewers often write in light of, or in response to, each other's reviews. Once a few negative reviews enter the public sphere, it can be difficult for reception to shift radically beyond this.

14. The "bad mousie" keeps coming back no matter how many times the girl and her family try and get rid of him (95).

15. Haaken and Reavy makes an intriguing statement about the role of narrative in memory and the significance of non-literal storytelling in narrativizing abuse:

Focussing on the narrative structure of memory and the social uses of stories, rather than on their veridical truth context does run the risk of downplaying the importance of factual claims. But in recognizing how victim and perpetrator images inhabit the human psyche in complicated ways, a richer realm of self-understandings unfolds than if we focus narrowly on factual claims alone. Once stories acquire social symbolic meaning and go beyond literal representation of past events, they also are open to multiple psychological and social uses [...] women [...] deserve the freedom to explore – to both create and discover – the dynamic flux that constitutes personal identity and the contours of history itself. (*Memory Matters* 228)

References

Bradbury, Lorna. "Review of *Tiger, Tiger* by Margaux Fragoso." *The Telegraph*, 22 Mar. 2011. 31 May 2012 <http://www.telegraph.co.uk/culture/books/bookreviews/8388282/Tiger-Tiger-by-Margaux-Fragoso.html>

Burroughs, Augusten. *Running With Scissors*. London: Picador, 2002.

Bywater, Michael. "Why this Real-Life Lolita has Nothing to Tell Us." *The Week*, 29 Mar. 2011. 23 Sept. 2012 <http://www.theweek.co.uk/news-opinion/6681/why-real-life-lolita-has-nothing-tell-us#>

Cooke, Rachel, Oliver James, and Anon. "Tiger, Tiger: What is the Point of Reading this Memoir of Abuse?" *The Guardian*, 27 Mar. 2011. 31 May 2012 <http://www.guardian.co.uk/commentisfree/2011/mar/27/debate-tiger-tiger-book>

Couser, G. Thomas. *Memoir: An Introduction*. Oxford: Oxford UP, 2012.

Diski, Jenny. "*Tiger, Tiger* by Margaux Fragoso: This Memoir Somehow Manages to Makes its Controversial Subject Matter Dreary." *The Guardian*, 9 Apr. 2011. 12 Dec. 2012 <http://www.guardian.co.uk/books/2011/apr/10/tiger-tiger-margaux-fragoso-review>

Douglas, Kate. *Contesting Childhood: Autobiography, Trauma and Memory*. New Brunswick: Rutgers, 2010.

Gilmore, Leigh. *The Limits of Autobiography: Trauma and Testimony*. Ithaca, NY: Cornell, 2001.

———. "American Neoconfessional: Memoir, Self-Help and Redemption on Oprah's Couch." *Biography* 33.4 (2010): 657–79.

Haaken, Janice. *Pillar of Salt: Gender, Memory and the Perils of Looking Back*. New Brunswick: Rutgers, 2000.

Haaken, Janice and Paula, Reavy, eds. *Memory Matters: Contests for Understanding Sexual Abuse Recollections*. London: Routledge, 2010.

Hampson, Sarah. "Deconstructing the Monster: Margaux Fragoso's Memoir of Abuse." *The Globe and Mail*, 23 Aug. 2012. 23 Sept. 2012 <http://m.theglobeandmail.com/life/family-and-relationships/deconstructing-the-monster-margaux-fragosos-memoir-of-abuse/article1927271/?service=mobile>

Harrison, Kathryn. *The Kiss*. New York: Random House, 1997.

———. "The Man Who Molested Me." *The New York Times*, 4 Mar. 2011. 31 May 2012 <http://www.nytimes.com/2011/03/06/books/review/Harrison-t.html?_r=1&pagewanted=all>

Jackson, Marni. "Fearful Asymmertry. Review of *Tiger, Tiger* by Margaux Fragoso." *The Globe and Mail*, 4 Mar. 2011. 31 May 2012 <http://m.theglobeandmail.com/arts/books-and-media/tiger-tiger-by-margaux-fragoso/article570038/?service=mobile>

Kitzinger, Jenny. "Transformations of Public and Private Knowledge: Audience Reception, Feminism and the Experience of Childhood Sexual Abuse." In *Memory Matters: Contests for Understanding Sexual Abuse Recollections*, edited by Janice Haaken and Paula Reavy. London: Routledge, 2010, 86–104.

Kois, Dan. "A Clinical, Searing Memoir of Abuse in 'Tiger, Tiger'." *NPR*, 3 Mar. 2011. 31 May 2012 <http://www.npr.org/2011/07/14/134194851/a-clinical-searing-memoir-of-abuse-in-tiger-tiger>

Liem, Shnane. "Review of *Tiger, Tiger* by Margaux Fragoso." *Vancouver Weekly*, n.d. 31 May 2012 <http://www.vancouverweekly.com/tiger-tiger-a-memoir-by-margaux-fragoso-book-review/>

Little Children. Dir. Todd Field. New Line Cinema, 2006

Lovrod, Marie. "Art/i/fact: Rereading Culture and Subjectivity through Sexual Abuse Survivor Narratives." In *True Relations: Essays on Autobiography and the Postmodern*, edited by G. Thomas Couser and Joseph Fichtelberg. Westport, CT: Greenwood, 1998, 23–32.

Sebold, Alice. *Lucky*. New York: Scribner, 1999.

Mackenzie, Craig. "'A Paedophile can make a Child's World Ecstatic': Anger at Girl's Book that Reveals Her Affection for 15-Year Abuser." *Mail Online*, 7 Mar. 2011. 31 May 2012 <http://www.dailymail.co.uk/news/article-1363538/Truth-fiction-A-young-girls-graphic-account-15-year-relationship-paedophile-age-seven.html>

Sebold, Alice. *The Lucky Bones*. New York: Little, Brown, 2002.

Tkacik, Maureen. "'Tiger, Tiger' by Margaux Fragoso: The Incandescent Memoir of a Real-Life Lolita." *The Observer*, 1 Mar. 2011. 31 May 2012 <http://observer.com/2011/03/tiger-tiger-by-margaux-fragoso-the-incandescent-memoir-of-a-reallife-lolita/2/>

The Woodsman. Dir. Nicole Kassell. Dash Films, 2004

Yang, Wesley. "Indecent Exposure: A Survivor Tests the Boundaries of Just How Far a Memoir of Child Abuse Should Go." *New York Magazine*, 13 Feb 2011. 31 May 2012 <http://nymag.com/arts/books/reviews/71625/>

Emma Maguire

POTENTIAL: ARIEL SCHRAG CONTESTS (HETERO-)NORMATIVE GIRLHOOD

Using the medium of graphic memoir, 17-year-old Ariel Schrag brings to life an alternative to heteronormative mainstream representations of girlhood, and in self-publishing at such a young age, she also takes charge of her own representation and the circulation of that representation as a teenage girl. With an emphasis on the enabling formal characteristics of comics medium, I consider how the young author addresses the representation of her girlhood sexuality in light of theories of girlhood and girls' media-making practices. Specifically, I position Potential *as "risk-taking self-representation" that creates space for marginal girlhoods to be articulated and explored via the "inventive textual practice" of comics (Chute 26) by articulating a lesbian identity in the symbolic and protected spaces of adolescent rites of passage. Drawing on Judith Halberstam's* The Queer Art of Failure, *I explore how representations of failure in Schrag's depictions of prom work to open up alternative possibilities for adolescent femininity and sexuality.*

Introduction

It is 1999. Ariel is a 16-year-old lesbian girl who loves to draw and who attends Berkeley High School in California. At lunchtime, she huddles over her latest autobiographical comic project in the art room at lunch times with her vegan girlfriend Sally, extracting advice on life, art, and lesbianism from their hip art teacher, Ms Salt. The relationship between Ariel's parents is tense and a divorce seems imminent but, more importantly, her high school prom is coming up and so is her 17th birthday. Her mission to lose her virginity must be kicked into gear – who wants to be a 17-year-old virgin, right? This is the world of *Potential* – the third instalment of a four-part autobiographical comics series by teenager Ariel Schrag entitled The High School Comic Chronicles of Ariel Schrag. Completed in her summer holidays each year, each instalment chronicles the events of the preceding school year beginning in 1997 with her freshman adventures and wrapping up with her senior year in 2000.[1]

As Ariel navigates the fraught territory of adolescent girlhood, her work visualizes her experiences for the reader in an orderly narrative that gives shape to the chaos of "growing up." Complex private tensions and intricate social relations are mapped out on the pages in black and white, contained within the neat rectangular frames of the comic. Hillary Chute has argued that the comics medium in particular works in women's autobiographical writing to recover histories of "absence and aporia" (2). The graphic memoir puts "contingent selves and histories into form" (Chute 3). In my work on the autobiographical practices of girls and young women, I am interested in how young women take up particular discourses, conventions, and modes of performance in their self-storying, and about what kinds of girlhoods emerge when girls take the opportunity to story their own lives. When Schrag engages with countercultural and anti-normative discourses in her graphic memoir series, she also responds to significant moments of American adolescence such as going to prom, losing one's virginity, experimenting with drugs and alcohol, and romantic obsessions and catastrophes. *Potential*, in particular, has a keen eye on these archetypal teen moments. I am interested in how Schrag negotiates the tensions between her countercultural indie/grunge ethic and a desire to participate in highly symbolic, mainstream teenage rites-of-passage. In this essay, I use *Potential* as a point of focus for thinking about the rituals of adolescent girlhood and to explore how the normative functions of such rituals might be challenged through girls' autobiographical practice. In particular, I argue that through the depiction of what Judith Halberstam calls the subversive "art of failure" *Potential* exemplifies a strategy for contesting heteronormative ideologies that shape dominant models of American girlhood and the rituals and rites of passage that are key to maintaining them.

Visualizing girlhood: girls' autobiographical practice and subversive self-representation

Mary Celeste Kearney, in *Girls Make Media* (2006), encourages us to think about how girls have forged a space for themselves as culture-makers within a society in which their stories are undervalued. Images and models of feminine adolescence are often created by adults who speak from a privileged position within the field of media production. Girls, however, are increasingly participating in the creation and distribution of their own girlhood narratives via blogs, vlogs (video blogs), published memoirs, graphic narratives, autobiographical visual art, poetry, personal zines, and online social media profiles and through such forms have been able to diversify available models of feminine adolescence. This is important because, as girlhood scholar Catherine Driscoll points out, the image of "the girl," wherever she appears, is a site where cultural debates around "the forms and functions of the feminine" are played out (8). The ability to circulate (potentially) nonnormative representations of young femininity in the public domain thus constitutes a vital, diversifying contribution to discussions of what women are capable of being, doing, and becoming. Images of girlhood are part of the way in which ideas about "the things girls can do, be, have, and make" are circulated and, for girls, these representations demonstrate a range of practices and behaviors in which they might engage in order to "do" girlhood (Driscoll 278).

As a mode of representation with particular claims to "the real," autobiography has a special significance in discussions about the relationship between representations of marginal groups and the material circumstances of those groups, and the recent surge in popularity of the genre has brought marginal stories to mainstream culture in a range of life narrative media (Whitlock 1–2, 3). Although the published literary memoir has been one form spotlighted by autobiography scholars, the graphic memoir has seen a surge of critical interest in the 1990s and 2000s following significant publications such as Art Spiegelman *Maus* (1991), Marjanne Satrapi's two part *Persepolis* (2000), and Alison Bechdel's *Fun Home* (2006). These texts, among others, have heightened the status of graphic life narrative as a sophisticated storytelling medium with the capacity to negotiate the complex work of life narration in rich and exciting ways via the interplay of text and images. For women, comics may have a special role in the visualization of "nonnormative" lives. Chute notes that women have become dominant producers of high-quality graphic life narratives, using the "cross-discursive" form to tell subversive, traumatic, and marginal stories that insist on women's presence and their life histories (2).

The last 15 years have also seen an increase in the publishing and popularity of girls' comics diaries and graphic life narratives. Amid an abundantly diverse comics market, the comics that girls create about themselves continue to attract a growing audience.

Chute notes the tradition of feminist comics in providing a format for representations of women that have been contentious, confronting, and progressive, where more mainstream media have retained dominant modes of representing femininity. Comics are certainly not the only form where women are able to articulate anti-normative selves, but they are "an aesthetically engaged format" that offers women cartoonists "the opportunity to visualize non-normative lives of women" (Chute 26). Here, the key idea is visualization: it is the *graphic* nature of comic texts which is central to the way in which the medium is able to give shape to aspects of women's lives and histories that have struggled to find form in more traditional or literary modes of life narrative (4). One example of this effect is in Schrag's depiction of both her lesbian sexual experiences and fantasies, which works against an absence of genuine representations of girls' lesbian sexual experiences. This absence, in part, works toward the continuation of the myth that women cannot have sex with each other because sex is understood as vaginal penetrative sex between a man and a woman. Schrag explores this heteronormative understanding of sexual intercourse in her memoir through Ariel's mission to "lose her virginity" to a boy.

In Chute's discussion of how "the work of (self-) interpretation is literally visualized" in autobiographical comics, she also comments on the way in which the "excessive expressivity" of the visual image can make this kind of representation "risky" (4, 92). I would emphasize here the practice of authors and artists who "literally visualize themselves beyond prescriptive models of alterity or sexual difference" which forms part of the risk of self-representation (Chute 92). Refusing to regurgitate predictable formulations of a liveable life, shaping new and alternative narratives, and contesting the universality and dominance of existing narratives are all risky exercises in representation. In Schrag's case this is a particularly salient point as, for a young girl whose body and sexual expression is already policed heavily in both public and private contexts, to visualize a narrative in which she not only depicts herself engaging in multiple sexual activities but in ways that contest the widely protected paradigm of heterosexuality is taking a risk indeed. But it is not only in the depiction of sex that *Potential* engages in risky self-representation. I want to argue that Schrag's text, in the depiction of teenage rites of passage from the point of view of a young lesbian girl, works to unsettle the naturalized association between teenage girlhood and heterosexuality and to illuminate (and contest) the heteronormative functions of such coming-of-age rituals.

Another element of the comics form that brings to bear on my reading of *Potential* as a subversive text is the medium's history, which is characterized by political engagement and an underground cultural ethic (Chute 13–15). The underground comics scene of the 1950s, 1960s, and 1970s had strong political and activist currents, where liberal activists used comics to communicate political messages (Abrams 435–6). Using provocative images and contentious subject matter, the comics community also fought against censorship for the rights of representation and artistic freedom (Chute 13–14). As part of the literary landscape, comics can be seen as an "underground" and politically engaged medium with an element of do-it-yourself (DIY) ethic, which has a record of telling stories that challenge norms, critique social conditions, and propose alternative lifestyles. Often devalued as childish or trivial in literary and popular discourse, comics have been used by artists seeking to counter the elitism of high art and culture. It is this history of resistance and boundary-pushing that makes the medium open to the articulation of subjectivities that might not find a place in more visible or prestigious modes of storytelling. By using comics as the vehicle for their life writing, girls can utilize the capacity of the medium to intervene in normalizing narratives of girlhood that circulate through more visible cultural media. That the medium has not been highly valued in mainstream culture also resonates with the kind of "indie" esthetic that Schrag cultivates in her series, and which reveals some tension between her resistance to, and desire to participate in, mainstream values.

From the outset, in Schrag's first instalment *Awkward*, she distinguishes her textual territory as sub- and countercultural, invoking markers of the alternative youth subculture of her day. She attends indie and alternative music concerts and experiments with illicit drugs and alcohol with her friends. She displays an extensive knowledge of the alternative music scene, including song lyrics, names of band members and identifying the connections between different musical acts. She loves Juliette Lewis, star of the violent and controversial film *Natural Born Killers* (1994), and acts out scenes from the movie with her boyfriend. She engages with other markers of youth subculture such as graffiti art and alternative fashion throughout the text. Schrag uses these markers to indicate her affiliation with the values of Generation X youth culture which defined itself against and also presented a critique of mainstream (adult) cultural values, particularly the greed, superficiality and social conformity that young people saw as the marks of the consumer culture created by their parents' generation the "baby-boomers" (Epstein 18–21; Mattson 58–9). One cultural ethic to emerge out of this kind of resistance to mainstream consumer values was independent or "indie" music culture. This kind of culture, still evident today, has as one of its key values the condemnation of "selling out," that is, trading the "authentic" or "real" quality of small, low-budget, community-driven music production and consumption habits for the financial gains available in the "shallow" and "artificial" mainstream (Fish 88–9; Hesmondhalgh 35–36).[2] In her *High School Comic Chronicles* Schrag's incorporation (even saturation) of the texts with markers of indie/alternative music and culture point to the author's desire to be received as countercultural and anti-mainstream. I am suggesting here that Schrag's indie esthetic and countercultural values go some way toward enabling her to articulate a lesbian identity through her comic. As she positions herself as anti-normative through her style and cultural tastes, her anti-normative formulation of adolescent sexuality is tied in with this. At several points in the memoir, Ariel goes to see alternative bands with her lesbian group of friends, and these occasions are a celebration of both their shared identity as lesbian girls and also their "cool" music taste. In *Potential*, Ariel presents her lesbianism as variously banal, exciting, and confusing but rarely problematic in everyday life. At Ariel's West Coast high school, the rules around accepted adolescent femininity and sexuality are relatively fluid, but in the heightened and more structured space of prom she encounters more resistance to her lesbian identity. That Schrag remains invested in the narratives of "prom perfection" and heteronormative definitions of sex, despite her attachment to otherwise counter-normative ethics, speaks to the way in which dominant gender ideology pervades youth cultures that might otherwise consider themselves "alternative" or anti-mainstream.

Schrag is not alone in trying to offer broader representations of girlhood that take into account diverse sexual identities. Recently, the US television series *Glee* has been praised for its representation of queer sexualities among the show's central characters, and UK teen drama series *Skins* has offered more complex representations of teenage sexualities to the small screen.[3] Despite these departures, however, many mainstream and marginal representations of youthful sexualities have historically been shaped by a normative heterosexual discourse. This is significant for Ariel Schrag, who was writing at a time when mainstream representations of young women's sexuality were largely heterosexual. Butler, in *Gender Trouble*, identifies the difficulties in articulating nonnormative sexual identities within an oppressive discourse of heteronormativity that would seem to occlude such expression. She maintains, however, that the "persistence and proliferation" of queer identities – despite the supposed "impossibility" of their existence – open up avenues within the matrix of heterosexual power for "rival and subversive matrices" of gender and sexuality that destabilize the very matrix in which they exist (24). The articulation of queer identities, although shaped by a normalizing heterosexual discourse, destabilizes the dominance of heterosexuality and pushes on existing boundaries of sexual identity. In this way, we can read Ariel Schrag's graphic memoir as an instance of queer identity articulated within a heteronormative discourse that, in its articulation, helps to destabilize this discourse and contest heterosexual dominance. In doing this, it opens up more space for further subversive narratives of girlhood sexuality.

One way that Schrag's representation thwarts the discourses of heteronormativity that underpin her representations of teenage rites of passage is in her depiction of "failure." Halberstam (2011), in her critique of the hegemony of success in North American culture, posits "the queer art of failure" as a kind of counterhegemony to the dominant narrative of success that underpins contemporary American life. She argues that behind the stories of success that abound within mainstream US culture, there lie rich histories of failure and negativity that offer a host of "more creative, more cooperative, more surprising ways of being in the world" (2–3). Citing the impossibility of queer subjectivities to "succeed" in a mainstream culture governed by heteronormative discourses, Halberstam positions failure as an art mastered by queers which creates possibilities for developing alternative modes of living. In representations of the failure of individuals to follow dominant trajectories of success, rich new avenues for living and ways of being open up. Rather than seeing the failure to carry out this or that task, achievement, convention, or path as an end point or closing off, Halberstam encourages us to view failure as simply another way of doing things. Furthermore, avenues of failure undermine the hegemony of success that often limits and narrows possible ways of being to those lionized by the dominant culture. In a consideration of how *Potential* transgresses more visible representations of girlhood through the representation of failure I now offer a reading of a significant rite of passage depicted in the book: Ariel's experience of attending prom with her girlfriend Sally as a lesbian couple.

"What will they think when they see the sheets tomorrow, Dylan?": Articulating lesbian girlhood in the heteronormative space of prom

The prom narrative is iconic in media about teenagers in high school and is crucial in heteronormative fantasies about teenage sexuality (Best, *Girls* 195). A typical prom narrative features a long preparation for the dance that hypes up the event and invokes the importance for the night to go off perfectly (often in the form of beauty routines and dress shopping for girls, and the securing of dates that are sexual "sure bets" for boys), followed by obstacles that appear unexpectedly and threaten the perfection of prom, the eventual arrival and entrance to the dance, another obstacle that threatens the ideal of prom perfection, the crowning of the prom king and queen, and then the after party or aftermath where the excitement of the dance has passed away, problems are resolved and characters convey the lessons that they have taken from the experience. For girls, the parallels to wedding narratives are difficult to miss: the focus on "the" dress, the pressure of constructing the perfect night, the rigid structure and rules of the ceremonious event, and the consummation of the night that is sometimes explicit and sometimes only alluded to. This connection between prom and weddings alludes to the heteronormative function of prom.

Although television and film have offered some queer interventions into the prom narrative, for example, *Glee*, *High School Musical*, *Degrassi High*, *Queer As Folk*, and *Dawson's Creek*, these are typically represented by two young *men* who endeavor to attend prom together. In terms of mainstream television or film representations of two lesbian girls going to prom together, there are even fewer instances.[4] There is a distinction to be made here between two heterosexual girls attending prom together as girl-friends (often because they have "failed" to obtain male dates), and two "out" lesbian girls attending as a couple. Representations of two straight girls attending prom together, because they do not destabilize the heteronormative narrative of prom, are more common and less controversial. These representations though, through the depiction of failure to get dates (and so perform the prom script successfully), do open up for girls an alternative to attending prom "on the arm" of a boy.

Schrag explicitly references the prom's exclusion of same-sex couples, as well as the threat of homophobic violence, in her memoir in a panel that shows Ariel and Sally preparing to have their professional prom photographs taken at the school gym before the dance. Sally frets, "I hope you know we're going to get our heads kicked in when we take our picture" (183). Sally goes to look for her sister Harriet and her friend Rowina whom she expects to "back them up" if they encounter violence, but returns furious: Harriet and Rowina have decided to leave, telling Sally they "don't wanna get beat up just because of you" (184). Although Ariel reassures Sally that they will "be ok," they do encounter homophobia that is both explicit (in the form of comments made by a group of students) and implicit (i.e., as a heteronormative rite of passage prom is implicitly exclusionary to same-sex couples). This feeling of exclusion is observed in the comic when Ariel and Sally meet up with their friends, also a lesbian couple, who tell Ariel they are leaving because, they say, "this sucks. There's nothing for gay people to do" (192).

As Chute reminds us, comics must be read on a visual as well as a textual level. In the panels that depict the dance, the prom-goers are shaded the same gray as the background and blend in as part of the atmosphere – they are, obviously, a part of the prom – while Ariel and Sally are rendered in high contrast white and black line. In the key "dance scene" panel beams of light crisscross the room, illuminating the boy–girl couples and groups of friends who are dancing and having fun. In these dance panels, Ariel and Sally are always shown in high relief, using the same technique of strategic shading; it is as though they are in their own spotlight, yet they are also excluded from the performance of the prom around them. The effect here is of a high visibility that comes with not "fitting in" and feeling self-consciously "other" as a result: as Ariel and Sally are shown, conspicuously sitting in silence while the crowd of boy–girl couples dance, Ariel narrates "I suddenly felt unbelievably ugly" (193). Ariel and Sally quickly decide to leave the prom.

In "The Production of Heterosexuality at the High School Prom" Amy L. Best notes the way in which prom privileges heterosexuality and forces queerness, if it is visible at all, to its margins: "The taken-for-granted rules of prom dating [. . .] sustain the link between the prom and romance and ultimately preserve a discursive and material arrangement in which heterosexuality is the privileged form" (196). Indeed, the overwhelming awkwardness that Sally and Ariel endure drives them to flee from the prom and to a friend's house where, with relief, Ariel notes "we were amongst friends" (194). Despite this eventual retreat, Schrag has, in an important way, used the comics medium to intervene in the iconic visual imagery of prom where queerness is made absent. By literally putting herself in the picture at prom, Schrag shows the prom as a space where queer subjectivities can and do exist – though tenuously. Panel after panel in the comic's prom sequence, Ariel and Sally stubbornly remain visible among the crowd, disrupting the heterosexual hegemony of prom. The effect is so important here because the powerful visual imagery of prom that is communicated repetitively via television and teen movies as well as girls' magazines rarely, if ever, includes a queer coupling as the focus of prom. As Best points out, in visual imagery of prom, queerness is usually only invoked on the fringes and in ways that reaffirm the heterosexual privilege of the event ("Production" 194). Here, though, the way in which teen-movies and girls' magazines circulate gendered fantasies around prom of heterosexual romance and prom perfection are interrupted by making a queer experience of prom the focus of the dance. That these hegemonic images of prom are so often circulated via visual media makes it particularly important that Schrag's representation is through the visual medium of comics.

Schrag shows how media representations of prom have shaped the meanings and expectations around this highly symbolic event, with a special focus on the visual. In the first panel of Chapter 7 – which is the "prom" chapter – Schrag depicts the characters Brenda and Dylan from the television show *Beverley Hills 90210* during a scene in which Brenda has just "lost her virginity to Dylan" in a hotel room during the prom. This first panel is a departure from the other chapters in the book, which all show Ariel in the first panel. Here, though, Brenda and Dylan stand in for Ariel as the first image that the reader encounters. As well as highlighting the relationship between comics and television as distinct visual mediums, this substitution of the author with characters from a mainstream television show signals a cluster of associations around performativity and prom that inform the rest of the chapter. Her replacement of a representation of her own body with that of television actors performing lines from a script signals the way in which ideology is circulated discursively through media images to inform the actions and behaviors of individuals – in this case adolescents who become familiar with the scripts of prom through television.

The performative aspect of prom is noted by Best who suggests that a key part of "doing" prom involves a "public performance" which relies on a highly scripted narrative of heterosexual romance that she terms "hetero-romance" ("Production" 196). A driving force behind girls' investment and participation in prom, hetero-romance relies upon a fantasy of heterosexual romantic love that is "deeply entrenched within American popular culture" (*Production* 197). Best argues that via its celebration of hetero-romance, "prom serves to draw young women and young men into a set of discursive relations that are central to the ongoing institutional operation of heterosexual dominance and the reproduction of gender identities and inequalities" ("Production" 195). In *Potential,* Schrag shows how her expectations of prom are shaped by such discourses in her preparation for prom where she tries to lose weight to be "pretty in prom dress, sexy for Sally," and to elicit a romantic proposal from Sally. The inclusion of the scene from *90210* points to the way hetero-romance as circulated through mainstream media has shaped Ariel's expectations and understandings of prom as it – along with many other similar representations – has shaped American teens' expectations and understandings of prom.

One of the mid-1990s television culture's most iconic teen hetero-pairings, the relationship between *90210* high-school sweethearts "Brenda and Dylan" was keenly followed by the show's fans. Schrag alludes to the iconicity of this particular television moment in the text of the panel, which reads, "Ever since the thrill of 6th grade's 90210 Season Finale with Brenda losing her virginity to Dylan, and Donna and her dress drunk downstairs, PROM had been the embodiment of all teenage classicism [sic]" (180). In Schrag's misuse of the word "classicism" we can read associations of the classic, the time-honored, and the mythic. The idea of the classic and of the classical resonates through representations of prom, and I suggest that the term classicism is perfect here, because it invokes ideas of tradition, formality, and archetype. Significantly, the text explicitly references the "embodiment" of the traditions and icons of the *teenage*. Prom, as an important rite of passage is a pinnacle of adolescence in America that is saturated by a heroic ideal of heterosexual romance.

Although the prom chapter in *Potential* begins with this iconic television moment, it swiftly moves away from this conception of prom and the heteronormative associations that it invokes. One important way that the text undermines the stability of the heteronormative nature of prom is by depicting the night as filled with disappointment and failure that is not wrapped up neatly and resolved by the end of the night. As the reader witnesses Ariel's painful and drawn out failure to enjoy prom, an alternative prom narrative opens up and undermines the hegemonic mandate for "perfection" that surrounds so much prom imagery and discourse. The invocation of performance, ritual, rite of passage, and heteronormativity as pictured in the chapter's first panel is imbued with optimism and a hopeful potential for fulfillment. This is indicated by the sparkling, bubbly visuals clustered around the word "PROM" that suggests an effervescent party atmosphere. Visually, the word prom is large, dominating the panel as the event dominates both media narratives of high school and the experience of adolescents in their junior and senior years.[5] This sense of hope is meaningful to a text which takes the word "potential" as its title. Moving now to the title page of the memoir, Schrag communicates her sense of expectation and excitement for the start of the school year. On the title page, the cartoon Ariel is shown in various poses with a chicken drumstick, and her speech bubbles read:

> Junior year and that means business. Times have been fun, I know it, but from here on out we're talkin': A's to plow for, virginities to lose, proms to attend, we're talkin' – potential so thick you can sink your teeth in it. (1)

In huge letters, the word "potential" overlays the other images; as the reader holds the comic in her or his hands, the word looks as though it has been placed on top of the work, hovering over its pages, weighing them down. It is below this word that Ariel is shown finally sinking her teeth into the chicken drumstick. Schrag threads the idea of potential throughout the chapters of her memoir, even repeating the word intermittently, as she does with the thematic titles of her other graphic memoirs *Awkward*, *Definition*, and *Likewise*. Schrag uses this technique of leitmotif to thread her experiences together and give structure to the chaos of her lived experience. "Potential" is the frame through which Schrag encourages readers to experience her stories, and the idea of potential or perfection, as noted above, is particularly significant in the mythology of prom.

Lurking, though, alongside the hope and possibility of potential is the implicit threat of disappointment and failure. As the panels that show Ariel's prom preparations develop across and down the page, a creeping sense of disappointment emerges. The last panel reads "however, despite my concentrated efforts on its perfection, problems for the best night of my life began to surface from very early on" (180). Ariel goes on to list the impediments to prom perfection that she encounters: such as Sally not wanting to go to the dance, difficulty purchasing tickets, and beauty routines gone wrong. As the narrative progresses, the threat of failure hangs over the extensive and drawn out difficulties in getting to prom which stem from both the slowly fracturing relationship between Ariel and Sally and Sally's concerns about going to prom as a lesbian couple. A continuous succession of errors which plays out over a full 39 panels impedes Ariel and Sally's arrival at the dance, and it seems as if they will never get to go to prom. After their brief and uncomfortable attendance at the dance, Sally and Ariel end up a small after party with a few friends where Sally rebuffs Ariel's attempts to have sex, and Ariel reacts emotionally. In the morning, the comic shows Ariel relinquishing her prom fantasy, symbolized by her surrendering her prom dress. In the final panel of the chapter, Ariel is shown walking away wearing day clothes instead of the dress that she is pictured in throughout the rest of the chapter. It reads simply, "I changed into some clothes and walked home" (205). While both thwarted expectations and setbacks in fulfilling the prom fantasy are all part of the drama of the prom narrative, most prom narratives preserve the event's sanctity of heterosexuality despite any challenges the characters encounter. In showing a failure to carry out the fantasy of prom night, Schrag shows that there is an alternative to the cheesy hetero-romance of mainstream prom narratives and makes room for a narrative of prom failure that contests the mandate for girls to live out the dream of the perfect prom night.

The focal point for Ariel's disappointment is the failure to fulfill both the prom's potential for romance and the "consummation" of the prom rite of passage through sexual intercourse with one's date, which is referenced in the chapter's opening panel with Brenda and Dylan. Often bound up in the prom narrative, the "losing" of one's virginity is another teenage rite of passage that is invoked in the first panel. The two characters are shown from the shoulders up, presumably naked in bed, and Brenda worries: "What will they think when they see the sheets tomorrow Dylan?" to which he replies "They'll think two people had a really good time last night" (180). In contrast to this scene's fulfillment of prom potential, Ariel and Sally's "bed scene" is markedly different suggesting through visual cues the opposition of the two representations. The panel containing Brenda and Dylan is drawn in clear black lines set against bright white, and the panel is clearly outlined in a perfect square that echoes the shape of a television screen. The brightness of the square panel evokes both the stage lights that illuminate actors on set and the glow of a television screen. Only the characters' heads are shown and they are seen from front on at an eye level. The overall effect is one of tidiness and straightforwardness – the narrative is easily contained within one square that communicates a familiar story to the viewer. In contrast, Ariel takes seven panels to show her and Sally in their bed scene in which everything is shrouded in gray shadows and set against a pitch black background. The borders are jagged and uneven, reminiscent of the effect of rumpled bed linen, and body parts protrude past the borders, intruding on other panels and across the uneven "gutters" (the blank space between panels).

Schrag uses this technique of uneven panels and irregular gutters throughout her memoir series to indicate both intoxication and a dream state. The gutters, a representation of time lapse, become unclear as Ariel loses her sense of time and place (McCloud 66–7). This disorderliness pervades the sex scenes as both girls' faces are made blurry, representing Ariel's drunken state, and are partially or wholly hidden in the action of their bodies. Like Ariel and Sally's journey to prom, their endeavor to have sex is riddled with obstacles. The panels read:

We stumbled onto her mom's bed and into a sloppy mass of swiping hands and legs. She started sucking hard and painfully on my neck and all I wanted were her fingers in my cunt my outstretched tights were in the way so I tried to reach down hers but instead grabbed some large protruding pad. I finally managed my hand past the mound and jubilantly jammed two fingers in. (195–6)

At this point Sally says "STOP" and Ariel continues to narrate, "She got up and stumbled out of the room, what was she doing?... period or something I dunno... I lay sprawled on the bed waiting for her to come back" (196). Four panels show Ariel lying on the bed alone, her face and body distorted. The last panel reads forlornly, "maybe she's not coming back" (196). Sally rebuffs Ariels other attempts to engage in sex, and retreats to the bathroom. Ariel is left to brood over their relationship problems, while both girls spend the remainder of the night apart. This fragmented, messy, and unpleasant experience complicates and diversifies the more visible narratives of successful (if anxious) prom "consummation" that exist. It shows an alternative way to "do" prom that, as I have been arguing, widens the scope for girls' prom narratives to include "failure" and alternative experiences to the iconic fantasies that center on perfection and success.

The "aftermath" or after-party in the prom narrative often sees the characters overcome some difficulty, learn a valuable lesson, or undergo some form of self-realization, but this does not happen for Ariel. The closest that Ariel comes to closure is a sleepy cuddle that she shares with Sally at the end of the chapter. Schrag shows herself slipping into a dreamy state where she talks nonsense and is confused about what is real and what is imagined. When she awakes Sally appears frightened and upset as she says to Ariel, "You're my girl, no one else's, and I'm yours, only yours" to which Ariel replies simply "ok" (205). Both girls are depicted looking worried and solemn, sitting apart from one another, and the next panel shows Ariel walking home alone with her back to the reader. The conclusion to the prom chapter shows a refusal to perpetuate the myth of hetero-romantic "success" stories bound up in prom narratives. In showing her failure to have a romantic prom, Schrag demonstrates resistance to this powerful driving force that shapes girls' expectations and experiences of prom, and serves to reinforce the heteronormativity of prom mythology. It is also telling that in Schrag's prom story, there is no mention of one of the most lauded of prom ceremonies: the crowning of the prom king and queen. Here, Schrag marginalizes this iconic symbol of heterosexuality by leaving it out altogether, thereby denying the narrative its usual climax and choosing instead to tell her own story of awkwardness, failure, and disappointment.

Conclusion

Schrag's graphic memoir destabilizes both established norms of girlhood and sexuality and conventional systems of media production that have constructed adults and men as authoritative producers of culture, and young people and women as consumers (Kearney 4). By taking control of her own representation and the way it is disseminated, Schrag empowers herself and other girls to participate in the creation of what it can mean to *be* a girl. Particularly in terms of girlhood sexuality, Schrag has created and distributed an alternative to more familiar narratives of "the girl."

Though embracing the markers of alternative identity available in music and fashion, Schrag negotiates the anxious terrain of teenage sexuality, foregrounding her lesbian identity as the catalyst for a personal reformulation of heteronormative stories of girlhood. Through Schrag's positioning of her narrative as subcultural, she engages in a critique of mainstream cultural ideals and uses this frame to articulate an empowered lesbian sexual identity.

In depicting the way heterosexuality defines the high school rite of passage of prom, Schrag shows how comics can "put contingent selves and histories into form" (Chute 3) and by putting herself and her sexuality in the picture, she contests the way heteronormative narratives have rendered queer stories and subjectivities invisible and excluded. Schrag, rather than creating a narrative that sustains the fantasy of prom, positions the fantasy as problematic and destructive, and as a script that she is unable to integrate into her identity as a lesbian girl. In doing so, she critiques the powerful mythology of hetero-romance that surrounds the dance. As Halberstam (3) might put it, Schrag's story of prom failure "poke[s] holes in" the normalized and naturalized stories of girlhood that work to sustain a heterosexual dominance that reinforces unequal gender relations. In this way, *Potential* offers what Halberstam (6) calls a "detour" around "tried and true paths of knowledge production," which in this context is what it means for girls to be girls. Schrag's representation of her girlhood sexuality offers an alternative to the recurrent heteronormative cultural representations of adolescent girlhood and in doing so widens the possible range of expression for other adolescent femininities and sexualities. By encouraging the reader to "look and look again" the comics form allows Schrag to explore the connections between heteronormative narratives of girlhood sexuality in mainstream cultural media to her own experience of lesbian sexuality.

Notes

1. Schrag self published her first autobiographical comic book *Awkward* at the age of 15. In 1997, the book was published by independent comics publisher Slave Labor Graphics, who also published her subsequent high school comic memoirs. In 2008 and 2009, the books were reprinted by Touchstone/Simon & Schuster. Under Touchstone, the two first books *Awkward* and *Definition*, which are much shorter than the final two works, were published as one book. So although Schrag's *Comic Chronicles* is a four-part series, the most recent form appears as three books.
2. It is ironic to note that the indie music scene became so popular that during the 1990s it became a part of mainstream pop music in the UK, and more commonly known as "alternative" music in the USA (Hesmondhalgh 1).
3. A US remake of *Skins* in 2011 followed the success of the original series, indicating a recognition of the demand for complex and controversial – often referred to as "gritty" and "real" – representations of youth for which *Skins* is celebrated (see Stelter 2010).
4. Not only are lesbian subjectivities made invisible in prom narratives, lesbian girls are also denied a place at prom by schools that police the dominance of heterosexuality via the school dance. A case in point as recently as 2010 is the Mississippi school that cancelled their senior prom rather than allowing student Constance McMillen to attend in a tuxedo with her girlfriend as her date. McMillen successfully sued the school with the help of the American Civil Liberties Union and her story was reported in mainstream news media. McMillen also appeared on *The Ellen Show* where Ellen DeGeneres encouraged public support of the teenager (see Adams 2012).
5. Prom is often described expectantly by teenagers as the "best night of my life," or "the most important night" (See Best 2004). This disproportionate importance is also reflected in Schrag's text when she describes prom as "the embodiment" of teenage mythology (180).

References

Abrams, Nathan. "From Madness to Dysentery: *Mad*'s Other New York Intellectuals." *Journal of American Studies* 37.3 (2003): 435–51.

Adams, Richard. "Constance McMillen Shall go to the Prom." *The Guardian.com*, The Guardian News and Media Ltd. 24 March.2010. Web. 9 January 2013.

Best, Amy L. "Schooling, and the Discourse of Self-Change: Negotiating Meanings of the High School Prom." In *All About the Girl: Power, Culture and Identity*, edited by Harris Anita. New York: Routledge, 2004, 195–203.

———. "The Production of Heterosexuality at the High School Prom." In *Thinking Straight: The Power, the Promise and Paradox of Heterosexuality*, edited by Ingram Chrys. London: Routledge, 2005, 193–213.

Butler, Judith. *Gender Trouble: Feminism and the Subversion of Identity*. New York: Routledge, 1999.

Chute, Hillary L. *Graphic Women: Life Narrative and Contemporary Comics*. New York: Columbia UP, 2010.

Driscoll, Catherine. *Girls: Feminine Adolescence in Popular Culture and Cultural Theory*. New York: Columbia UP, 2002.

Epstein, Jonathan S. "Introduction: Generation X, Youth Culture and Identity." In *Youth Culture: Identity in a Postmodern World*, edited by Jonathan S. Epstein. Malden: Blackwell, 1998, 1–23.

Fish, Duane R. "Serving the Servants: An Analysis of the Music of Kurt Cobain." *Popular Music and Society* 19.2 (1995): 87–102.

Halberstam, Judith. *The Queer Art of Failure*. Durham: Duke UP, 2011.

Hesmondhalgh, David. "Indie: The Institutional Politics and Aesthetics of a Popular Music Genre." *Cultural Studies* 13:1 (1999): 34–61.

Kearney, MaryCeleste. *Girls Make Media*. New York: Routledge, 2006.

Mattson, Kevin. "Talking About My Generation (and the Left)." *Dissent* 46.4 (1999): 58–63.

McCloud, Scott. *Understanding Comics: The Invisible Art*. New York: HarperPerennial, 1994.

Schrag, Ariel. *Awkward and Definition: The High-School Comic Chronicles of Ariel Schrag*. New York: Touchstone, 2008.

———. *Likewise: The High-School Comic Chronicles of Ariel Schrag*. New York: Touchstone, 2009.

———. *Potential: The High-School Comic Chronicles of Ariel Schrag*. New York: Touchstone, 2008.

Stelter, Brian. "MTV is Looking Beyond 'Jersey Shore.'" *The New York Times.com*, The New York Times. 24 October 2010. Web. 9 January 2013.

Whitlock, Gillian. *Soft Weapons: Autobiography in Transit*. Chicago, IL: U of Chicago P, 2007.

Pamela Graham

ALICE PUNG'S *GROWING UP ASIAN IN AUSTRALIA*: THE CULTURAL WORK OF ANTHOLOGIZED ASIAN-AUSTRALIAN NARRATIVES OF CHILDHOOD

This paper examines the 2008 literary anthology Growing up Asian in Australia, *edited by the young Australian writer and award-winning memoirist, Alice Pung. Featuring a collection of auto/biographically based prose, poetry, and comics by "Asian-Australian" authors, each short text within the anthology focuses on coming-of-age in modern-day Australia. Informed by auto/biography and Asian-Australian studies, this paper explores the cultural work that Pung's anthology aims to do. Through a reading of the anthology's paratexts as well as the short, individual childhood autobiographies, the discussion considers the strategies Pung employs in order to attract a broad readership, and how the anthology mobilizes life narratives of childhood to intervene in debates about Australian national, local, and personal identities at the start of the twenty-first century. I argue that Pung's text skillfully balances politics and populism, critiquing fundamental issues of national identity and self-representation while simultaneously appealing to a broad readership.*

In Australia in the first decade of the twenty-first century, issues of identity, belonging and citizenship have featured prominently in the public sphere. From the 2005 Cronulla race riots in a beachside suburb of Sydney to recent parliamentary debates surrounding asylum seeker policy, arguments regarding who belongs to the nation, or who has the right to apply to belong, have consistently taken center stage in the media and in the political arena.

Such national preoccupations are not new. As a former British colony, Australia has a long and infamous history of excluding people regarded as "other" to the "ideal" (white and culturally British) Australian. As Regina Lee points out, "in the construction of the [Australian] national self, the exclusion of non-white communities has performed a crucial role" (214). This exclusion is conspicuous in both popular cultural representations of those deemed "other," as well as in institutionalized exclusion via legislation such as the country's notorious 1901 *Immigration Restriction Act*, colloquially known as The White Australia Policy.[1]

One particular cultural group that has consistently been positioned as "other" in Australian national discourse is people described as being of "Asian" heritage.[2] Graham Huggan has suggested that "Asia" – a catch-all phrase for countries as diverse as China, India and Indonesia – has frequently been constructed in a negative way in the prevailing Australian national story, providing "a gallery of outlandish racial stereotypes, ranging in intensity from inept comic villains to ravening barbarian hordes" (132). As Jacqueline Lo, Olivia Khoo, and Helen Gilbert note, "The foundational role of the White Australia Policy in the formation of nationhood has meant that, in the popular imaginary, 'Asians' are usually located outside the nation space" (2).

However, despite this history of exclusionary discourse, on an institutional level at least, Australia's attitude toward Asia is changing. Largely due to the economic significance of the "Asian-Australian" relationship, a range of Australian Federal Government programs and initiatives have been designed to acknowledge and reconceptualize Australia as a country in the Asian region.[3]

Change is also occurring on a cultural level. In recent years, Asian-Australian cultural production has been progressively increasing. Arguably, there is now a critical mass of work – including literature, film and visual arts – by and about Asian Australians. Asian-Australian cultural studies is quickly developing into an established academic field and there are numerous blogs and websites dedicated to the discussion of Asian-Australian cultural production.[4] As Olivia Khoo recently observed, "From distanciation to fascination and engagement, Australia's relationship with Asia continues to inform the culture and politics of the nation" ("Regionalizing Asian Australian Identities" 461).

This paper looks at one recent literary response to emerge from this cultural climate: the 2008 literary anthology, *Growing up Asian in Australia* (2008), hereafter referred to as *Growing up*. Edited by Alice Pung, a young Australian writer and award-winning memoirist, *Growing up* features a collection of auto/biographically based prose, poetry, comics, and interviews by "Asian-Australian" authors.[5] Each short text within the anthology relates, often in a humorous way, the author's experience of coming of age in contemporary Australia, and contributors include over 50 established and emerging writers such as Benjamin Law, Simone Lazaroo, Hop Dac, Sunil Badami, Amy Choi, and Leanne Hall.

Informed by Asian-Australian cultural studies, and auto/biography studies, in this paper I explore how *Growing up* works as cultural intervention aimed at reconsidering prevailing representations of Australian national identity in the early twenty-first century. What strategies does Pung, as editor of the anthology, employ in *Growing up* in order to achieve particular cultural aims? How does *Growing up* mobilize life narratives of childhood to intervene in Australian national identity debates? To address these questions, I focus on two interconnected aspects of the anthology.

Firstly, I turn to the form and packaging of *Growing up*. I consider the significance of the anthology genre and explore the role it plays in perpetuating the text's ideological aims. In particular, I read *Growing up* in light of Huggan's suggestion that, in the context of Australian identity politics debates, there are two types of anthologies: those that are integrationist and those that are interventionist (118). For Huggan, the "primary function" of the integrationist anthology is "the celebration of national cultural diversity" (118). Such texts are "conciliatory rather than confrontational" and are constructed in a "spirit of reconciliatory universalism" (118). In contrast, the interventionist anthology "takes a much more critical view of the notion of diversity and the construction of the nation itself" (118). Although Huggan constructs his binary distinction to discuss a previous generation of anthologies – those produced during the "multicultural" anthology boom of the late 1970s, 1980s, and 1990s – his model nevertheless provides a useful framework in which to consider how *Growing up* is positioned and marketed.

Pung's aim in compiling *Growing up* was to have it circulate widely, thereby engaging in debates about what constitutes "Australian-ness." In a note on her website, she explains

> the thing I wanted to accomplish with this book—first and foremost—was to infiltrate our popular culture—our common culture, our everyday culture—with stories about how integral Asian Australians are to our national identity. This meant getting the books into the mainstream bookstores. ("Original Introduction")

I argue that to facilitate these aims, Pung strategically uses elements found in both interventionist and integrationist anthologies in order to aid the circulation of her text to as wide an audience as possible. This ambiguous positioning, complicating Huggan's binary integrationist/interventionist model, provides a way for *Growing up* to reach readers who may find "conciliatory" integrationist texts more accessible than purely interventionist ones.

Secondly, as *Growing up* is as much a literary work as it is a socio-political one, I turn to the literary representations offered "inside" the anthology to analyze how such depictions narrate childhoods that resist dominant representations of Asian people in Australia. I suggest that the choice of childhood as the theme for the anthology is a significant one; one that appeals to universal notions of coming-of-age, yet simultaneously allows for specific expressions of cultural diversity. I explore how the act of narrating a childhood self via the use of a relational narrative mode, as well as the device of humor, enables contributors to critique the socially available scripts for writing Asian-Australian experiences now. Bringing these two strands together, I aim to show how *Growing up* complicates prevailing notions of both "Asian" and "Australian," unsettling dominant narratives of national identity in contemporary Australia.

Literary anthologies and identity politics

Over the past 30 years or so, the literary anthology has emerged as a productive tool for destabilizing value-laden ideas of "national literature," as well as for intervening in identity politics debates. Critics in North America have long argued that the anthology is an important vehicle for the representation of marginal voices and experiences. Joe Lockard and Jillian Sandell have described what they call "citizenship-by-anthology" (246), while Cynthia Franklin has shown the anthology to be a "privileged site" for important cultural work in "creating communities" of writers, and making visible those previously marginalized in academic and mainstream cultures (29).

In Australia, anthologies have also been used as tools of literary activism. Patricia Eliades, writing in 1995 about what was then referred to as "minority writing," showed how anthologies were used by Australian feminists "from the late 1970s onwards [. . .] to demonstrate the diversity of women's writing and to undermine those male-dominated literary hegemonies and reviewing practices which historically favored male writers" (74). Informed by Eliades' work, more recently Huggan has highlighted how, fuelled by newly developed policies of multiculturalism and accompanying public funding, the years from the late 1970s through to the early 1990s saw a surge in the production of "multicultural anthologies," a publishing phenomenon that Eliades labels "anthologmania" (Huggan 117; Eliades 75).[6]

In both North American and Australian contexts, the anthology form has been viewed as a useful tool primarily because it provides a way for a range of "voices" to be represented in the one text.[7] Anthologies may contain work by numerous authors, who may vary according to gender, class, sexuality, age, and cultural heritage. Therefore, the anthology is a very direct and immediate way to communicate literary and cultural diversity.

The "demonstrating diversity" effect that anthologies have is arguably heightened when the anthology is positioned as life writing. Despite the fact that the constructed, performative nature of all life writing has been acknowledged for some time now, many recreational readers remain drawn to the genre for its status as non-fiction.[8] Writing that is marketed and positioned as auto/biographical promises access to "authentic experience" in a way that writing marketed as fiction generally does not. Therefore, anthologies of life writing act as testaments to "real life" diversity in a way that non-life-writing anthologies do not.

However, Eliades has pointed out that while anthologies have the potential to do important cultural work, they also run the risk of re-marginalizing those they seek to make visible (74). Anthologies that aspire to cultural intervention are inevitably constructed around a central identity marker such as "gender," "race," or "class." While this labeling is simply part of an anthologizing process, and plays a significant role in the marketing of a text, grouping a disparate range of work under an all-encompassing identity is not without its problems.

Simone Lazaroo, whose work features in *Growing up*, has voiced concerns that the term "Asian Australian," for example, has the capacity to lead to reductive readings of a writer's work as "yet another example of 'ethnic minority' or 'migrant' writing" (109). For Lazaroo, these readings obscure the ability for publishers, reviewers, and readers to consider "arguably more significant issues" in a writer's work (109). The term is also critiqued by author Merlinda Bobis, who contends that "'Asians' cannot be lumped into one heap, like a hyphenated brand of jeans, because Asia is a large continent of diverse cultures" (119). So for these commentators, the term's potential to universalize the identities of a wide range of people is clearly a problem.

At the same time, many scholars understand the political advantages of an umbrella term such as "Asian Australian." For example, Lo, Khoo, and Gilbert suggest that, "as a provisional category of identification to be mobilized strategically in the face of racist politics, 'Asian Australian' is a portmanteau term that unites peoples of various 'Asian' ethnicities, enabling a degree of political solidarity and critical purchase" (2). Likewise, Ien Ang contends that the term Asian Australian is a "hybrid category [. . .] a contradictory site of cultural struggle for membership in the wider society"

("Introduction" xvi). In other words, although a label like Asian Australian has the potential to homogenize, universalize, and possibly re-marginalize the many identities it seeks to include, it is also politically useful.

For Pung, it is clear that an Asian-Australian identity is necessary in order to engage in cultural work that resists traditional constructions of Asian people in the Australian public sphere. In *Growing up*, Pung uses the label for political purposes, explicitly positioning her text as "writing back" to prevailing representations of people of Asian appearance in Australia.

Paratexts: intervention and integration

A reading of *Growing up's* paratexts – its blurb, introduction, contents page and cover – reveals a dialectic of integration and intervention. The book's blurb, for example, features interventionist elements. It reads, "Asian Australians have often been written about by outsiders, as outsiders. In this collection they tell their own stories with verve, courage and a large dose of humour" ("Introduction" 1). This statement explicitly acknowledges the historically marginal position of Asian-Australian people in Australian public life, and proclaims the anthology's aim of correcting misrepresentations.

Yet the blurb also tempers overt politicization by appealing to apparently universal notions of coming of age. The book promises the reader "tales of leaving home, falling in love, coming out and finding one's feet" ("Introduction" 1). Such broad tropes, a summary of any coming-of-age narrative, rather than specifically Asian or Australian, or even Asian Australian, appeal to the notions of "reconciliatory universalism" and "celebration of national cultural diversity" that Huggan suggests are a feature of integrationist anthologies (118).

The text's introduction also reveals a productive and strategic tension between integration and intervention. Pung promises readers that the stories in the anthology will "show us what it's like behind the stereotypes," and she adds, "growing up is a funny time. During no other period will we experience so many firsts: first day at school, first friend, first love, first fear, first heartbreak, first loss, first epiphany..." (1–2). With these statements, Pung addresses a universal readership ("us") who are assumed to share the "firsts" of "growing up" as a common experience. This builds intimacy with the reader, who is invited to consider his or her own childhood, rather than the anthology's political agenda. Yet at the same time, the mention of stereotypes is implicitly interventionist and political, acknowledging a history of Asian-Australian misrepresentation.

Pung opens the introduction with an anecdote about her own childhood, where she reveals she was the subject of racist comments by other children. She says

> When I was growing up, we were called Power-Points. I thought it was because we were so smart and dweeby in a Microsoft-magnate sort of way. All that untapped potential! All that electrifying brain power! Then someone pointed to an Australian power-socket, and told me to take a closer look. Imagine it was a face, they said, think about what kind of face it would be. They saw two sloping lines and one straight down the middle and thought it was hilarious. ("Introduction" 1)

In this anecdote, Pung signals to the reader that *Growing up* may not be the mere "celebration" of cultural diversity that integrationist anthologies offer. Her childhood sketch serves as an implicit rationale for the project, justifying its existence and indicating the anthology's antiracist aims. Yet at the same time as declaring her text's intentions, Pung uses humor to lighten the tone. By evoking the image of a "smart and dweeby...Microsoft magnate" she makes fun of the "model minority" stereotype that is so frequently used to represent Asian people in Australian discourse: the idea that Asian people are high-achieving, model citizens, who work hard to gain professional status.[9] The use of humor here undermines the authority of the racist sentiments Pung encountered in her childhood and works to build the reader's complicity in the anthology's interventionist project.

When considering how this text uses aspects of both interventionist and integrationist anthologies as a way of reaching the widest possible audience, it is interesting to note that the introduction that appears in the final published copy of *Growing up* was not the introduction Pung initially wrote.[10] She had written a more strident introduction that was more explicitly interventionist, positioning the book in terms of race politics, where she asks

> So what was it like for a yellow or brown person growing up in a country where "Advance Australia *Fair*" was taken literally to mean "advance, pale-faced patriots," while those of a different colour should be effaced? ("Original Introduction")

In this original introduction, Pung's childhood anecdotes are decidedly more assertive:

> In secondary school, the only representations I saw of our early Asian settlers— people with faces like my relatives—were in illustrations as pigtailed caricatured demons or hanging dead from trees in the goldfields; even though the early pre- mining-boom Chinese were known to be carpenters, merchants and free-settler farmers. ("Original Introduction")

Pung revised the introduction after being warned that readers directly confronted with explicit references to Australia's history of racism would avoid buying or reading *Growing up*. Pung explains

> After [...] the introduction was completed and edited, I was told by a trusted adviser who had decades of experience in the book publishing industry, that this type of heavy introduction might not make people want to pick up the book at Borders. She was [...] absolutely right. Academics and students might be interested in the history of Asian-Australians, but we as a popular culture are perhaps not ready. ("Original Introduction")

Pung is clearly aware of the difficulties involved in attracting an audience for a text that is literary, yet has clear sociopolitical aspirations. This awareness is embodied in the selections made for the anthology, as well as Pung's "Introduction," and it is visible in structural choices, such as the table of contents, which are drawn from archetypes of Australian national identity. For example, the first section of the anthology is entitled "Strine," the colloquial term for "Australian" English language (vii) and focuses on experiences of learning either English or a family language. Other sections include "Pioneers," "Battlers," "Mates," or "Legends" (vii–xi). These archetypes of "Australianness" are ones traditionally associated a white, male, heterosexual figure.[11] By using these categories here, Pung suggests that the qualities of stoicism, tenacity, and loyalty embodied in the "pioneer," "battler," or "mate" can also apply to Asian Australians, and that they are not, as she puts it in the introduction, "confined to those with white faces and First-Fleet heritage" (2).

While the structure of the anthology is directly interventionist, the book's cover returns to a more ambiguous mode. On one hand, the cover makes an appeal to the apparently universal experience of childhood and adolescence. Kate Douglas notes that until relatively recently, childhood and adolescence in an Australian context has traditionally been regarded nostalgically as a utopian, "Edenic" time (10). The cover of *Growing up* includes a key feature that is consistent with this observation. It depicts a school photograph that shows three rows of primary-school-age children posing with their teacher, and a board that reads "Gabrimagrie Primary School, Grade Prep, 1970."[12] For readers who grew up in Australia over the past 40 years or so, the yearly (color) school photograph would presumably be a familiar sight, one that might prompt a nostalgic remembrance of childhood. In this way, the photograph is designed to be a universal symbol of childhood, provoking readers to view growing up as something experienced by everyone in the same way.

On the other hand, the cover literally highlights that this is not the case, thereby indicating Pung's interventionist agenda. The single child of "Asian" appearance, seated in the front row of the class, is subtly tinted a contrasting yellow color. In the context of Australia's history of positioning people of Asian heritage as the "yellow peril," a clear statement is being made about the "Asian" child being singled out because of his racialized appearance. Such detail disrupts a purely nostalgic reading of childhood as an "Edenic time," signaling the book's position as a text that addresses the role of "race" in Australian national and individual identity constructions.[13]

Childhood and the figure of the child, then, are central to Pung's project of literary activism. From the cover of the book to the individual autobiographical narratives inside the text, the theme of childhood provides a way for Pung to appeal to a wide range of readers in a way that other themes may not.

On the one hand, childhood narratives appeal to the apparently universal experience of coming-of-age, implying that the anthology is "not just for Asian Australians," but for "everyone," thus broadening the text's potential readership. As Douglas highlights, over the past two decades, in the wake of the 1990 United Nations Convention on the Rights of the Child, the figure of the child has been "highly visible at all levels of Western cultural life from art and literature through advertising, popular television programs and films" (4). In an Australian context, childhood and adolescence, then, is presumed to be a time of life that all readers are familiar with and may relate to regardless of individual cultural heritage.

On the other hand, while childhood broadens an appeal to readers, it also provides Pung with a way of demonstrating a range of Asian-Australian experiences. As she explains, in planning the *Growing up* project, "I concentrated on the period of 'growing up' because that's the period when most of life's 'firsts' happen and I also wanted the definition of Asian Australian to be as diverse and inclusive as possible" ("Q&A with

Alice Pung"). In this way, childhood becomes political strategy: a way actively to assert presence and diversity.[14] Douglas contends

> childhood is recognizable synecdoche for history – a means of explaining and interpreting the past, revising and correcting the mistakes of history. Concurrently, childhood continues to be a symbol of the future and its potential – a means for sanctioning an autobiographical narrative and for drawing attention to politics (9).

In *Growing up*, the figure of the Asian-Australian child functions as a cultural site, where Australia's racist and exclusionary history may be revised. The Asian-Australian child selves presented in the anthology also serve as symbols of the future, signifying a shift away from colonial Anglo-American-centric conceptions of Australia to a more complex vision of the country that includes, rather than excludes, Asia.

Rewriting the received scripts of childhood: relational narratives

Moving from an exploration of the anthology's form and paratexts, I now consider how the individual autobiographical narratives "inside" the anthology contribute to *Growing up's* project of literary activism. Here, I specifically consider two of the most prominent ways that individual authors narrate their childhood selves: via relational narrative modes and through the use of humor.

In recent years, the idea of an autonomous autobiographical subject has been dismantled. In place of this idea has come the notion that autobiographical representation is inevitably relational, that, as G. Thomas Couser puts it "one person's autobiography is inevitably someone else's biography. That is, it is generally admitted that one cannot write about oneself without representing others..." (140). This approach is evident in *Growing up*, as the most prominent mode individual authors use to represent themselves is a relational approach. Many of the stories begin with the autobiographical author introducing what John Paul Eakin has termed a "proximate other" (86), and a number of the stories open with reference to family members such as parents or grandparents. For example, six of the authors begin their stories by introducing his or her father. Bon-Wai Chou begins, "My father grew up in the country" (133); Diem Vo starts "My father owned a Vietnamese video store" (155); Phillip Tang's first line states, "My father had a sixth sense" (173); Cindy Pan says "Daddy took my hand in his firm capacious one" (179); Chin Shen begins "My Dad grew up in Shanghai" (183) and Pauline Nguyen starts "Like his peers, my father wanted desperately to raise four high achievers" (291). Many of the authors also begin with information about their grandfathers or great-grandfathers. Amy Choi's story, for example, opens with the line "I was never particularly kind to my grandfather" (7). Ken Chau begins most of his poems – which are interspersed throughout the anthology – by introducing his great-grandfather. His bitterly ironic poem, *The Early Settlers* starts, "Great-Grandfather arrived in 1897 to grow corn cabbage tobacco in Wahgunyah" (25).

Mothers and grandmothers also feature as proximate others in many of the stories. Sunil Badami uses his mother as a way to relate the racism he experienced as a child and his embarrassment at having an Indian name. After being called a range of offensive terms at school Badami's mother counsels: "Stones and sticks and such-like can only shake skeletons. Just rise over it!" (9). In Diana Nguyen's narrative, her mother plays a central role in showing the demands of parental expectation on a first generation Australian (287), and, in her story entitled "Destiny," Shalini Akhil's grandmother functions as a proximate other who guides Akhil to accept and be proud of her Indian Australian identity (176).

In her comprehensive study of Asian-American intergenerational family memoirs, Rocío G. Davis suggests that the relational narrative mode provides a way for the autobiographical narrator to "reconfigure" his or her identity whilst acknowledging a "cultural debt to family" and exploring the "meanings that the family history might have for the writer's present or community" (*Relative Histories* 13). She argues that this "process activates [. . .] a recognition of the power of personal narratives inserted in the public forum to engage historical and cultural issues, in order to challenge dominant mainstream versions that have often hidden, misrepresented or invalidated these stories" (*Relative Histories* 13).

While the short autobiographical narratives in *Growing up* are not the full-length, North American intergenerational memoirs that Davis is talking about, Davis' observations are useful to consider here. In relating their childhood selves through the biographical lens of a proximate other, the authors in Pung's anthology reconfigure the identities prescribed them via the misrepresentation or marginalization of people of Asian heritage in Australian public life and remind readers of the historical presence and contribution of Asians in Australia. In doing so, these individual narratives challenge prevailing versions of "Australian-ness" and therefore further the anthology's interventionist aims.

Rewriting the received scripts of childhood: humor

In addition to a relational mode of narrating childhood, many of the individual authors use humor. In this context, humor might be interpreted as a desire for acceptance and read as contributing to a "celebratory" integrationist agenda. However, a close reading of a number of individual autobiographical narratives in *Growing up* shows that humor works in a more sophisticated way for these narrators, and it is a feature that Pung herself has commented on. At the 2008 launch of *Growing up*, in a speech describing her experience of speaking at public events such as book launches and writers' festivals, Pung said that whenever she would stand up to speak, she would sense that the audience had particular expectations of the stories she would tell. Pung suggested that, because of her visibility as an "Asian-Australian" young woman, audience members expected particular "migrant narratives": tales of survival and "triumph over adversity," rather than the humorous anecdotes Pung had prepared. As a result, Pung often felt that she had to adjust her approach. She says

> I thought shit, I'd better scrap my jokes [. . .] people saw a small Asian girl who had written a book and you could almost feel the women in the audience getting ready to open their bags and get out the tissues. ("The Launch of *Growing up*")

Pung's keen sense of audience expectation is consistent with Sidonie Smith and Julia Watson's assertion that as readers of auto/biography "we expect particular kinds of stories to be told by those who have a direct and personal knowledge of that experience" (*Reading Autobiography* 173). When it comes to Asian-Australian narratives, it seems that many readers expect a standard "rags-to-riches, overcoming adversity" story: one that relates difficulties of migration, followed by a narrative of apparent success, where success is generally measured in economic terms.

This model of expectation is understandable, given two factors. Firstly, the prominence in Australia of Asian-American and Asian-Anglo diasporic literature, such as Jung Chang's *Wild Swans* or Adeline Yen Mah's *Falling Leaves*. Such "blockbuster" texts have been powerful in shaping readers' expectations and providing a template for writers who follow in their wake.[15] As Pung herself suggests, when it comes to Asian-Australian writing,

> people really expect a certain kind of narrative, and that's because we've had a lot of Asian-American literature. I read so much of it when I was growing up. But it didn't really reflect my experience. I wanted to create something distinctly Australian. ("The Launch of *Growing up*")

Secondly, Smith and Watson suggest that "people tell stories about their lives through the cultural scripts available to them, and they are governed by cultural strictures about self-presentation in public" (*Reading Autobiography*, 176). When it comes to narrating childhood in contemporary "Western" contexts, Australia included, Douglas suggests that two of the dominant "scripts for remembering" are "nostalgia and trauma" (14). The prevalence of these scripts of nostalgia and trauma means that readers have arguably come to expect these modes of narration in childhood autobiographical writing. The narrative templates available for Asian-Australian writers may be even more narrow and prescriptive and, for writers like Pung, neither the nostalgic nor the traumatic, "overcoming adversity" model adequately reflects their experiences.

In *Growing up*, while some of the individual authors narrate their childhood selves in ways that fit these existing templates, a number of the authors choose alternative methods, such as humor. In doing so, these authors contribute to *Growing up's* interventionist agenda, by rewriting or subverting the existing autobiographical and national scripts about Asian-Australian identity. This is particularly significant in an Australian context, where humor is often cited as a characteristically Australian trait. For example, an Australian Federal Government website devoted to outlining "Australian humour" explains

> Australian humour has a long history that can be traced back to our origins as convict colonies [...] This unique sense of humour is recognised [...] the world over as being distinctly Australian. Our humour is dry, full of extremes, anti-authoritarian, self-mocking and ironic. ("Australian Humour")

In the context of Pung's anthology, authors who use a humorous narrative mode signal their "Australianness" and position their literary work as Australian. Further, literary critic Wenche Ommundsen has suggested that the "latest generation" of Asian-Australian writers, including Pung, seek to distance themselves from prescribed Anglo-

American "refugee story" templates ("Of Dragons and Devils," 509). Humor provides a way, then, for many of the *Growing up* authors to do this and to assert a new generational identity.

For example, Tom Cho's piece, "Learning English," begins with the lines "when I first arrived in Australia, I did not know a word of English. I began English lessons through a migrant settlement program soon after I arrived but found it all very difficult" (15). These opening sentences, with their realism, and discussion of the linguistic obstacles faced by many migrants, raise reader expectations that what follows will be a "migrant story" according to the dominant "overcoming adversity" script. However, Cho confounds these expectations by adopting a surreal, humorous mode

> things did improve when I learnt the trick of replacing words I did not know with phrases like "'bla, bla, bla" or "yada, yada, yada," "whatever" or the name of a celebrity [...]. I was born in a town called Rod Stewart. Back in those days Rod Stewart was a very busy town. The major industries were David Hasselhoff and coal (15).

Peppering his story with the names of celebrities, such as "Bruce Willis" and "Oprah," Cho explains how watching American television influenced his language learning to the extent that he "now answer[s] to the name 'Ricardo Montalban,'" although a friend suggests Cho is more like a "Chinese Heather Locklear" (16).

In "Learning English," Cho uses surrealist humor to disorient the reader. Form and content work together to communicate the bewilderment Cho's child-self experienced learning an unfamiliar language. The insertion of *non sequiturs* into Cho's basic biographical "facts" disrupts a purely realist autobiographical reading and, more significantly, unsettles a simplistic "migrant narrative" interpretation. Therefore, the use of humor here is far from integrationist. On the contrary, it works to further the anthology's interventionist aims. Cho constructs his childhood vignette to be a reminder about how expectations about identity can be restrictive and exclusive, and he prompts the reader to reconsider his or her assumptions.

Another author who uses humor in the anthology is Tanveer Ahmed. In his autobiographical story, "Exotic Rissole," Ahmed compares his own family life with that of his childhood friend, Daryl Lynch. Ahmed admires his friend, saying "I loved everything about my best friend Daryl. I called him Lynchy, performing the Australian practice of elongating someone's name with an 'o' or a 'y'. I admired his crew cut and was riveted by his rat's tail [hairstyle]" (96). Meanwhile, Ahmed's father cuts his son's hair, thereby "channelling 1970s rural Bangladeshi fashion through" young Ahmed (96). Ahmed is envious of the fact that Lynchy has "an airconditioner and a soda-stream machine," explaining, "I was amazed. My parents would never buy such a wonderful thing" (97). While Ahmed's mother, much to his embarrassment, makes spicy food, Daryl complains that "all his family ate were rissoles, steak and baked potatoes" (97). Ahmed says "I would look at him with envy, wishing my mother would cook such things" (97).

Humor in this story comes primarily from the way Ahmed uses a comparative device of a "Bangladeshi Australian" and an "Australian" household. The fact that Ahmed admires his friend's conventional hairstyle of a crew cut and a rat's tail, one that is associated with a white working-class identity, would arguably seem oddly amusing to many Australian readers. Likewise, the idea that Ahmed is envious of such pedestrian "Australian" foods such as rissoles and potatoes seems absurdly funny to those readers who find such foods familiar, ordinary, and bland.

Yet this comparative framework functions not only to amuse the reader, but to shift prevailing ideas of who and what is viewed as exotic. By viewing an "ordinary," everyday "Australian" food as exotic and valuable, Ahmed shrewdly subverts the discourse of exoticism frequently present in representations of "Asia." Ahmed's childhood narrative turns the ethnographic lens away from his own family and onto his quintessentially Australian school friend, Lynchy. Therefore in "Exotic Rissole," the Australian "way of life" becomes "other," something for young Ahmed to discover and sample.

One final autobiographical story that demonstrates the use of humor in *Growing up* is Shalini Akhil's "Destiny." In "Destiny," Akhil uses both humor and a relational narrative approach to show how her grandmother helps her to explore her identity as an Indian-Australian girl. Akhil tells the reader how when she was young she would watch *Wonder Woman* on television and imitate her, sure that it was her destiny to one day *be* Wonder Women. However, when Akhil's grandmother arrives to stay with the family, things change. Her grandmother reminds Akhil of her Indian heritage, and Akhil realizes "I could never grow up to be exactly like Wonder Woman. My skin was the wrong colour, my eyes were the wrong colour, and my legs just weren't long enough" (177).

As the story progresses, Akhil's relationship with her grandmother helps her to accept her appearance and adjust her idea of destiny. She says her grandmother "didn't like the way Wonder Woman dressed" and that "she thought it looked like she'd left the house in her underwear – like she'd forgotten to put her skirt on"(177). Her grandmother warns, "You can fight all the crime in the world [. . .] but if you leave the house without putting your skirt on, no one will take you seriously" (177). Her grandmother subsequently suggests that Wonder Woman could wear "a lungi" – traditional Indian dress – and Akhil and her grandmother go about making a Wonder Woman costume out of traditional Indian dress and jewelry.

Akhil's naïve child-self watches her grandmother prepare an Indian lunch of "superhero food," including "magic rotis" to accompany "super-hero eggs" with "onions and some chillies" (178). Her grandmother assures her that this food will help her run faster and see better in the dark. As the story progresses, Akhil develops pity for the television Wonder Woman, saying that rather than Indian superhero food, Wonder Woman only had "peanut-butter and jelly sandwiches" to eat (178). She says she is sorry that Wonder Woman does not have a "magical grandmother to suggest wearing a lungi over her embarrassing sparkly nappies" (178). By the end of the story, Akhil is so convinced that Wonder Woman is less privileged than her that she decides to change her destiny; she says that "When I grew up, I was going to be *Indian* Wonder Woman" (178).

In this story, Akhil's child self looks to the future and to her imagined destiny – becoming a powerful "superhero" of dual cultures. Her grandmother's wisdom guides young Akhil to explore other "superhero" options – ones that include, rather than negate, Akhil's cultural identity. Her grandmother's criticism of Wonder Woman's clothing influences Akhil to see the iconic, idealized female "superhero" as absurd and her choice of "peanut butter and jelly sandwiches" as woefully inadequate.

Conclusion

In many ways, *Growing up* appears to be an integrationist anthology. With its appeals to childhood as a universal theme, and the use of self-deprecating humor – often viewed as a quintessentially "Australian" characteristic – by Pung and many of the book's contributors, *Growing up* may at first seem to be an example of "happy hybridity," an assimilationist gesture towards celebratory models of cultural identity (Lo, "Beyond Happy Hybridity" 166).[16] The use of childhood autobiographical narratives also appeals to a diverse range of readers. Pung has said, "Although this collection is titled *Growing up Asian in Australia*, I wanted to bring out the common humanity of our authors, so that any reader could pick up the book and be amused, amazed, moved and heartened" ("Q&A with Alice Pung").

Yet, as this discussion has indicated, *Growing up* is more complex. A reading of the anthology's paratexts shows that Pung draws on both integrationist and interventionist elements, complicating Huggan's binary "multicultural anthology" model. Childhood autobiography is a cultural site where histories and identities may be reconfigured. Pung's choice of such narratives is not simply about universal appeal but is an astutely political gesture. Davis argues, in her study of Asian-North American autobiographies of childhood, "when ethnic subjects write autobiography, they control the representation of the American or Canadian subject, instead of allowing themselves to be passively represented by the received scripts of the dominant culture" (*Begin Here* 10).

Although Davis is speaking of a North American context, Pung and the authors featured in her anthology have similar aims. The autobiographies of childhood in the anthology function as a collection of "strategic performances," what Ang has described as the "deliberate, rhetorical construction of a self for public, not private purposes: the displayed self is a strategically fabricated performance, one which stages a useful identity, an identity which can be put to work" (*On Not Speaking Chinese* 24). The anthology format provides a way to present a number of these "strategically fabricated" performances and to indicate to a wide readership the presence of a diverse range of identities within contemporary "Australian-ness." *Growing up* thereby complicates prevailing notions of both "Asian" and "Australian," unsettling dominant narratives of national identity and creating a new "Australian" identity as the "Asian century" dawns in contemporary Australia.

Acknowledgements

I would like to thank Tully Barnett, Kylie Cardell, Rocío Davis, Kate Douglas, Hannah Kent, Leena Kurvet-Käosaar, Claire Lynch, and Julie Rak for their helpful feedback on this paper at the Flinders University Life Narrative Research Group's "Autobiographies of Childhood" symposium in July 2012.

Notes

1. In an Australian context, the term "Asian" tends to be used to refer to people who are from East or South East Asia, or have such heritage. Representations of Asian people in various Australian media have mostly consisted of stereotypes that present Asian people variously as exotic, devious, or ridiculous. Some of the most prominent representations include nineteenth-century images like the "Mongolian Octopus" cartoon or the pigtail-wearing character of "cookie" on the goldfields, to more contemporary stereotypes like reality television William Hung's Australian equivalent, "whacky Asian" Zhuo "Flynn" Lui, who appeared on *Australian Idol* in 2004. For an up-to-date discussion and analysis of Asian Australian representation on Australian television, see Law (2009).

2. It is important to note that the White Australia Policy also functioned to marginalize and dispossess Aboriginal people, whose cultures were, and continue to be, doubly impacted by immigration to Australia. See Morton-Robinson (2003, 23–40).

3. For example, in November 2012, the Australian Government released the findings of its report entitled *Australia in the Asian Century* where it outlined numerous recommendations aimed at making Australia "a more Asia-literate and Asia-capable nation." See Australian Government. *Australia in the Asian Century*.

4. See, for example, the Asian Australian Studies Research Network website, the Asian Australian Film Forum, and the online magazine, *Peril*.

5. Pung writes for a range of Australian publications, but is probably best known for her 2006 memoir, *Unpolished Gem* (2006) that relates Pung's childhood and adolescence growing up in a Chinese-Cambodian family in suburban Melbourne. She has also recently written a second memoir, *Her Father's Daughter* (2011).

6. For a discussion of Australian "multicultural" anthologies, see also Gunew (1994, 6–10).

7. Jillian Sandell, citing Barbara Benedict, says: "anthologies have been an important genre for minority literatures because it allows for what Barbara Benedict calls a 'heteroglossia of diverse voices' to be published within a single text." Benedict (1996, 29) qtd. in Sandell (2005, 293).

8. On the constructed nature of autobiographical acts see, for example, Smith and Watson (eds.) (1998).

9. "Model minority" refers to the way Asian people in countries like the USA and Australia are frequently represented as 'good', model citizens, who work hard, gain professional status, and live according to so-called "traditional family values". As Maria Lo points out, "model minority discourse. . .is essentially a discourse of containment." It is a way of fixing an identity for anyone who looks "Asian." Lo (2008, 97). For a discussion of the "model minority" stereotype in Australia, see T. Khoo (2003, 33).

10. For Pung's explanation of this process, see Pung's, "Original Introduction."

11. Robyn Morris highlights that "In constructions of 'Australianness', the cast is historically male dominated. . .heroic, hyper-masculinised, white and heterosexual—figures such as the stoic bushman, brash bushranger or the fearless ANZAC solider are routinely resurrected in cultural celebrations of Australian nationhood" (152).

12. For a detailed discussion about the covers of autobiographies of childhood, see Douglas (2010, 44).

13. For a discussion and analysis of school photographs, see Marianne Hirsch and Leo Spitzer's "About Class Photos."

14. Following Henry Jenkins' work, Douglas contends that "the child figure has been, and continues to be important in a range of political and ideological battles. . . 'almost every political battle of the twentieth century has been fought on the backs of children.'" See Douglas (2010, 4).

15. Wenche Ommunsen notes that "the success of diasporic Chinese writers such as Maxine Hong Kingston, Jung Chang and Adeline Yen Mah produced a receptive audience throughout the Western world and spawned numerous imitations. The '*Wild Swans* factor' has also returned to haunt other writers, creating an arbitrary standard against which they have been judged, reinforcing cultural stereotypes for Western consumption." Ommundsen (2002, 68)

16. Jacqueline Lo's concept of "happy hybridity" argues that there are models of hybridity that deny the complexity of hybrid identities in favor of a celebratory view. According to Lo, "the happy hybridity model celebrates the proliferation of difference" with "the end result" being "harmonious fusion" Lo (2000, 166).

References

Ang, Ien. "Introduction: Alter/Asian Cultural Interventions for 21st Century Australia." In *Alter/Asians: Asian-Australian Identities in Art, Media and Popular Culture*, edited by Ien Ang, Sharon Chalmers, Lisa Law and Mandy Thomas. Sydney: Pluto Press, 2000, xiii–xxx.

———. *On Not Speaking Chinese: Living Between Asia and the West*. London: Routledge, 2001.

Asian Australian Studies Research Network. 2012. Web. 21 Sept. 2012

Asian Australian Film Forum. 2011. Web. 21 Sept. 2012

Australian Government. "Australian Humour." 17 Dec. 2007. Web. 2 Oct. 2012

———. "Australia in the Asian Century." Canberra: 2012. Web. 30 Oct. 2012

Benedict, Barbara M. *Making the Modern Reader: Cultural Mediation in Early Modern Literary Anthologies*. Princeton, NJ: Princeton University Press, 1996.

Black Inc. "The Launch of Growing up Asian in Australia at the Sydney Writers' Festival." n.d. Web. 24 Sept. 2012

Bobis, Merlinda. "'Voice-Niche-Brand': Marketing Asian-Australianness." *Australian Humanities Review* 45 (2008): 119–125. Web. 5 Aug. 2012.

Chang, Jung. *Wild Swans: Three Daughters of China*. London: Harper Collins, 1991.

Couser, G. Thomas. "Genre Matters: Form, Force, and Filiation." *Life Writing* 2.2 (2005): 139–156.

Davis, Rocío G. *Begin Here: Reading Asian North American Autobiographies of Childhood*. Honolulu: University of Hawai'i Press, 2007.

———. *Relative Histories: Mediating History in Asian American Family Memoirs*. Honolulu: University of Hawai'i Press, 2011.

Douglas, Kate. *Contesting Childhood: Autobiography, Trauma, and Memory*. New Brunswick: Rutgers University Press, 2010.

Eakin, Paul John. *How Our Lives Become Stories*. Ithaca: Cornell University Press, 1999.

Eliades, Patricia. "Anthologising the Minority." *Hecate* 21.1 (1995): 74–97.

Franklin, Cynthia G. *Writing Women's Communities: The Politics and Poetics of Contemporary Multi-Genre Anthologies*. Madison: University of Wisconsin Press, 1997.

Gunew, Sneja. *Framing Marginality: Multicultural Literary Studies*. Melbourne: Melbourne University Press, 1994.

Hirsch, Marianne and Leo Spitzer. *About Class Photos*. Nomadikon: The Bergen Center of Visual Culture, Oct. 2009. Web. 16 Dec. 2012.

Huggan, Graham. *Australian Literature: Postcolonialism, Racism, Transnationalism*. Oxford: Oxford University Press, 2007.

Khoo, Olivia. "Regionalizing Asian Australian Identities." *Continuum: Journal of Media & Cultural Studies* 25.4 (2011): 461–4.

Khoo, Tseen-Ling. *Banana Bending: Asian-Australian and Asian-Canadian Literature*. Montreal: McGill-Queen's University Press, 2003.

Law, Benjamin Yuk Nung. "The New Lows: Representing Asian-Australians on Television." Ph.D. thesis. Queensland University of Technology (2009). Web. 22 Sept. 2012.

Lazaroo, Simone. "Not Just Another Migrant Story." *Australian Humanities Review* 45 (2008): 109–118. Web. 5 Aug. 2012.

Lee, Regina. "'Flexible Citizenship' Strategic Chinese Identities in Asian Australian Literature." *Journal of Intercultural Studies* 27.1 (2006): 223–7.

Lo, Jacqueline. "Beyond Happy Hybridity: Performing Asian Australian Identities." In *Alter/Asians: Asian-Australian Identities in Art, Media and Popular Culture*, edited by Ien Ang, Sharon Chalmers, Lisa Law and Mandy Thomas. Sydney: Pluto Press, 2000, 152–68.

———. "Disciplining Asian Australian Studies: Projections and Introjections." In *Locating Asian-Australian Cultures*, edited by Tseen Khoo. London: Routledge, 2008, 11–28.

Lo, Jacqueline, Tseen Khoo, and Helen Gilbert. "Introduction: New Formation in Asian Australian Cultural Politics." In *Diapora: Negotiating Asian-Australia*, edited by Helen Gilbert, Tseen Khoo and Jacqueline Lo. St Lucia: University of Queensland Press, 2000, 1–12.

Lo, Maria. "Model Minorities Models of Resistance: Native Figures in Asian Canadian Literature." *Canadian Literature* 196. Spring (2008): 96–114.

Lockard, Joe and Jillian Sandell. "National Narratives and the Politics of Inclusion: Historicizing American Literature Anthologies." *Pedagogy: Critical Approaches to Teaching Literature, Language, Composition and Culture* 8.2 (2008): 227–54.

Morris, Robyn. "Growing up an Australian: Renegotiating Mateship, Masculinity and Australiannesss." In *Locating Asian-Australian Cultures*. edited by Tseen Khoo. London: Routledge, 2008, 151–66.

Morton-Robinson, Aileen. "I Still Call Australia Home: Indigenous Belonging and Place." In *Uprootings/Regroundings: Questions of Home and Migration*. edited by Sara Ahmed, Claudia Castañeda, Anne-Marie Fortier and Mimi Sheller. Oxford: Berg, 2003, 23–40.

Ommundsen, Wenche. "Of Dragons and Devils: Chinese-Australian Life Stories." *Journal of the Association for the Study of Australian Literature* 1 (2002): 67–80.

———. "'This story does not begin on a boat': What is Australian about Asian Australian writing?" *Continuum: Journal of Media & Cultural Studies* 25.4 (2011): 503–13.

Peril: Asian Australian Arts and Culture Magazine, 2006–2012. Web. 21 Sept. 2012

Pung, Alice. *Growing up Asian in Australia*. Melbourne: Black Inc., 2008.

Pung, Alice. *Original Introduction to Growing up Asian in Australia*. Sept. 2009. Web. 10 Aug. 2012.

Pung, Alice. *Growing up Asian in Australia: Q&A with Alice Pung*. June 2008. Web. 10 July 2012.

Pung, Alice. *Her Father's Daughter*. Melbourne: Black Inc., 2011.

Pung, Alice. *Unpolished Gem*. Melbourne: Black Inc., 2006.

Sandell, Jillian. "This Bridge Called My Book: Anthologies of Women's Life Writing and the Problem of Community." In *Women's Life Writing and Imagined Communities*. edited by Cynthia Huff. Abingdon: Routledge, 2005, 278–98.

Smith, Sidonie, and Julia Watson. *Reading Autobiography: A Guide for Interpreting Life Narratives*. Minneapolis: University of Minnesota Press, 2001.

Smith, Sidonie and Julia Watson, eds. *Women, Autobiography, Theory: A Reader*. Madison: University of Wisconsin Press, 1998.

Yen Mah, Adeline. *Falling Leaves: The True Story of an Unwanted Chinese Daughter*. New York: John Wiley & Sons, 1997.

Tully Barnett

"READING SAVED ME": WRITING AUTOBIOGRAPHICALLY ABOUT TRANSFORMATIVE READING EXPERIENCES IN CHILDHOOD

In recent years, the "memoir boom" coupled with an explosion of "books about books" has seen members of the literary establishment writing about their experiences of reading in their childhoods and adolescences. Readers are impacted by what they read and their sense of self can be both constituted and signified by the texts they have read, and when and how they read them. Memoirs of literary figures underscore ways in which this can happen. This article considers bibliographic nonfiction works by Michael Dirda, Alberto Manguel, and Karla Holloway, as three very different kinds of autobiographical expressions about reading in childhood, in order to explore how these narratives are put to use. These authors construct their childhood reading experiences in different ways. In all three, however, the value of books and the act of reading serve to frame their autobiographical recollections and to solidify a position in the literary establishment. Ultimately, memoirs of reading can advance conservative constructions of childhood that locate acts of reading and book appreciation in opposition to, and as a means of escaping, a social class.

"Reading and life are not separate but symbiotic," declares Julian Barnes, Booker Prize-winning author and fixture of the British literary establishment, in *The Guardian*. The act of reading is tied, he asserts, to the act of living. But Barnes is not referring to just any act of reading. He is not talking about workaday reading such as reading the back of a cereal box, or a sign at the train station, or the information sheet in a box of prescription antibiotics. Rather, he is referring to a higher, more sacred understanding of reading reserved for literature and for reading experiences that are personally transformative, especially fiction and non-fiction that deeply transport or impact the reader. Alberto Manguel furthers this association of reading with the sublime when he writes that "we are, at the core, reading animals and [. . .] the art of reading, in its broadest sense, defines our species" (*A Reader* ix). In this statement, Manguel elevates reading from an act to an art, infusing it with a sense of grandeur; for him, the practice of reading is what separates humans from animals. But in suggesting this, Manguel stratifies different kinds of humans; if reading is what makes us human then those who enjoy the act, who revel in it, or who produce reading experiences for other people might be more human than those who do not.

These statements about reading demonstrate the extent to which members of the literary establishment – by which I mean people who work in roles associated with the writing, collecting, or editing of literature, in publishing and bookish taste-making, or in professing literature in Academia and related roles – locate in the act of reading, and in the objects of the book and the library, a symbolism, even a sense of the sublime, that has implications for culture and cultural consumption. Such contentions are woven with high-culture assumptions not just about the paramount importance of reading, but its inherent value as a measure of life, of humanity and the human, and of identity. These are public statements made in "cultural gatekeeping" publications – the former in *The Guardian*, a newspaper with a high-culture reputation – and the latter in Manguel's *A Reader on Reading*.[1] These authors are speaking directly to readers, to people at that very moment immersed in the act of reading and thus arguably biased toward such discourse.

The current boom in autobiographical writing about books and reading must be related to and considered alongside the memoir boom more broadly. A number of memoirists from different backgrounds have charted the growth of their intellects and subjectivities, their educations, and their journeys to writing their life story, through the books they read in their childhoods.[2] Many more infuse their early reading experiences with a sense of the magic that set them on the path to becoming lovers of, and contributors to, and gatekeepers of, literature. What makes Barnes and Manguel stand out from the great many memoirists who reference childhood reading is that they are also veterans of the literary community and, to some extent, gatekeepers of literature. There are vested interests and agendas here, most obviously, to negotiate literature's place within culture.

This article considers the relationship between reading and the life story by looking at the ways in which cultural gatekeepers like Michael Dirda, Alberto Manguel, and Karla FC Holloway depict books and reading in their narratives of childhood. Dirda, a long time book reviewer for the *Washington Post*, Manguel, an internationally renowned writer, anthologiser, and publisher, and Holloway, an English professor, construct their reading experiences in childhoods in specific ways. For both Manguel and Dirda, reading is tied to escaping social class, while, for Holloway the act of reading is an experience tied to race and racial prejudice, a perspective which invests her work with greater political weight and significance. Ultimately, in all three instances, the book and the act of reading serve dual functions, not just as the crux of these autobiographical recollections and life narratives, but as the foundations of careers and livelihoods. This, I argue, significantly informs a common construction of transformative reading experiences in childhood.

Childhood as a site of self-construction

Nostalgic and sublime recollections of past reading experiences are inextricably integrated with another site of nostalgia: childhood. In *Childhood*, Chris Jenks offers a sociological perspective of childhood, pointing out that childhood politically charged. Henry Jenkins concurs when he writes that childhood – which, he points out, is always a "temporary state" – "has become an emblem for our own anxieties." Thus, how authors write autobiographically about their childhoods and about childhood in general is frequently linked to ideals of childhood that are in the contemporary moment. Kate Douglas argues that autobiographies of childhood "reveal more about the present than they do about the past" (6). Douglas contends that "twentieth-century autobiographers sought not only to understand childhood developmentally and socially – to understand their experiences of the world – but also to explore how experiences of childhood impact upon adult life" (9). Douglas's project in *Contesting Childhood* is to transcend a narrow focus on the *Bildungsroman* frame as the primary purpose for recounting childhood in memoir and in the scholarship of such memoirs – necessary given the popularity of trauma memoirs, for instance. However, it is clear that this model still has a powerful role, particularly in conservative contexts, for example, as seen in works by cultural gatekeepers. This is to make a distinction between the kinds of memoirs produced by established literary names and memoirs produced by the so-called ordinary people. In the 1990s, memoir

> did not prominently feature elder statesmen reporting on how their public lives neatly paralleled historical events. Instead, memoir in the '90s was dominated by the comparatively young whose private lives were emblematic of unofficial histories. (Gilmore 28)

This moment, that Gilmore terms the "memoir boom," is characterized by a focus on stories of trauma, addiction, abuse, lives lived on the edge of acceptable society, and on recoveries, as both Gilmore and Douglas show. For example, Jaycee Lee Dugard's memoir of her life after she was abducted as a child, *A Stolen Life: A Memoir*, acknowledges the place of books and reading in her attempt to stay sane in a horrific situation. Andrea Ashworth, similarly, speaks about reading in her abusive childhood in *Once in a House On Fire* (2004). More recently, *The End of Your Life Book Club* (2012) focuses on reading as a shared experience between mother and son during treatments for terminal cancer in the final months of her life. These works speak of books and reading that serve to transport the reader away from horrific lives or experiences, if only for a short time, as well as providing a reminder that a different future is possible, or, as in the case of *The End of Your Life*, that serve to give shape to the life lived and to build acceptance of death.

Autobiographies of cultural gatekeepers also appropriate the *Bildungsroman* frame and show the ways in which reading and books provide a means of enrichment, education, and escapism. Yet precisely because these authors are cultural gatekeepers as well as readers and autobiographers, there is another dimension to their recollections of childhood reading, namely to solidify the sense of the self as a deserving, faithful, and productive member of the literary establishment. That is, instead of testaments to the transcendence of an abusive, traumatic, or inevitable situation, these autobiographical acts are aimed at legitimating the place of the author in the literary establishment. While all memoirists narrate their childhoods through the lens of their adult selves, I am suggesting that in the memoirs of people employed in the broad field of literature, the implications require specific consideration.

Michael Dirda's memoir of a readerly child

Where some authors simply wish to chart their growth as readers, or their transition from reading to writing, or to communicate their love of books amongst a readership with, almost wholly, shared interests, others use the memoirs of reading in childhood for more specific purposes. Michael Dirda, a Pulitzer Prize-winning literary critic with a Ph.D. in comparative literature, published his memoir, *An Open Book: Coming of Age in the Heartland*, in 2003. This title conflates life and human experience with books, in the mode of Barnes and Manguel as discussed above, and constructs life as text. In addition, the title establishes that this mode of being – that is, being with books – is in direct or even brutal opposition to the non-bookishness of his home town of Lorain, Ohio, a blue collar, steel worker town.

This is not Dirda's first book about books. As a literary critic with the *Washington Post*, Dirda has published his musings about books in works such as *Readings: Essays and Literary Entertainments*, a collection of (mostly "personal") essays. It is also not the first time Dirda has written autobiographically about his youthful experiences with books. He opens *Readings* with an essay called "The Crime of His Life." In the second line of this essay he writes:

> One afternoon some thirty-five years ago, a 13-year-old boy was lingering in the book section of O'Neil's department store, surreptitiously turning the pages of *Tarzan the Untamed* [. . .] and read through an entire novel in the course of a lazy summer day [in the store]. (1)

Despite the use of the third person here, that boy is, of course, his own self. In this essay, Dirda dramatizes the experiences of his childhood reading activities and opportunities. He uses books as a means to frame or hang the narrative he wants to tell. The "crime" mentioned in the title of the autobiographical essay is the circumspect opening, in store, of prepackaged bundles of discounted books in order to create the particular set of books he wants to purchase. Dirda is a readerly child, a passionate, and determined one, a construction that serves his adult identity as a writer well.

It is not difficult to find examples of memoirists who want to list, even catalogue, the books of their childhood shelves and in their youthful hearts. Authors frequently link the rise of fledgling identities to the books they found in their early environment. In some of these narratives there is an inherent judgement as well, a positioning of the self as guardian of books in a culture that devalues them, and Dirda provides an illuminating case study of this avenue of self-portraiture. In *An Open Book*, Dirda writes:

> Mine, it now seems, may be the last generation to value the traditional bound book as the engine of education, culture and personal advancement. The future belongs to screens and keyboard. Though that may sound direly elegiac, I know people will always need stories and that any era's external packaging of them hardly matters: Oral formulas, scrolls, codices, paperbacks, e-texts—they all get the narrative job done. Nonetheless, what follows may often appear a kind of memorial, a minor monument to a time of softly turned pages, when the young entered libraries

hungry for books to devour rather than information to download, when printed matter still. (14)

In this way, Dirda constructs himself as a last sentinel watching the sun go down on the long and important history of the book. The use of the word "Elegiac" explicitly raises a connection with Sven Birkerts' 1994 *The Gutenberg Elegies*, a lament for what he sees as the unequivocal end of the book, and establishes both projects as memorials to the book as a dying art form as well as to the role of Dirda and Birkerts in safeguarding the reputation of the book in its dying moments. In this way, Dirda pursues a conservative project, one that assumes that the technology of the e-reader will necessarily see the demise of the printed book. This elegy for the book is coupled with the elegy for childhood. Indeed, the back cover of *An Open Book* contains "praise" for this work and for others by the author, including an endorsement by Harold Bloom, who calls this book "an elegy for childhood, youth, and first loves – both sexual and literary." The book's packaging contains other markers of book culture. The front cover contains two photographs. The first is a black and white picture of the author on the front porch of, one assumes, his house, aged about five or six with two younger children (most likely siblings) visible through the screen door behind him. The second is a color aerial photograph of the main street of Lorain, Ohio where Dirda grew up. Although undated on the dust jacket, this photograph displays markers of the 1950s or early 1960s in the models of cars on the road, the buildings, and their signage and other adornments. Steelworks are visible in the background. Both of these photographs communicate nostalgia consistent with memoirs of childhood.

The inside flap of the book's dust jacket also explicitly positions Dirda's love for reading in opposition to the class expectations of his "factory town" by opening with a statement of tension that defines the work: "'All that kid wants to do is stick his nose in a book,' Michael Dirda's steelworker father used to complain, worried about his son's mystifying passion for reading" (inside front jacket). However, as the narrative unfolds we learn that Dirda senior recites fragments of Edgar Allan Poe to his sick son (32), reads to his son (32), regularly takes him to the public library (34), builds bookcases for the family home (34), and later makes bracket shelves for his son's room (99). Yet, Dirda credits "serendipity" for furnishing "the Dirda household with a number of surprisingly good books" (35) instead of his parents, glossing his father's evident dissatisfaction with his blue collar job and expressed wish for his son to have a better life fuelled by literature and academia. Dirda's construction of reading literature allows him to construct an origin myth that foregrounds his own inherent "nature" as the ingredient that saved him from a steel worker life, rather than the nurturing role of his parents – clearly narrated on the page – as facilitators of his bookishness.

Dirda's book is a conventional memoir of childhood, covering the period of the author's life from age 4 to 19 and encompassing the usual topics and scripts for remembering such as meals, routes to school, chores, and parents' moods in the home. However, the book is divided in its table of contents into four sections titled "Learning to Read," "Turning the Pages," "Adult Material," and "A Liberal Education." This structure serves to further conflate reading with life. "Learning to Read" contains material about the author's life from about the age of four years old and commences the memoir, initiating a structure in which the depicted life begins not with birth but with the process of learning to read. "Turning the Pages" picks up the story from the beginning of junior high. "Adult Material" concerns the author's high school years, and "A Liberal Education" marks his life at Oberlin College from 1966. In "Michael Dirda's Book List," after the "Epilogue," Dirda shares with the reader two lists of books. The first is retrieved from a journal kept at the time, a list of books read by the time he was sixteen. The second is of books read by the end of high school. The inclusion of these lists at the end of this book serves to ensure that the reader knows how precocious a reader Dirda was in his teens by listing the highly literary, difficult books he sought out. The list also serves another purpose. Of the 55 books, just 4 are by women. While this is to some extent a reflection on cultural and environmental factors beyond the author's control, it also perpetuates, whether consciously or otherwise, the stereotype of the literary canon as the domain of white male authors. It also furthers a high art/low art agenda underpinning Dirda's writing. Throughout the book there is discussion about Dirda's love for comics in his childhood (54). He describes in detail the euphoria he felt when, after trading comics with a classmate, he is spontaneously given 30 extra comics for free:

> Utterly light headed, I pedalled home around six P.M. and en route noticed guys playing late-fall baseball in the field next to our elementary school, could even hear the *thwack* of the bats and the *thunk* of the balls against leather. At that moment, as when the dove descended upon the apostles, I felt the unmistakable presence of grace: The world was truly good and life a blessing. (57)

This use of sublime and religious language situates the experience of reading and (comic) book ownership within the icons of Christian tradition and American heartland identity (baseball). However, there is no list of comics read by the author at the end of this bookish memoir. Comic-book reading is positioned clearly as an early step toward the "real" reading he would embark upon later, as are other works of pulp fiction. Dirda reminisces that "if Agatha Christie provided my introduction to 'grown-up' fiction, then Fyodor Dostoyevsky deepened the casual relationship into a serious love affair" (126).

There are thus several undercurrents of elitism at work in Dirda's memoir: his positioning of himself as last sentinel standing watch over the dying print medium; his fashioning of his own autonomy in pursuing a career as a reader and writer in spite of evidence that his parents aided him in this journey; and his assertion of literature as a high art form and perpetuation of a high/low hierarchy. In doing this, Dirda further cultivates and validates his own worth and worthiness as cultural gatekeeping and the final two paragraphs of the Epilogue advance these threads further:

> Long ago my father used to warn me: "A writer writes. A reader reads." For most of my life, even that as a staff book reviewer and essayist for *The Washington Post*, I have thought of myself as primarily a reader. An enthusiastic, well-informed reader, to be sure, and one with a minor talent to evoke the particular excitement and quiddity of a novel, a collection of poems or a work of intellectual history. Nonetheless, I really should have listened to my dad and would give a lot to hear him yell at me just one more time: "Get your nose out of that book and go do something useful."

Yes, Dad. You may not, as you used to say, always be right, but you're never wrong. I now wish I had sat down with pen and paper more often than with an old paperback, had titled my days more towards being a Writer than a Reader. Still, who knows? Perhaps even now it's not altogether too late (322).

While this may seem a peculiar note to conclude on, potentially undermining the meaningful conflation of reading with life that was pursued so thoroughly over the preceding pages, it also demonstrates that a life of reading has enabled Dirda to pursue a life of writing. Despite his self-conscious protestations to the contrary, he is a "Writer," and the body of writing he has produced is the culmination of a life of reading. Dirda is not just last sentinel of the printed book: he is a contributor to that hallowed canon of work. The subtext is clear: reading saved Dirda from a working class life in a steelworker town. This is a narrative of success clearly meant to resonate with his readership, though it is markedly different to, for example, Jaycee Lee Dugard's account of reading as a means of coping with abuse after her abduction or Andrea Ashworth's account of reading as a means of dealing with childhood abuse, despite the fact that all three advance a thesis of reading as a means of salvation. Have studies of memoir and autobiography, encouraged by the boom in subaltern and traumatized voices, left us unprepared to deal with the conservative narratives of self that also populate the shelves of life writing? Dirda's recollections of his childhood are obviously shaped to convey a poverty of cultural wealth as well as material wealth. In doing so, and in chronicling the intellectual enlightenment bequeathed by the books he digested, he situates his life narrative within the *Bildungsroman* framework, albeit tinged with heroic fantasy: his autobiography chronicles his journey from economically and culturally disadvantaged working class upbringing to burgeoning connoisseur of the written word to his current station as respected literary critic commemorating and standing vigil over high-culture objects. In attending to narratives like Dirda's, we see the influence of the survivor narrative in memoir, though we also see how it can be co-opted for more abstract, less traumatic circumstances.

Alberto Manguel's holy erotics of reading

Though Dirda sanctifies his reading childhood in his memoir, Alberto Manguel repeatedly mystifies and makes sublime, indeed holy, the reading experience throughout his oeuvre. This is explicit in the way he begins *A History of Reading* – a nonfiction book about reading interspersed with accounts of his own personal experiences of books – with images, and descriptions of images, of saintly readers from Aristotle to Erasmus, Saint Dominic to Francesca, and Paolo to Mary Magdalen to Charles Dickens to Jorge Luis Borges. He muses that "All these readers, and their gestures, their craft, the pleasure, responsibility and power they derive from reading, are common with mine. I am not alone" (5), clueing us in to the community experience of reading. At this point, Manguel gives an account of his own learning to read (age 4) as an "act of conjuring" (6). Here, "shapes [...] metamorphosed from black lines and white spaces into a solid, sonorous, meaningful reality" (6). He characterizes reading as not just magical but crucial: "We all read ourselves and the world around us in order to glimpse what and where we are. We read to understand, or to begin to understand. We cannot do but read. Reading, almost as much as breathing, is our essential function" (7).

In this way, Manguel reiterates what he sees as the connection between reading and being human. Manguel also evokes the *Sefer Yezirah*, the sixth century Hebrew text that outlines God's creation of the world through "a written Book made of letters and numbers" (8). The reading of books becomes an act of religious devotion. Furthermore, Manguel argues that his own books were "transcriptions or glosses of that other, colossal Book" (8). Again, the book is conflated with the human and the act of reading with a moment of the divine. Collectively, these anecdotes and allusions position the act of reading as the loftiest, weightiest of pursuits: saintly activity, magical process, and the stuff of life itself. It is also, for Manguel, a criterion through which we can distinguish between humans and non-humans, where the non-human consists not only of animal but also of lesser incarnations of the human. Unlike Dirda and Holloway, Manguel repeatedly casts reading as a crucial element of the human project.

The first chapter of *A History of Reading* is devoted to Manguel's personal history as a reader, from learning to read at age 4, to becoming a "professional" reader, turned toward collecting other people's personal experiences of reading into a history.

> And so I ambitiously proceed from my history as a reader to the history of the act of reading. Or rather, to *a* history of reading, since any such history—made up of particular intuitions and private circumstances—must be only one of man, however impersonal it may try to be. (22)

There are correspondences and commonalities between Dirda and Manguel's writing – both perpetuate the reading experience as a sanctified occupation, especially Manguel, in dignifying readers with the label of the human which circuitously implies non-readers are intrinsically lacking in humanity – but Manguel's personal incursions into the text are not the conservative and self-congratulatory statements Dirda offers about his own reading experiences. Manguel is not trying to wedge open the door to the literary establishment with a pile of lauded books, though the relationship between book culture and higher social classes is apparent in the way he describes his father's plush library. Manguel writes:

> Before returning to Argentina, my father had asked his secretary to buy enough books to fill the shelves of his library in our new house; obligingly, she ordered cartloads of volumes from a secondhand dealer but found, when trying to place them on the shelves, that many of them wouldn't fit. Undaunted, she had them trimmed down to size and then bound in deep green leather, a colour which, combined with the dark oak, lent the place the atmosphere of a soft forest. [...] Reading these circumcised books required the extra effort of supplanting the missing bit of every page. (279)

Like Dirda, Manguel responds to his father's literary habits and draws both to and away from them in equal measure. Reading also serves a marker of status, albeit differently: in the Manguel household, literature is abundant and "cartloads of volumes" are bought – and subsequently mutilated – solely for aesthetic reasons, where in the Dirda household it is books that elevate Dirda above his blue collar compatriots. The link between books and sex, reading and eroticism – hinted at here by Manguel's use of the term "circumcised" to describe the trimmed books – arises repeatedly throughout

Manguel's discussions. In *A History of Reading*, he gives another account of the trimmed books, without describing them as circumcised:

> Later as an adolescent in my father's largely unused library in Buenos Aires [. . .] I made another discovery. I had begun to look up, in the elephantine Espasa-Calpe Spanish encyclopedia, the entries that somehow or other I imagined related to sex: "Masturbation," "Penis," "Vagina," "Syphilis," "Prostitution." I was always alone in the library, since my father used it only on the rare occasions when he had to meet someone [. . .]. I was twelve or thirteen; I was curled up in one of the big armchairs, engrossed in an article on the devastating effects of gonorrhoea, when my father came in and settled himself at his desk. For a moment I was terrified that he would notice what it was that I was reading, but then I realised that no one— not even my father, sitting barely a few steps away—could enter my reading space, could make out what I was being lewdly told by the book I held in my hands, and that nothing except my own will could enable anyone else to know. (12)

Like Dirda, Manguel here appropriates the *Bildungsroman* narrative, with a particular focus on sexual awakening via literature. Reading construed as a private space of auto-eroticism is extended in Manguel's 2010 memoir, *A Reader on Reading*, where Manguel talks about reading explicitly erotic fiction in that same room in Buenos Aires (173). The conflation of reading with life advanced by Dirda is thus apparent in Manguel, not just psychologically and psychically but physically and physiologically too. This conflation is also evident in the writing of Holloway, though her interests are more aligned with race and racial prejudice than the class concerns of Manguel and Dirda.

Karla Holloway and the politics of being marked by books

Karla Holloway's 2006 work, *BookMarks: Reading in Black and White. A Memoir by Karla FC Holloway*, is clearly, by virtue of its subtitle, marked as a memoir, and indeed it begins with and contains throughout vignettes of personal experience of books and reading in her youth and then in the childhoods of her children. However, much like Manguel's work, the autobiographical elements supplement a much broader story. Although Holloway begins with an experience in her adolescence – an English assignment asking her to nominate a list of periodicals she read, and her growing awareness that she would be interpreted, if not exactly judged, according to that list – the work is not chronological but flips back and forth throughout her life and bookish experiences. In chapter 7, "The Children's Room," she relates her romantic and magical experiences of discovering books and reading them in the county public library with its turrets and other trappings of an "enchanting space" (118). This is in contrast to an earlier discussion of "the Negro library" as a continually contested space, and where Holloway looks at a range of issues affecting the circulation of books in African-American families. However, Holloway begins her memoir by describing her own personal library, looking for words to "suggest something lovely, lofty, and serene, and that capture the feeling I have there when the afternoon sun lingers and stretches across from the antique library desk in the window to the chair where I sit reading" (32), before she goes on to report the state of libraries under policies of segregation. She quotes from Ralph Ellison's experiences of using libraries in his childhood (44), Maya Angelou's book lists in *I Know Why the Caged Bird Sings* (95), and Malcolm X's discussion of the transformative experience of reading in prison (81–85) and then uses this narrative to frame her own heartbreaking experiences of providing books to her son in jail in the hope that they might provide a transformative experience or comfort.

For Holloway, books are not something to save her – they didn't save her son from his terrible fate, after which Holloway finds her ability to engage with books and reading eroded (53). She reflects:

> The thing that had been a lifetime of solace and escape and seduction into another space too is gone, with him? [. . .] It took me years to hold a book again in the way that would allow its story to displace my own. (53)

Holloway's account is of an intimate connection between a child and their books:

> I do have left the sense that books and our memories of them and their spaces have a potential for both marking and mourning a far greater intimacy that we might at first imagine could come from our touch of its pages. (53)

Manguel too acknowledges that a personal library is a "sort of multilayered autobiography, each book holding the moment in which I read it for the first time" (*A Reader* 278). But for Holloway, libraries, both public and private, contain political barriers. Holloway details not only a history of black people's access to libraries in the pre-civil rights U.S. but also discusses the advice given in 1931 in the newsletter of the National Association for the Advancement of Colored People for building up of a personal library on a limited budget in austere times (33).[3]

Holloway's work is markedly different in focus and purpose than that of Manguel and Dirda. All three authors revere books and reading, and locate in their childhood access to books a magic that infuses their lives and careers – though for Holloway this is tempered by a tragedy that does not appear in the works of Manguel and Dirda. The childhood stories of all three are informed by their professional careers as gatekeepers of literature – Dirda as book reviewer, Manguel as publisher and anthologist, Holloway as professor – and thus each have a stake in the preservation of literature and the industry. But there are differences here too. Like Manguel, Holloway is painting a historical portrait of reading and literary consumption beyond her own personal experiences, while Dirda's recollections are rooted predominantly in his own private history. But, like Dirda, she is painting a portrait of reading as an act impacted on by social and environmental factors, unlike Manguel for whom reading is both necessity *and* luxury. Ultimately, however, Holloway is not simply a chronicler of and advocate for reading: she is an advocate for the freedom to read and learn, and does not take for granted that reading is not as freely available as others like Manguel and Dirda seem to assume.

Conclusion

The narratives of childhood reading discussed in this paper provide three similar yet distinct case studies of authors with strong ties to the literary establishment – critical, industrial, scholarly or otherwise – reconstructing their childhood literary engagement. Moreover, they all present some form of self-fashioning, following Stephen Greenblatt's use of the term (1980), around books and literary culture, but in different ways. Here, books become a shorthand through which life writers can establish their credentials as fully fledged members of the literary establishment, can validate and reinforce their inclusion in that establishment, and can nostalgically recall their indoctrination into a mystical world of books. It is a world that in some cases comparatively few people in their immediate environments were cohabiting, a world that was essentially isolated because of the solitary nature of most reading experiences outside of being read to in infancy and at school. At the same time, personal stories of youthful reading attach book history to humanistic arcs of birth and death, growth, maturation, seen most obviously in Dirda's division of his own life story into different stages of reading, making explicit that human identity – at least in the case of active readers – can be both constituted and signified by the texts we read and when we read them. Ultimately, memoirs of reading can advance conservative constructions of childhood that locate acts of reading and book appreciation in opposition to, and as a means of escaping, a social class. For Dirda, books and acts of reading are fashioned as the portal through which the author escaped his lower class of origin destined for a position in the upper middle classes of the literary establishment. For Manguel, books are affiliated with his conservative impulses and form a barrier between the human and the nonhuman in ways that stratify beings, even humans, into more human (those that read) and less human (those that do not). In contrast to these, conservative memoirs, however, are the politically progressive work of Holloway, who advocates not only for the importance of literature but the very right to access books, taken for granted by many establishment-based celebrants of the written world. Her work shows that literary memoirs by literary establishment do not only reinforce the status quo.

In addition to providing case studies of the reading reminiscences of these authors, these three memoirs of the transformative power of childhood reading can serve other functions also. However, in the contemporary life writing zone of cultural production and criticism there are few tools to help us unpack the conservative memoirs of authors like Dirda and Manguel. Contemporary life narrative seems understandably preoccupied with the experience of the subaltern; the marginalized; the voiceless; and the victimized, traumatized, and suffering tropes that Dirda and Manguel only superficially attempt to mobilize. This is not only understandable but also vital work in the field. However, its volume comes at the expense of critiques of contemporary conservative memoirs that proliferate largely unexamined. These memoirs or memoir-moments may be boring, trite, infuriating to scholars of life narrative, and trivial given the range of human experiences, expressed elsewhere in the medium of life writing, but they are in many ways stealthy and somewhat sinister in the role they play, in that they confirm and perpetuate the stereotypical views of class politics, and thus they are worthy of attention and analysis.

Although much of this article identifies the conservative trajectories of nostalgic remembrances of reading in childhood, it also points to the effective component of reading and the link between affective reading and the material object of the book. This affect is not restricted to canonical literature, or to authors who use their memories of reading to legitimate their position in the literary establishment, like those discussed here. In this way, these narratives also form part of the larger discussion around the future of the book and the future of reading in "the late age of print" (Bolter; Striphas). The view (or perhaps the threat) that children born today will never read print, perpetuated by the likes of Dirda and Birkerts, is absurd for precisely these reasons: the love of the material book is communicated through material bodies in shared reading experiences with strong affective components. And yet, as the discussion of Holloway, and to a lesser extent Dirda and Manguel, demonstrates, a range of cultural and environmental factors can and do impede literacy, access to and consumption of books: these three authors managed to overcome these factors, but legions of potential readers and writers have not and do not. Conversely, this invests their reminiscences with even greater weight and value.

Acknowledgements

This article was written with the support of the Flinders University Life Narrative Research Group. Thanks to the LNRG, its co-directors Kate Douglas, and Kylie Cardell, and to the participants of the Telling Tales symposium hosted at Flinders University in July 2012.

Notes

1. Alberto Manguel, Argentinian-born writer, editor, anthologist, and translator, has worked in the book industry for decades. His 1996 book *A History of Reading* outlines his view of the history of reading and book collecting from 4000 BC to the present day, though little attention is paid to current debates on how technology might be changing reading. Manguel's 2010 book *A Reader on Reading* is a collection of essays, lectures, and other occasional writings tied together with quotes from Lewis Carroll's *Alice in Wonderland* and *Through the Looking-Glass*. Both contain detailed personal stories in which Manguel discusses his personal reading history from learning to read aged four (*History* 5) to his extensive book collection. Manguel's books are aimed at a general reading audience of book lovers. Although Manguel has written two novels in Spanish, the majority of his works are not fiction.
2. Examples of books about books that contain a significant autobiographical component include works by Lewis Buzbee, Anna Quindlen, Francis Spufford, Pat Conroy, and Patricia Meyer Spacks. Leah Price's coffee table book *Unpacking my Library: Writers and Their Books*, includes not only the anecdotes about writers' connections to their personal libraries but also Price's own recollections of her own and others' libraries. Scholarly work considering books about books has come recently from Nicola King, who looks at memoirs by academics, and Ana Vogrincic who considers the broad field of books about books.
3. However, Manguel also describes the politics of reading under the military dictatorship of Argentina in the 1970s (*A Reader* 279).

References

Ashworth, Andrea. *Once in a House on Fire*. New York: Metropolitan Books, 1998.
Barnes, Julian. "My Life as a Bibliophile." *The Guardian*, 29 Jun. 2012. <http://www.guardian.co.uk/books/2012/jun/29/my-life-as-bibliophile-julian-barnes>. [Accessed 1 Jul. 2012].

Birkerts, Sven. *The Gutenberg Elegies*. Boston: Faber and Faber, 1994.

Bolter, J. David. *Space, The Computer, Hypertext and the History of Writing*. Hillsdale, NJ: Erlbaum Associates, 1991.

Buzbee, Lewis. *The Yellow Lighted Bookshop: A Memoir, A History*. St Paul: Greywolf Press, 2006.

Conroy, Pat. *My Reading Life*. New York: Doubleday, 2010.

Dirda, Michael. *Readings: Essays and Literary Entertainments*. Bloomington: Indiana University Press, 2000.

————. *An Open Book: Coming of Age in the Heartland*. New York: W.W. Norton, 2003.

Douglas, Kate. *Contesting Childhood: Autobiography, Trauma and Memory*. New Brunswick: Rutgers, 2010.

Dugard, JayceeLee. *A Stolen Life: A Memoir*. New York: Simon and Schuster, 2011.

Gilmore, Leigh. *The Limits of Autobiography: Trauma and Testimony*. Ithaca: Cornell University Press, 2001.

Jenkins, Henry. N. D. "The Innocent Child and Other Modern Myths." <http://web.mit.edu/cms/People/henry3/innocentchild.html>. [Accessed 31 Oct. 2012].

Jenks, Chris. *Childhood*. New York: Routledge, 2005.

King, Nicola. "Uses of the Past: Hindsight and the Representation of Childhood in Some Recent British Academic Autobiography." *Rethinking History* 13.1 (2009): 95–108.

Manguel, Alberto. *A Reader on Reading*. New Haven: Yale University Press, 2010.

————. *A History of Reading*. New York: Viking, 1996.

Price, Leah. *Unpacking my Library: Writers and Their Books*. New Haven: Yale University Press, 2011.

Quindlen, Anna. *How Reading Changed My Life*. New York: Ballantine, 1998.

Spacks, PatriciaMeyer. *On Rereading*. Cambridge, MA: Harvard University Press, 2011.

Spufford, Francis. *The Child That Books Built: A Memoir of Childhood and Reading*. London: Faber, 2002.

Striphas, Ted. *The Late Age of Print: Everyday Book Culture From Consumerism to Control*. New York: Kindle file Columbia University Press, 2009.

Schwab, Will. *The End of Your Life Book Club*. New York: Knopf, 2012.

Vogrincic, Ana. "Pleasure and Shame: Books on (not) Reading (An Overview of the Field)." *The International Journal of the Book* 7.3 (2010): 57–67, <http://ijb.cgpublisher.com/product/pub.27/prod.363>. [Accessed: 18 Nov. 2012].

Claire Lynch

ANTE-AUTOBIOGRAPHY AND THE ARCHIVE OF CHILDHOOD

This essay examines the concept of children's autobiography via several autobiographical extracts written by the author as a child. Although only a small proportion of people will compose and publish a full-length autobiography, almost everyone will, inadvertently, produce an archive of the self, made from public records and private documents. Here, such works are seen as providing access to writing both about and by children. The essay explores the ethics and poetics of children's writing via the key debates in life writing; in particular, the dynamic relationship between adults and children, both as distinct stages of life and dual parts of one autobiographical identity. The term "ante-autobiography" is coined to refer to these texts which come before or instead of a full-length narrative. They are not read as less than or inadequate versions of autobiography, but rather as transgressive and challenging to chronological notions of the genre.

Strange, that while so many years of schooling merge into long forgotten hours, some lessons latch hold of the memory forever. I remember being told about the constant renewal of cells, rebuilding the body piece by piece, so that over a period of years a whole new person stands in place. The same you but different. The lesson haunts me now as I read myself as a child. The same me but different.

As they prepared to move from their home of twenty-seven years, my parents made a number of visits to my house, bearing dusty boxes containing what I came to think of as the archive of my childhood. Sifting among the preserved objects, favorite toys, first shoes and sports trophies, I was struck by the number of texts which, if collated, would produce a narrative portrait of a childhood. Birth and baptismal certificates, health records and school reports, combined to provide a narrative of my childhood, composed by the adults who observed and cared for me. So far, so typical of many a family attic. But alongside these, I was surprised to find, were numerous autobiographical documents I had evidently written as a child. For all my adult reluctance to engage in the autobiographical act, it appeared I had already long been doing so.[1]

The accidental archive

Archives are enticingly flexible. They are at once a location (the place where things are collected), a collection (the things themselves), and a symbolic link between the past and present (the implied value of the things). The scale of archives ranges from the national to the personal, preserved in various levels of formality. On an individual scale, some lives are catalogued in major reference libraries, others preserved haphazardly in a shoebox under the bed. The quantity of archived lives continues to grow, since in the current period, more so than ever before, lives generate documents both in print and online. The popularity of family history is a clear indicator of this as enthusiasts gather up birth and death records, faded photographs and maps of distant towns to produce an archive of their own. These archives, both formal and informal, share what Philip Larkin famously described as "magical" and "meaningful" components. For Larkin, the "magical value is the older and more universal," providing the tangible and precious connection to the "paper he wrote on" and the "words as he wrote them" (99). The "meaningful" by comparison, emerges by way of the signifying power of those words. While a published text conveys its purpose to the reader in clean-copy typescript, an archived autobiography also acts as a historical artifact. For Larkin, it is not simply the content but the nature of archives that matters in revealing the presence of the writing life, hinted at in handwriting and errata. Acknowledging the materiality of the archive is particularly relevant in a life-writing context. While the meaning conveyed through language retains primacy, the physical document also provides non-linguistic information. Writing which comes before or instead of the polished and published text contains revelatory mistakes untouched by a proofreader and the idiosyncrasies unseen by an editor. At the same time, the handcrafted object of the daily journal or bundle of letters conveys meaning about those who produced and preserved them. Although only a small proportion of people will ever compose and publish a full-length autobiography, the production of a personal archive is almost as inevitable as it is inadvertent. While official records and institutional documents collate the bare facts of a life, diaries, photograph albums, love letters and social networking sites both conceal and reveal the "magical" and "meaningful" aspects of a life story. On their own, such documents might be seen as mere fragments, inadequately detailed to be validated as life writing, but in combination – as an archive – they have a value and significance greater than the component parts.

The human urge to narrate manifests itself in multiple written formats across times and cultures.[2] Nevertheless, my argument here, that the haphazard textual outputs of any life can constitute an archive depends on numerous assumptions, not least of all the idea that the subject has lived long enough to accumulate them. This is not simply a matter of quantity. A well-documented life may indicate success through numerous preserved correspondence, press-clippings, and certificates. Alternatively, a traumatic life may be recorded in medical records or prison reports.[3] The theme of this paper grew, at least in part, from the happenstance of discovering a box of artifacts from my childhood. Among the usual nostalgic memorabilia, I was surprised to find several documents in which I had, as a child, written about myself. For the most part these were mediated by adults, the product of activities designed to develop literacy, handwriting, and other skills. Nevertheless, they also seemed to form part of a wider project of encouraging the child to construct a developing life narrative. Dates indicate that the documents were written between the ages of four and eight, and the contents range across the factual recording of height and hair color to the more subjective matter of favorite smells and ambitions for the future. While limited and fragmentary when read apart, in combination, they provide very clear examples of Larkin's "magical" and "meaningful" archival tropes.

One of the most striking documents in this accidental archive is a faded red exercise book bearing the title "My Self." It is evident that this document was not conceived of as an autobiography per se, but rather a series of tasks to help 8-year-olds understand their senses, preferences and an embodied selfhood (Figure 1). It is in one way an empirical record (I find I was 116 cm tall in March 1989) and at the same time a subjective list of preferred smells and textures (petrol and snow, respectively, it seems). The project has clear cross-curricular aims; I have made bar graphs about the number of children in each family for the class, favorite foods, and types of house. As a preserved document, it comments both on the individual author and more generally on the surrounding sociocultural context. While much of the content is mundane, there are also unexpected elements that force me to consider questions of poetic license and accuracy. Although long forgotten by the adult me, I have documentary evidence here of my childhood preferences. Should the archive take precedence over the memory? I am, for instance, both amused and surprised to find such a cliché of monocultural Britishness lurking between the pages. According to the bar chart here, the class's favorite food is a Roast Beef dinner, followed closely by Fish and Chips. Had I tried to write of my childhood retrospectively, I could not have remembered this, nor would I have imagined it. Yet it is also equally likely that I would not have chosen to include this information as a child had it not been a task set by the teacher. These texts are always, already, written for adults, as they are assessed and evaluated for handwriting quality and spelling accuracy. More tellingly, they provide adults with a way to read children's lives. Similarly, reading this text again as an adult creates an uncanny sense of recognition and dislocation, since this text is both written by me and by someone else.

Reading these documents from the perspective of a literary scholar raises important ethical questions since the drawings, language, and handwriting mark the author (me) as a child, with all the attendant temptations to read them as amusing, trivial, or nostalgic.

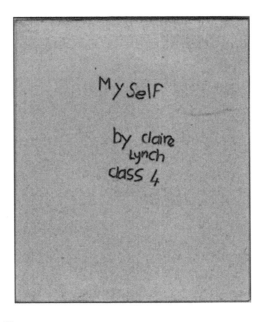

FIGURE 1 "My Self".

In other words, the apparent "magical" element here might easily overshadow that which is potentially "meaningful." Carolyn Steedman's approach is unrivalled in this matter when she reminds us that any archive is "made from selected and consciously chosen documentation from the past and also the mad fragmentations that no one intended to preserve and that just ended up there" (68). Simply, the survival of these texts is as much by accident as design. Any interpretation, therefore, must also take into account the possibility that they are neither necessarily representative nor particularly unique. An archive is only evidence of its own survival, and whether that survival matters remains the prerogative of the reader. In the case of these notebooks, self-portraits, and personal descriptions, both the production and rediscovery of the archive are matters of chance. Archives are both constructed and preserved serendipitously, just as those who work on them are fated victims of an archive's gaps and limitations. The material identified here provides a rare opportunity to act simultaneously as subject, author and researcher. Perhaps uniquely, the documents under consideration are as alien as they are familiar. As accounts of childhood, they preserve forgotten experiences as well as reinforcing well-established ideas of selfhood. While adult life writing depends upon the act of retrospect, divining meaning from what has been, children, by necessity, write about lives in the present and future tense. These are not documents of a remembered past, but rather an imagined future.

Children's autobiography

Humans are narrative creatures; we grow in understanding by recounting our experiences, both to ourselves and to others. This is particularly the case with the so-called formative experiences of childhood and youth. Early experiences are often awarded symbolic value, forming an established part of the narrative we tell ourselves through memory and others via anecdotes and autobiography. The teenage years commonly emerge as dominant in this sense. Frequently understood as a time of acute self-awareness and identity crisis, generations of teenage diaries and preserved juvenilia have acted as source material for subsequent adult auto/biographies. This article, however, focuses on life narratives produced at an earlier stage, before the author develops the teenage capacity for introspection. Children's autobiography, as it will be referred to here, represents a different engagement with genre expectations as understood by teenage and adult counterparts. This is not to say that children's autobiography is free from the expectations of genre. Indeed, such writing is typically produced in an educational environment and, therefore, instigated and monitored by adults. As a result, the work may be shaped and influenced by the teacher's guidance at the same time as being dependent on the child's developing skills of self-expression and limited by the time allocated to the task and the author's patience. Since there is an element of inevitable coercion here, the motivation to narrate oneself is necessarily different from that observed in adult autobiographies, where cathartic release or powerful self-expression may be sought. While there are, self-evidently, differences between autobiographies written by children and adults, they should not be understood as weaknesses. Those who would question children's capacity to narrate their own experience are at risk of missing the representative power of the text as well as unfairly undermining the author's agency. In regard to this, Peter Alexander's landmark work is key when he theorizes how and why the child writer, particularly the autobiographer, can be understood. Building on the insights of Foucault, who so astutely analyzed the treatment of children as an indicator of a society's wider priorities, Alexander highlights the impact of children's powerlessness, which "renders them peculiarly vulnerable to being observed and silenced" (79).

It is notable that children and childhood are routinely the dominant focus of adult autobiography as authors seek to understand their current sense of self through retrospection. Both popular and literary narratives cluster around the Wordsworthian imperative in which the child protagonist is repeatedly cast as progenitor of the adult author. As such, it seems only mildly provocative to describe autobiography as a form of children's literature. Although the phrase is used predominantly to denote work written exclusively for children to read, I suggest a double application in the sense that we use women's literature or Victorian literature that is written by them. In fact, the study of writing for children offers a number of useful precedents in this matter such as raising the ethical concern as to "whether adults can or should interpret the voices of child readers" (McDowell 245). McDowell's query forces us to reconsider assumptions of difference and power, a matter clearly pertinent to the examples under consideration here, reduced (but not eliminated) by the fact that I attempt only to interpret my own writing. The self-portraits, descriptions, and lists that form this archive of childhood are writing by a child about a child. Again, established frameworks from children's literature are useful since it is typically here, as Mitzi Myers notes, that we may find "work about, for, and as a child" (3). While genres directed to children as readers may, unsurprisingly, tend toward a child-centered narrative, they are nonetheless not by a child.[4] Many of the most successful adult authors who write for children are adept at imitating or replicating a child's perspective in order to reduce the gap between the writer and the reader. Such an approach should not be read as patronizing, but rather an attempt to reverse an established power imbalance between the producer and the consumer of the text. Knoepflmacher takes this even further so that instead of thinking of adult writers as entirely distinct from those they write for and about, they are seen as "former children" attempting to engage in "an adult reactivation of childhood selves" (xiv). In Knoepflmacher's reading, adult authors must function simultaneously as their past and present selves, simultaneously the child they were and the adult they are. It is a process replicated in autobiography where the adult author must also attempt to reconnect to the child protagonist's perceptions. In this sense then, the genre of autobiography can be said to reclaim the possessive apostrophe in children's literature, allowing it to rationally be described as literature both about and in a sense by children.

The wisdom of ages

Considering both the ethics and poetics of writing about and by children magnifies some of the key debates in life writing. Where questions are raised over the consistency or reliability of the narrator, for example, we are reminded of debates over autobiography's relationship with "truth." Similarly, those who would reject children's autobiography on the basis of perceived lack of sophistication recall discussions of a spectrum of work ranging from what Mary Evans designates as the "'serious' and 'good' auto/biographies" (4) to the implied trivial and poor. There is also, of course, the matter of timing; have children lived long enough to write about life? Again, this is a recurring question in which young autobiographers are criticized for publishing too early (before experience and hindsight have revealed the lasting significance of events) and older writers condemned for convenient amnesia or self-serving nostalgia. The combination of these misgivings seems to implicate children's writing as the last taboo. As Alexander puts it:

> The range of literature in English, at least that routinely studied by academics, has expanded markedly over the past few decades, as disciplines from post-colonial studies to women's studies have widened literary horizons. But it remains striking how little attention is paid to the writing of children. The truth seems to be that child writers have been so effectively silenced that we seldom think of them (77).

Certainly, in autobiography the glut of children is an illusion. When we read children in autobiography we are really reading the adults they have become, not the children they were. Convincing and engaging as the portraits of children in autobiography may be, as Nicola King reminds us, "this can only ever be an effect of the language used by the adult self who is doing the remembering and reconstructing" (97). In other words, praise for the so-called authentic child's voice in autobiography might equally be seen as misplaced admiration for those best able recreate the voice we expect to hear. As King so helpfully points out, this is, to a large extent, a result of linguistic tricks such as "the present tense, short sentences and simple, direct language" (98).

The distinction here between children as the consumers but not producers of literature, is crucial. This is not simply a case of mislabeling, but also a pernicious power dynamic in which children's literature is designated "to be not by children but only for them—and to be written by almost anyone but children" (Alexander 77). The documents I discuss here are writing by a child, but my ability to understand them is limited by adult preconceptions. Comparisons on the grounds of accuracy and fluency are less than enlightening and the context too is troubling. An indicative example is a "News Book" from the year I was seven. In a popular classroom task, repeated across generations and locations, pupils are asked to recount the activities of the weekend at the start of a new school week. In my rereading, I am aware of an underlying sense that these are narratives of gently coerced disclosure, used by adults to gain insights into the child's experiences, ambitions, and environment. They serve a protective function certainly but also, inevitably, a prurient one. As expected, the "News Book" recounts domestic and local experiences such as birthday parties and family visits. At the same time, background events place the author in a highly specific geographic and temporal location when, for instance, recalling having seen Concorde's "pointy nose" flying overhead.[5] Although the "News Book" contains writing by a child, the writing remains validated by adults and is ultimately adult-orientated. As adults maintain power over children, couched in the language of protection and nurturing, they also define and teach the terms through which children describe and understand themselves. This withstanding, these are clearly empowering documents at some level. After all, as Rachel Robertson puts it, "Writing your life gives you immense power in one way and almost none in another" (314). The child subject is experimenting with expressions of identity, using the first person to describe a world in which she occupies the central position. Nevertheless, adulthood is valorized here, both in the events described and the act of narrating experiences to the teacher in writing.

Settling on an analytical approach to this material is not simple. The value of these texts is based on the point that they are unremarkable and widely recognizable. Certainly the well-filled pages of the "News Book" are evidence of a child kept busy assessing her place in the world. Similarly, opening the "My Self" notebook in the middle, I find my class frozen in the act of measuring our surroundings against ourselves: the coat trolley, the blackboard, and the rug, measured out in handspans and footsteps. I am compelled to compare this information with the desk I sit at as I write this. It is also six handspans wide, although I write and measure with different hands. In this text too, it is not only the content but the context which conveys meaning, highlighting the circumstances of the child autobiographer. I read now, printed on the back cover that my exercise book is "manufactured and supplied by the county council" and think of all the other children in towns and villages from the south east edge of London down to the cliffs of Dover, writing out their lives. The object here expresses a significance that the text alone could not. The paper provided by the state, the task too, approved by educationalists shifts this from an act of individual self-expression to a fragment of a far larger archive of children's autobiography.

Practice makes perfect

As is so often the case in discussions of autobiography, agency and opportunity form the foundations of the argument here. When Eakin considers the "prerequisites in our culture for being a person, for having and telling a life story" (114), referring to debates of social status, gender, class, sexuality, and so on, it remains implicit that the "person" be an adult. One of the most striking revelations about the rediscovery of these texts, therefore, was the sense in which they formed part of an implied social conditioning in how to have and tell a life story. The fact that these documents span several stages of early years education is also indicative of their perceived significance within a specific sociocultural moment. The writing provides evidence of a tradition, or perhaps even an imperative, of training children to compose and rehearse experiences and memories into a narrative of selfhood. It is of course entirely appropriate that this be discussed in relation to writing since "the modern view of childhood was a literary development" (Alexander 80). In the disciplines most closely concerned with child development including the social sciences and educational policy, recent decades have witnessed a boom in the attention given to juvenilia and its capacity to reproduce the voices of children in an historical context. While sociocultural factors frequently prohibit children from acts of self-expression, words committed to paper may allow oppressed voices to be heard in retrospect. As Alexander astutely argues, using language and ideas borrowed from postcolonial theory, children's right to write has revealed a "rather different view of the child-adult power disparity [...] most clearly in children's autobiographical writing" (82).

While it is evident that efforts toward considering children's autobiography more seriously are growing, it remains typical to only legitimize the childhood writing of established adult writers. In other words, it is only once an adult author has established a literary reputation that their juvenilia are awarded retrospective interest.[6] For genuine equality of opportunity, of the kind postcolonial and life narrative approaches have lobbied for, the child writer needs to be analyzed and evaluated without deferral to the subsequent work of the adult. It is perhaps only in children's autobiography where such an approach is possible. While in adult autobiography childhood is represented as "a privileged site of experience and memory" (King 97), the child autobiographer, by contrast, does not have the dominant experience of adulthood with which to form a comparison. In adult-authored texts, childhood is frequently seen as significant in shaping the adult autobiographer, yet the child self, purportedly by necessity, is always narrated and mediated through the adult author. In child authored texts, however, "the mythology of Childhood" and the related "real or imagined age of innocence" (Guy 177) are put under pressure since the child is not yet embroiled with the competing narrative of adult retrospect.

The inconstant autobiographer

The complexity of distinct adult/child perspectives is multiplied here in the joint roles of child author and adult reader. Is it ever possible for an adult author to read back to the child self? Can I legitimately claim to have applied the objective eye of a researcher to first person writing signed in my name? At the very least it seems useful to submit these texts to the shared concern of autobiography and children's literature, namely that the "former self-as-child is as alien to the adult writer as it is the adult reader" (Coe 1). The revelation of these childhood documents in a scholarly context is unnerving and I am reminded of Eakin's warning that "we are all of us judged when we tell the stories of our lives" (113). Using them as I have is no doubt perilous, ethically and theoretically, since both the subject and the approach step outside the traditional academic remit. This is in no small part due to the already transgressive nature of autobiography. As Jeremy Popkin explains:

> Autobiographies, or so the romantic image of the genre would have it, are flamboyant assertions of individuality and subjectivity, whereas serious scholarly endeavour [...] is often collective, and its results are supposed to be unaffected by researchers' private interests and emotions ('Autobiography' 30).

This project snares me in contradiction. The texts are very clearly "assertions of individuality" and although I do not remember writing them, I know that I did. How then can I balance the presumption of "subjectivity" if I choose to identify myself as an autobiographical author, at the same time as maintaining the "serious scholarly endeavor" as I seek to analyze them? The real contradiction, as it emerges, is not between the autobiographer and the scholar, but the adult and the child. This then is the real site of potential revelation, while not every adult will have access to preserved copies of their childhood autobiographies, immeasurable numbers of people across a range of educational traditions and timeframes will have likely written something like this. Texts such as these, I contend, whether reread or lost forever form part of the internal autobiography of us all. They are texts that come before, or frequently instead of, autobiography as we traditionally understand it.

Ante-autobiography

In his memoir of childhood, *The Gatekeeper*, Terry Eagleton describes "anti-autobiography" as writing an autobiography "in such a way as to outwit the prurience and immodesty of the genre by frustrating your own desire for self-display and the reader's desire to enter your inner life" (57). This reticence to comply with the expectation for "self-display," both for oneself and the imagined reader is examined here, not as "anti-autobiography" but rather ante-autobiography. While the former is written in self-conscious rejection of the genre, the latter comes before an awareness of any such rules. Eagleton's "anti-autobiography" is rebellious and hyper-aware; ante-autobiography has no knowledge of the rules it disrupts. Although written out of different standpoints, both approaches are successful in highlighting the norm by diverting from it. Indeed, as Alexander argues, children's engagement in autobiography can be read as "a resistance to the power of the adult world to observe and silence" (82). Ante-autobiography then is not less than or inadequate to mainstream autobiography, but rather, transgressive and challenging to our notions, not just of what autobiography is, but what it is for.

Since these texts are understood as coming before autobiography, the term is equally applicable to an unfinished or fragmented autobiography. In other words, the material that has the potential to become an autobiography, the personal archive, might also usefully be understood as ante-autobiographical. Sifting through the documents left by her late father, Carolyn Kraus observes that the papers offered "traces of a life, frozen realities" (252), not yet an autobiography, but the capacity to be if only a narrative structure is applied. Yet as Kraus goes on to note, it is not the content of these documents which matters so much as the material objects themselves as she observes that their "visual 'truth' spoke louder at times than the words on the page" (252). Reading through my own found documents, I am struck by the same sense. The document pictured here, entitled "A Description of Me" is still stapled to the faded backing paper which attached it to the classroom wall; this is an autobiographical sketch made public, literally put on display (Figure 2): I am struck by the privileging of gender

FIGURE 2 "A Description of Me".

(I am a girl first and foremost) my name is last, set apart and corrected by the teacher who has capitalised it in red pen. As with all archival documents, meaning is found in what is left unsaid. As I have written here, to distinguish myself from others: "I have navy blue shoes and wear a red and white checked dress with a red jumper." But what I wear here is what I must wear every day. This is not a description of my individuality, but in the most banal sense, my uniformity as well as my school uniform.

Since "A Description of Me" is ostensibly a list of physical characteristics, it both connects and divides the me now from the me then. Although I still have the same color eyes, I can no longer sit on my hair; we are different people both in what we choose to write and how we write it. Yet it is precisely in this difference that "juvenile autobiography parallels the writing of other marginalized groups writing back to the Centre" (Alexander 86). These texts are disruptive of adult standards and expectations, therefore, the adult me is necessarily alienated from their priorities. As I read the description, I resist the urge to correct or rewrite, keeping in mind Meg Jensen's concern over the "damaging distance between practice and theory in the field" (299). One way or another, this is my autobiographical practice; but can it really be said to contribute to an understanding of the theory?

Children's lives in public view

In cultures where childhood is now relentlessly documented, the first portrait obtained *in utero*, followed by diligent parents writing, photographing, filming, and uploading, young lives are recorded in greater detail than ever before. From the private archives of family photograph albums to the official collation of medical records and census returns, children's lives are perpetually narrated by adults. While we are familiar in the age of new media with older children and teenagers engaging in self-narration through Facebook, Twitter, PostSecret, and so on, younger children's autobiographical impulses are, perhaps understandably, often overlooked. Since it is only from the end of the nineteenth and start of the twentieth century that childhood has been viewed as "a qualitatively different period of life than adulthood" (McDowell 241), it may be unsurprising that nostalgic, traumatic, or unreconstructed versions of childhood have dominated in autobiographical writing. Furthermore, while childhood is now widely understood to differ from adulthood, adult autobiographical accounts of childhood are often weakened by presenting the period as homogenous. Basil Guy draws attention to this disparity by asking whether "all Childhoods [are] equally valid? Do not some stand out more than others? And why?" (179). It is all too evident that all childhoods are not considered "equally valid" by those responsible for the provision of healthcare, education, and pragmatic support on a global scale. Quite clearly, the very materials under scrutiny in this article indicate a privileged childhood in which an informal archive has been constructed by adult carers. A parallel article in which no documents exist, either through wilful neglect or indifference would offer a valuable counterpoint to the case made here. Again, the parallel with postcolonial and life narrative theory might be drawn; the undocumented life remains invisible.

In adult autobiography, both traumatic and nostalgic childhoods gain legitimacy in a shift from private to public formats. What value then can be attributed to these texts that remain within familial readerships? The concern is a common one, echoed by

Popkin who has enquired of his own family archive, why anyone else "should take any interest in these materials?" ("Life Writing" 179). Certainly, I make no claims for the originality or significance of these texts beyond the fact that they have been preserved and are, therefore, available for analysis. By its very nature, the material lacks the elements that would usually qualify it for such attention. These texts stand outside of the standard genre framework because, until now, they have remained private. Since an essential element of autobiography involves bringing the inner self into public view, this development is essential. Questions of power are central here, since children do not have the same means to distribute their stories through traditional channels of publication. Access to the public sphere is either through adults or later through themselves as adults. So while I know I wrote these narratives, I cannot claim any superior ability to infer meaning from them. If I could remember anything that might explain them, my adult self would no doubt rationalize or reduce the significance with which such ideas were held at that time. The me of then cannot adequately communicate to the me of now; we do not know each other, much less understand one another. How then might these texts be read without simply sidelining the child author as a rough draft of the finished adult identity?

Narratives of convenience

Examining the letters which remain as records of her father's life, Kraus notes that they were:

> Composed, for the most part, without documentary intent – un-filed, unmediated by strangers – 'private documents' speak with the special authority of overheard confessions. Their 'truth' is unrehearsed, direct. Coming upon each one was like lifting the corner of a dusty curtain (258).

As with Kraus' example, it is precisely the accidental nature of these childhood documents and the haphazard way they have been collated and preserved which awards them meaning. They are in the purest sense ante-autobiographical since they reveal things they did not know they were hiding. As Kraus notes, the "un-filed" and "unmediated" are revelatory in themselves but also as a result of the gaps they accentuate; the missing letters are always the most important in an incomplete correspondence. The significance of inconsistency and incompleteness is all the more evident for child writers, supporting Eakin's concept of autobiography as not just a "literary genre" but "an integral part of a lifelong process of identity formation" (2001: 114). While the framework outlined here has allowed me to read my childhood texts in combination as ante-autobiographical, it cannot adequately extend to the texts that are absent.

At the age of 10, I was given a diary with a padlock which I kept in a secret hiding place. I wrote and sometimes drew about events in my life, but I was never happy with the result. It seemed to me at that point that I was so different day-by-day that yesterday's entry was already too juvenile, a misrepresentation of today's me by the treacherous me of the day before. So I would tear out the pages and start again. I maintained this pattern of self-destructive diarist throughout my late childhood and teenage years, starting a diary, then, looking back over and tearing out pages, an impatient and vain autobiographer. Before this age, if the archive is to be believed, I was able to write unselfconsciously about myself in the public setting of the classroom. Not, as has already been argued, from an innate impulse, but rather, because the education system in this particular time and place prioritized children thinking and writing autobiographically. Yet, as Popkin warns, documents can acquire "new relationships to each other that their creators could not have imagined" (2010: 174). In this case, there is an uncomfortable sense that the real autobiography has been destroyed in the missing pages of the diary. What caused the discomfort and self-consciousness that led me to destroy that narrative even as I wrote it? Was there perhaps an awareness of the rebellion implied in reflecting on one's own life outside of the teacher's remit? Two years before I had started the diary I had completed another task in school, this time thinking of myself in a future context by listing the things I wanted to do once I had "grown up" (Figure 3).

There is nothing particularly remarkable about the list. All of the sought after activities are notably out of the child's reach either because they are seen as too dangerous ("making a cup of tea" or "cutting the grass") or because they confer authority and agency ("going to work," "staying up late"). Some of these I must surely have already done, ("going shopping," "taking a train"), but clearly the aspiration here is to do these things independently. The one seeming anomaly in the list is the desire to "read a hard book." Certainly my 8-year-old self could not have imagined a future life as an academic, at least not if the adjacent wish to "have lots of money" is any indication. Yet the inclusion of this ambition provokes the temptation to construct narratives of convenience, to "imply inevitability, the assumption that the past was bound to lead to the future which is our present" (King 97). Reading this list, for instance, it is tempting to focus on my childhood ambition to "read a hard book" at the exclusion of the other points mentioned in order to construct a narrative around my subsequent career.

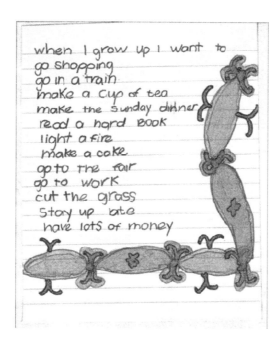

FIGURE 3   "When I Grow up I Want to".

Had I become a chef, no doubt the plan to "make the Sunday dinner" would seem equally significant in retrospect.

The list itself makes manifest the adult compulsion to ask children what they want to be. In this way, ante-autobiographical documents draw out power dynamics in which adulthood is represented as yearned for. As Alexander explains, there is in children's autobiography:

> [A]n assumption, the more powerful for being generally unspoken, that the child perceives the adult world as superior, and adulthood as a desirable state to be aspired to, a state towards which the child writer is willingly shaped by forces of socialization which show themselves in the writing (81).

This interpretation of the dynamic in which children long to be adults is frequently reversed in traditional autobiographies where authors are inclined to recall even difficult childhoods with some element of nostalgia. Simply put, while the canon of adult autobiography abounds with portraits of children, it seems children are more inclined to write autobiographies about adults. My contention here runs contrary to the standard argument that adults stand in a position of uncontested power over children. As Christensen has argued, children are frequently written about and imagined "as archetypal victims," creating the paradox in which the image of an unhappy child is upsetting, but also welcome, due to the feelings of protection and compassion it arouses in adult readers, ultimately confirming the notion of "adult power" (42). Writing about themselves as vulnerable children, autobiographers frequently recall the "adult power" of those who dominated them but also express the same power over their child selves, whom they now seek to protect in the text. It is only where children are able to write autobiographically themselves that the imbalance may be disrupted.

The former-child and pre-adult

As the discussion above suggests, the perceived distinction between the adult and child self might be most usefully seen as a biographical not autobiographical relationship. While the child self is necessarily separated from the adult self by the chronology of life, the adult is equally distanced from the child by the vagaries of memory and the distraction of subsequent experience. What the ante-autobiographical provides then is an opportunity to examine writing before and after the impact of scholarly presumptions. As Rocío Davis so helpfully puts it:

> We comprehend that academics function not only as 'scholars,' committed to objective reality, but as 'authors' who somehow project themselves in their texts which, in important ways, may become negotiations of their personalities and intellectual positions (2).

Returning to the writing produced before an adult understanding of genre or theory was gained raises the question of when "intellectual positions" can be said to begin. Such re-readings highlight the inevitable contradictions between the respective ambitions and priorities of childhood and adulthood. More than this, they create a space for bringing together past and present selves. Reflecting on life after the publication of her acclaimed autobiography *Chernobyl Strawberries*, Vesna Goldsworthy maintains a distance in language as she separates her past self from her present. Listening to an actor reading her work in translation, she observes the image of her younger self on the cover of the book, remarking: "I remember her well enough to suspect that she prefers Julia [the actor] to me" (2). This sense of separation between the past self (the author and subject of the autobiography) and the present self (observer and reader) seems particularly informative; they are the same but different. While Goldsworthy's comparison is based on the recollection of the preferences of the past self, it is also vital to acknowledge the nuances from the past which are inevitably forgotten. When Rachel Robertson, for example, reads back over the forgotten words of an ex-lover, she is surprised to find them "personal, generous and not at all pretentious. I hadn't remembered that he had sent me 'love and gratitude'" (314). So often, reliance on memory, or the absence of evidence, can disrupt both past and present understanding. As Robertson's encounter so neatly captures, what one forgets is, very obviously, as significant as what one remembers.

While adult retrospect necessarily corrupts the representation of a child's lived experience, just as a child's still-developing vocabulary determines the limits of his or her self-expression, the ante-autobiographical remains flexible, encompassing fluid representations of children and childhood across life writing forms. The concept maps onto core questions in the field, not least notions of memory, fiction, and representation. Childhood remains key in either case since, as King points out: "Writers of autobiography have to make choices about chronology, and these are choices partly informed by the importance they place upon childhood as formative of later identity" (97). These "choices," however, are so often presumed to be reliant on the author's memory. As childhoods are increasingly narrated, recorded, and preserved, the resultant archives and the ante-autobiographical material they provide have the potential to introduce another dimension to the way children and childhoods are written. Alexander's crucial point that "One of the clearest markers of powerlessness is enforced silence" (77) stands as a reminder that we must not only encourage children to write autobiographically, but also accord them enough value that they are read.

Notes

1. The primary texts around which this article is shaped are, by their nature, unpublished. A small sample has been reproduced here in facsimile form to allow the reader to consider the materiality of the object as well as the textual content. The matter is further complicated by the fact that the same author has produced the primary texts (as a child) and the analysis of them (as an adult). Throughout, great care was taken to remain attuned to the ethics of writing about oneself, paying particular attention to the fragile intimacies and insecurities of relating to oneself as a child.
2. Indeed, the absence of official life documents can be a source of extreme hardship and exclusion. Those who are considered "sans papiers," such as illegal immigrants, are all too aware of the perceived illegitimacy of the undocumented life.
3. Material circumstances are patently relevant here. Poverty and displacement are among the factors likely to preclude the production and preservation of childhood documents.

At the same time, recent developments in technology have enhanced governmental capacity to preserve public records on an international scale.

4. There are, as ever, exceptions. In fiction, Christopher Paolini wrote his popular *Eragon* books, at the age of 15. The most lauded child writer of the last century was Anne Frank whose wartime diary established a precedent for the power and lasting significance of such narratives long after her death.

5. Concorde was an iconic supersonic jet, the result of collaboration between the British and French aviation industries. Since only 20 were built in its limited lifetime of 1976–2003, spotting its distinctive shape in the air may well have seemed newsworthy in 1988.

6. The major text on this topic supports this contention even in its very title (Alexander and Juliet).

References

Alexander, Christine and McMaster Juliet. *The Child Writer from Austen to Woolf*. Cambridge: Cambridge University Press, 2005.

Alexander, Peter. "Another Oppression: Juvenilia as Alternative Colonial Narratives." *English Academy Review: Southern African Journal of English Studies* 22.1 (2005): 77–88.

Christensen, Pia Haudrup. "Childhood and the Cultural Constitution of Vulnerable Bodies." *The Body, Childhood and Society*. Ed. Alan Prout. Basingstoke: Palgrave Macmillan, 2000. 39–59.

Coe, Richard N. *When the Grass Was Taller*. New Haven: Yale University Press, 1984.

Davis, Rocío G. "Introduction: Academic Autobiography and/in the Discourses of History." *Rethinking History* 13.1 (2009): 1–4.

Eagleton, Terry. *The Gatekeeper: A Memoir*. New York: St. Martin's Griffin, 2003.

Eakin, Paul John. "Breaking Rules: The Consequences of Self-Narration." *Biography* 24.1 (2001): 113–27.

Evans, Mary. *Missing Persons: The Impossibility of Auto/Biography*. London: Routledge, 1999.

Goldsworthy, Vesna. "The Present of Intimacy: My Very Public Private Life." *Biography* 34.1 (2011): 1–10.

Guy, Basil. "*When the Grass Was Taller: Autobiography and the Experience of Childhood* (Review)." *Biography* 10.2 (1987): 177–9.

Jensen, Meg. "Separated by a Common Language: The (Differing) Discourses of Life Writing in Theory and Practice." *a/b: Auto/Biography Studies* 24.2 (2012): 299–314.

King, Nicola. "Uses of the Past: Hindsight and the Representation of Childhood in Some Recent British Academic Autobiography." *Rethinking History* 13.1 (2009): 95–108.

Knoepflmacher, U. C. *Ventures Into Childland: Victorians: Victorians, Fairy Tales, and Femininity*. London: University of Chicago Press, 1998.

Kraus, Carolyn. "Proof of Life: Memoir, Truth, and Documentary Evidence." *Biography* 31.2 (2008): 245–68.

Larkin, Philip. "A Neglected Responsibility: Contemporary Literary Manuscripts." *Required Reading: Miscellaneous Pieces 1955–1982*. London: Faber & Faber, 1983, 98–108.

McDowell, K. "Toward a History of Children as Readers, 1890–1930." *Book History* 12.1 (2009): 240–65.

Myers, M. "The Erotics of Pedagogy: Historical Intervention, Literary Representation, the 'Gift of Education' and the Agency of Children." *Children's Literature* 23 (1995): 1–30.

Popkin, J. D. "Is Autobiography Anti-Academic and Uneconomical? Some Thoughts on Academic Autobiography." *History of Political Economy* 39.1 (2007): 30–47.

———. "Life Writing in the Family." *a/b: Auto/Biography Studies* 25.2 (2010): 172–85.

Robertson, Rachel. "Carving, Forging, Stealing." *Life Writing* 7.3 (2010): 305–15.

Steedman, Carolyn. *Dust*. Manchester: Manchester University Press, 2001.

Anna Poletti

AUTOBIOGRAPHY AND PLAY: "A CONVERSATION WITH MY 12 YEAR OLD SELF"

This article considers how auto/biography scholarship might read and understand the use of the archive of play by contemporary autobiographers. Drawing on the work of the pediatrician and psychoanalyst Donald Woods Winnicott, I examine how documents generated from play can be read as instances of self-life-writing, and demonstrate the interpretive approaches that we might use to consider texts which incorporate the archive of play in self-representation. Taking an autobiographical video posted to YouTube that "went viral" in December 2012 as an example, I argue that Winnicott's distinction between the content and the activity of play offers not only a way of understanding the role of playing in developing and understanding a sense of self but also a way of reading autobiographical texts that re-mediate materials produced through childhood play.

Introduction

Given that this issue of *Prose Studies* is concerned with life writing and childhood/youth, I take this as an opportunity to think about the material that might be found in any individual's archive of their childhood or youth, which may both constitute life writing and life writing project undertaken in adult life. As Claire Lynch's contribution to this collection has fruitfully explored, one common site for the production of life writing by children and young people is the education system. In this article, I will consider another space where children and young people regularly produce documents relating to themselves: play.

In what follows, I will make some suggestions regarding how auto/biography scholarship might read and understand the use of the archive of play by contemporary autobiographers. Drawing on the work of the pediatrician and psychoanalyst Donald Woods Winnicott, I will make some preliminary suggestions regarding how documents generated from play might be read as instances of self-life-writing, and the interpretive approaches that we might use to consider texts which incorporate the archive of play in self-representation.

In referring to "the archive of play," I here describe the materials produced and left behind by the activity of playing. Of course, not all play produces a material trace. That play that does, however, results in material that is – as the case study I discuss demonstrates – a rich resource for self-representation and life narrative. Materials in the archive of play are diverse and can include: stories, hand-drawn and digitally produced illustrations, letters, videos, photographs, puppets, costumes, collage, and automatic writing. Indeed, the *kinds* of materials in any individual's archive of play is themselves informative and of interest, as I will discuss later. The materials, and the archive itself, may or may not be cherished by the autobiographer. The archive of play may not be valued or recognized *as* an archive. Many, one suspects, are thrown away during spring cleaning or the purges of objects that regularly occur in societies with high levels of consumption. Where such archives do persist, they may constitute the flotsam of a previous life that is stored in out of the way places and rarely accessed, or stored by members of one's family or childhood friends. The value of the archive of play becomes apparent once an autobiographical project is initiated or, as in the case of Dan Eldon, the Reuters photographer stoned to death in Somalia in 1993 aged 22, a young life is memorialized (Eldon).[1] In some cases, the archive itself demands remediation or engagement in the contemporary moment, as I will explore in the examples of "A Conversation With My 12 Year Old Self" and the auto/biographical film *Tarnation* (Caouette 2003).

In "The Rumpled Bed of Autobiography," Sidonie Smith and Julia Watson consider the role of the archive (broadly conceived) in the production of life writing in contexts where younger autobiographers are using a variety of material and textual remnants from the past. Inspired by Tracey Emin's infamous exhibition of *My Bed*, they ask "how do we describe the difference between selected quotation of one's past moments in such memorabilia as objects and diaries, and the performance of one's past as memory work?" (4) Smith and Watson extend this by raising a question regarding methods of reading in the field: "to what extent are literary, or narratively based, theories of autobiography useful for inquiring into self-reflexive narratives that interweave presentations of self across multiple media. . .?" (13)

In my recent work on the auto/biographical documentary *Tarnation*, I have taken up these issues by examining how filmmaker Jonathan Caouette's use of home movie footage from his childhood challenges the practice of reading solely for narrative in self-representational texts. I argue that play recorded on home video both invites and troubles an indexical reading of the relationship between the content and the context of the play, and the larger narrative into which the archival document is sutured (Poletti "Reading"). Caouette's film can be read as a relational life narrative, as defined by Paul John Eakin and Nancy K. Miller, exploring both his close relationship with his mother and his relationship with popular culture as an archive and resource for self-expression facilitated by the technology of the moving image camera (Poletti "Reading" 58–59). What I did not have the chance to explore in that article, and that I would like to take up here, is how we might think about the relationship between play and the self, and how this could be extended to reading documents produced through play that appear in autobiographical texts. In that article, I suggested that increased access to recording equipment through domestic computing and audio-visual technology will result in more auto/biographical texts making use of such archival material, and Caoutte's film is not the only text that asks that we develop a framework for reading the archive of play. The journals of Dan Eldon and the viral hit video "A Conversation With my 12 Year Old Self", among others, demonstrate the rich potential of the archive of play for autobiographical practice, and its appeal to audiences.

In what follows, I outline elements of Winnicott's theory of the self and playing, suggesting a framework it might provide for reading documents from the archive of play in adult-authored self-representational texts. In doing so, I hope to contribute to the larger project of this special issue by indicating some unique characteristics of texts that use child and youth-authored material in auto/biography.

Relational identity and the self

As a pediatrician and psychoanalyst, Winnicott was uniquely placed to observe and theorize the role of play in identity development. According to Jan Abram, editor of *The Language of Winnicott*, "Running through everything that Winnicott writes is a preoccupation with *the human condition* and *what it means to be a subject*. All his questions, from very early on, are to do with the meaning of life and what it is within that makes life worth living" (emphasis in original 5). Along with Melanie Klein, Winnicott extended and revised the key components of Freudian psychoanalysis in the area of infant psychological development, that crucial early period where the individual moves from the realm of experience and impulse to self-awareness (Abram 103). A distinctive characteristic of Winnicott's theory of the self is his emphasis on the relationality of this process; his focus was on the necessary interaction between the infant's formation of a sense of self and the environment constituted by their primary care relationship with the m/other (Abram 5). Subjectivity, for Winnicott, is constituted relationally. It is through a supportive relationship with an empathetic m/other that the infant is able to achieve a separation between inner and outer worlds, to understand that they are separate from the world, *in* the world, and what expectations they can have *of* the world (Abram 10–12). The self comes into being in infancy through a process of developing an awareness of a Me, separate from a Not-me (Abram 103, 296). "The term 'self,' therefore, describes a subjective sense of being" (Abram 296), a feeling of one's self as real that is achieved in the movement from the state of unintegrated being to self-awareness (Abram 295).

Winnicott's emphasis on the relationality of subjectivity formation shares terrain with dominant paradigms of subjectivity in auto/biography studies. Recent work on patriography, for example, as well as the long trend of feminist criticism in the field has persuasively argued that the self produced through autobiographical practice is more often than not one formed in and through relationships with significant others (or the Other). An explicit engagement with Winnicott provides us with two things. First is a much-needed conceptual tool for considering what, if anything, is distinctive about autobiography produced by young people. The second is to help us understand what these texts communicate and imply about the importance of others in the development and maintenance of a sense of self. Although other strands of psychoanalysis may also provide such tools, the centrality of playing to Winnicott's theory of the relationship between the self and the world appears to me (at the moment at least) to provide an important conceptual tool because it allows us to examine the activity of playing alongside life writing itself – that is used by the individual to experiment with and experience a sense of self.

The importance of play in developing and experiencing a sense of self

Although the development of the self in Winnicott's theory appears dependent on a binary of Me/Not-me, he was deeply interested in theorizing how this dichotomy was productively and usefully held in tension and explored throughout life. His conceptualization of "transitional phenomena" describes the space between the internal world and the objectively external: "it is the place that both connects and separates inner and outer" (Abram 337). Transitional objects (such as a loved teddy) are one means of safely, and in Winnicott's words creatively, entering that space to experience a feeling of the self. Playing is another. The importance of transitional phenomena to our experience of ourselves is fundamental to the relationality of subjectivity: the space connecting and separating our sense of self from the world, and our ongoing ability to access it, is vital to his understanding of health. Transitional phenomena is a space facilitated through a trusting and holding relationship with the primary care giver, who supports, through play, the child's learning about and encounters with their separateness and connectedness to the world (Winnicott 47–48). For Winnicott, playing is an activity that allows one to enter the third space of transitional phenomena to "process self-experience and, at the same time, communicate" (Abram 248). While children use a variety of activities for playing, in adults, Winnicott suggests, playing "manifests itself, for instance, in the choice of words, the inflection of the voice, and indeed in the sense of humour" (40).[2] Thus, playing is evident in the *aesthetics* of living and communicating in adults, and it is this suggestion that invites us to consider how autobiographical texts that draw on the archive of play are themselves instances of the adult autobiographer *playing*. Let us look at an example.

"A Conversation With My 12 Year Old Self": the archive of play and the 'True Self'

On July 5, 2012, actor and regular YouTube contributor Jeremiah McDonald uploaded a video titled "A Conversation With My 12 Year Old Self: 20th Anniversary Edition". The video incorporates video footage he made when he was 12 years old. In the YouTube video, the 32-year-old McDonald finds a VHS cassette tape made by his 12-year-old self. On the tape, the 12-year-old Jeremiah asks his older a self a number of questions, which the adult answers. The interaction results in the adult Jeremiah rediscovering his love of drawing, a narrative arc which I will address in more detail shortly. The video received nearly 4 million hits in 4 days (*Today*), and at the time of writing, it has been watched over 9 million times in 7 months since its release. McDonald's video "'went viral" and was reposted on sites such as *The Huffington Post* and the *LA Times*. McDonald gave interviews to the *Today* show and *NBC News* who reported on the viral success of the video.

Part of the video's success, McDonald acknowledges in interviews, lies in the aesthetic and discursive strategies he uses to situate the video within autobiographical discourse and establish the tape as an authentic item taken from his archive of play. The video opens with intertitles that read "20 years ago I left a tape for myself." The 12-

year-old child, framed by a television set, appears saying to camera "I think I'd like to talk to myself in the future... yes that's something that I'll do." A montage of images of McDonald follows, which establishes the continuity of self between the 12-year old and the 32-year old. In an earlier reworking of the archival video, McDonald had not provided this context. In an interview, he discusses how this decision impacted on people's responses: "So I did do an early version of the same video, and I learned some things from that first attempt. When people would watch it, they'd say, 'Oh, who's that kid playing you?' I would say, 'Well, that's me.' They'd be confused. Looking at the [original] video on its own merits, it just wasn't that good" (Strecker). The opening 24 seconds of the YouTube video is essential to the success of the second version because it more clearly establishes the video, as possessing an autobiographical narrative ("20 years ago *I* left myself a video") and authenticates the tape itself as an archival document by showing the 32-year-old Jeremiah placing the tape in the VHS player. "Even though it's a surreal concept, that you pop in a VHS and you're having a conversation with the image, but (sic) I had to create a context that made sense. In the old version, my 12-year-old self just pops up on my laptop and we're talking, and we don't know why. Yes, I had to create a narrative," McDonald explains (Strecker). The use of the first person in the intertitles and the montage of self-portraits position the "12-year-old self" referred to in the title of the YouTube video as belonging to the filmmaker, thus inviting the viewer to take up the autobiographical pact (Lejeune).

However, it is also important to note that this second version of the video explicitly situates the existence and the materiality of the archive by *showing* a VHS tape (who knows if it is *the* tape) upon which is handwritten "do not watch until future."[3] Although the earlier version of the video remediated the document of play onto the laptop screen, reactions from McDonald's viewers suggested that this digitization worked against the document being read as coming from the archive. Reference to and representation of the materiality of the archive – in this case, a pile of VHS tapes from which *this* tape is selected – confirms the importance of materiality as an authenticating strategy in autobiographical practices beyond the book, both online such as in *Post Secret* and in zine culture.[4] Such strategies are never complete, however, and McDonald continues to defend the authenticity of the video of his child-self in the comments section of the video on YouTube, evidencing what Leigh Gilmore has argued is autobiography's unique ability to produce juridical readings concerned with evidence (Gilmore).

By situating the archive of play from which it emerges, "A Conversation With My 12 Year Old Self" is a celebration *of* playing. The 12-year-old Jeremiah is clearly enjoying the extension of his interest in time travel stories and love of Doctor Who, context given by McDonald in an interview (*Today*). The VHS video is both a document of a particular play – the content of the playing provides the narrative hook for the YouTube video – and a record of the activity *of* playing, where the 12-year old enters the transitional space between inner and outer worlds to creatively explore his relationship with his own future. The possibility *of* Jeremiah's future life is neither a purely internal phenomenon, his future is not "made up" by him, nor is a tangible feature of the external world, although it will exist there when it arrives. The video is a viral success because the VHS the 12-year-old Jeremiah produced has a uniquely prescient symmetry between form (playing) and content (the play). The content of the play (imagining a future self) and the activity of playing (entering the third space that connects and separates the individual from the world) both involve the excitement and precariousness which, for Winnicott, are defining features of playing:

> Play is immensely exciting. It is exciting not primarily because the instincts are involved, be it understood! The thing about playing is always the precariousness of the interplay of personal psychic reality and the experience of control of actual objects. (Winnicott 47)

In one sense then, the 12-year old's video is a testament to him receiving good-enough mothering,[5] that allows him to extend into the third space without fear of annihilation of his subjectivity, and that supports the formation of illusion of omnipotence. As an autobiographical document, McDonald's YouTube video could be read as a celebration of that environment – a testament to the parenting he received. Although his parent/s feature nowhere in the video, a reading informed by Winnicott could read "A Conversation With My 12 Year Old Self" as a celebration of the environment produced and maintained for the child Jeremiah by his primary care giver/s. An element of the success of the video comes from how it relies upon, but does not narrate, good-enough parenting that supports and is the context for the playing we see in the archival material. Our pleasure in watching the video is in imagining the supportive environment in which the play takes place, and which, according to Winnicott, is fundamental to the development of a sense of self.[6]

Viewers also enjoy and find meaning in the video, email it to their friends, and post it on social networking pages, because by drawing on the archive of play, McDonald creates a text that represents the magical and precarious joy of playing which, Winnicott suggests, is universal (41). "A Conversation..." involves archived play and records the adult Jeremiah playing with his own archive. Some of the charm of the video is in the playful interaction between the 12-year old and the 32-year old, they play together, and McDonald – as editor – organizes this playing into a narrative with a satisfying arc in two distinct acts. The first act is defined by a light-hearted banter between the two Jeremiahs; 12-year old asks the 32-year old questions ("Are all your questions going to be about pets?" the adult Jeremiah drolly asks when the 12-year old asks whether family pets are still living). This act follows a fairly predictable character dynamic: the maturity of the 32-year old and the immaturity of the 12-year old are established and juxtaposed, and this is crystalized when the 12-year old burps and the 32-year old mutters "charming." This dynamic shifts in the second act, when the adult begins to interview the child. "What were you doing before you made this video?" the adult Jeremiah asks. "Ah," says the child, and holds up a large hand-drawn picture of a rabbit that fills the screen. "There you go," the child says from behind the picture. At this point, the tone changes and shifts to a moment of revelation that is held to the end of the video. The 32-year old looks long and hard at the picture. "Is that Roy?" he asks. "Yes. Do you still draw Roy?" the 12-year old responds from behind the picture. "No. I don't draw much anymore," the adult says. Here begins the conclusion of the video, the 32-year old is reconnected with his love of drawing and narrates his childhood desire to be an animator, revealing that as a child (the child we see on the screen) he would draw a whole cast of characters regularly. The child Jeremiah shifts from being a distant, unfamiliar, and immature self to a representative of what Winnicott would call the True Self, the subjectivity that feels real, that is the kernel of the sense of self, and is experiences as the source of spontaneous gesture (Abram 306).

This moment of revelation, where the child-self creates the opportunity for the adult-self to reconnect with his True Self, fits neatly with dominant discourses that inform and structure representations of childhood in contemporary print autobiography, particularly nostalgia (Douglas). This is undoubtedly one reason for the immense popularity of McDonald's YouTube video. This is also one of McDonald's stated intentions for making the video, which was partly designed to work as viral marketing for his business of producing illustrations to order. This strategy worked, and resulted in McDonald being inundated with orders for his drawings (Lazar). In this case, the archive of play provides documentation for the re-presentation of a True Self through autobiographical discourse that authenticates (while narrating) an identity that is, in part, a vehicle for making an artistic practice financially viable, perhaps profitable. (And we should acknowledge here that McDonald is by no means the first to use autobiography in this way.) Since the enormous success of "A Conversation With My 12 Year Old Self," McDonald has continued to draw upon his archive of play for both ideas for future artwork, and to authenticate his identity as an artist. For example, see two recent video updates posted to his Tumblr, "Some projects I'll be working on in 2013" and "I wanted to be animator, but then I got lazy and went into filmmaking" where a line spoken by the adult Jeremiah in the revelatory act of "A Conversation. . ." is used to re-frame the short film *A Lot of Loss*, made in 2009.

However, the archival video also provides McDonald the opportunity to allow the child Jeremiah to resist this positioning. Although the adult is in reverie about his True Self and his lost relationship with drawing, the 12-year-old Jeremiah asks: "Don't you realize you're kind of. . .messing up time?"[7] I would like to linger on this question to consider both the potential meanings within "A Conversation. . ." and what it might tell us about childhood playing as autobiographical practice more generally.

This statement, when made by the 12-year old at the time of filming, expresses his enjoyment of the precariousness Winnicott suggests characterizes playing: the precariousness of the interplay of personal psychic reality – imagining his future life – and the experience of control of actual objects – in this case the recording equipment which allows the 12-year old to leave an object (a tape, but also a text) in the objective world, in what I am calling the archive of play, for his future self to find. The second person address in the statement "you're kind of messing up time" exists in the precariousness and pleasure of the third space of playing; the "you" is both the "I" making the recording, inspired by Doctor Who and time-travel stories, and the imagined future "I" who will be the recipient of the video. In saying "you are kind of messing up time," the child speaks both to himself and to his future self, warning both selves about the ramifications of interfering with the future, a common theme in popular culture narratives of time travel, and enjoying the precariousness of that potential interference. In imagining he *might* interfere with time, the child momentarily experiences the omnipotence that is a characteristic phase of the development of the self (Abram 305–306). The bold imagining of his video changing time itself is precisely the kind of fantasy of power that bolsters a strong sense of self in childhood development.

We could also read against the grain a little here, and see this warning from the 12-year old as cautioning against an idealization of the child-self as a representative of the True Self. Winnicott, in suggesting how psychoanalysts might engage playing in their therapeutic practice, sounds a similar warning regarding the analyst's temptation to interpret the content of play: "the significant moment is that at which *the child surprises him or herself.* It is not the moment of my clever interpretation that is significant" (Winnicott 51, emphasis in original). Thus, the 12-year-old Jeremiah reminds his adult-self that the video he has made is a result of the process of communicating about the self that serves a developmental purpose for the 12-year old which cannot be co-opted by the narrative imperative invented by the 32-year old in *his* play. The VHS tape is a trace of the playing by the 12-year old, and the content, Winnicott suggests, is of secondary importance to the activity itself. As a means of concluding, I will briefly point to how remediation, and particularly the suturing of the archive of play into a larger narrative of identity, is, somewhat paradoxically, what makes this importance tangible for audiences.

On December 6, 2012, Jeremiah McDonald posted "A Conversation With My 12 Year Old Self: The Prequel" to YouTube. This video uses another document from McDonald's archive of play, a video he purports to have found *after* the making and release of the twentieth Anniversary Edition. In the "About" section accompanying the YouTube post, McDonald says:

> Months after posting A Conversation With My 12 Year Old Self, I stumbled on another tape that contained the second half of the footage I shot in 1992, which I thought was lost. These are some highlights.

> Using footage I shot when I was 10, I attempted to do what I later did more successfully with the other video. It's clear the 10-year-old footage wasn't intended for this purpose, which is undoubtedly what inspired me to make a tape for my future self. I hope you enjoy it for what it is. Cheers.

The prequel video consists solely of a video made by the 12-year-old Jeremiah. In this archival document, the 12-year-old Jeremiah is standing in front of a television. "Hello," he says, "and welcome to a very special edition of the Jeremiah show. See today I will be talking to my former self." The 12-year-old Jeremiah then enters into a dialogue with a video made by his 10-year-old self, which screens on the television behind him. The 12-year-old host finds his 10-year-old self a little unsophisticated and frustrating. He treats the 10-year old *as* a child. "Now I will speak to myself in the present," the host says, and plays a video of himself. The two 12-year olds engage in banter: "You're better than my other self," the 12-year-old host tells his 12-year-old interview subject, "I mean, we're much better now right?" The 12-year old on the screen agrees, "Oh yeah." In the archival video posted as a prequel, elements of the twentieth Anniversary video are repeated in a different context of play. The prequel post acts to further authenticate the archival footage in the more popular twentieth Anniversary video, and to demonstrate that McDonald has been playing with the moving image of himself from a very young age. This video, and the other videos of play uploaded by McDonald under his "weepingprophet" alias on YouTube, present an archive of play not dissimilar in the form to that presented by Caouette in *Tarnation* – the use of domestic audio visual equipment to present and experiment with subjectivity. However, the raw archival footage – even when edited into "highlights" of 2 min 44 s in length – does not appear to be as interesting to audiences, if the hits are any gauge of traction (just over 48,000 for the prequel, compared with over 9 million for the twentieth Anniversary edition). I would suggest that this is because without the framing footage seen in the Anniversary edition, the text does not, at the level of form, explicitly establish the dynamic between the inner and outer that is connected by the transitional phenomena of playing. We see the trace of playing, but we focus on the content of the play rather than play itself because a lack of framing leaves the viewer without an explicit frame for interpreting the content *or* the activity. This very strategy is used, I have argued, to profound effect by Caouette in *Tarnation*, which has the room and flexibility of the feature length documentary form to create more complex relationships between archival material and the autobiographical practice taking place in the present. In both *Tarnation* and "A Conversation With My 12 Year Old Self: 20th Anniversary Edition," we see that that archive of play functions autobiographically when it itself is the subject of playing by the autobiographer, when they themselves are drawn into the precarious and enjoyable third space by the material, and in doing so, connect with a feeling of the self as *real*.

The source of this feeling, for the adult autobiographer using childhood material, is of course partly historical. The archive of play, like all archives, places its subject in time. What I have attempted to demonstrate here is that this placement can be read as occurring at the level of form (the act of playing) rather than content (the material produced in play). Autobiographical texts such as these engage audiences because we see in the activity of playing the trust established in the primary care relationship that enables it, a relationship we all experienced but in infinitely variable degrees, *and* a confirmation of the importance of playing for our sense of who we are throughout our lives. Moreover, autobiographical texts that draw on the archive of play are themselves the result *of* playing, the autobiographer entering into a relationship with the archival material that allows them to encounter (temporarily) their past selves in a space that is precarious, exciting, and satisfying and which ultimately reinforces a feeling of the self as real.

Acknowledgements

My thanks go to Kate Douglas and Kylie Cardell for the invitation to participate in a stimulating and collegial event in Adelaide in July 2012. Thanks also to Amanda Kerley, who posted "A Conversation With My 12 Year Old Self" to my Facebook wall, and Johannes Klabbers for early conversations on Winnicott and playing, and for being a first reader of this article.

Notes

1. Eldon's adolescent journals — notebooks in which he developed sophisticated collages involving original photographic prints, ephemera, and writing — were edited by his mother and published in a hardback full cover in 1997 under the title *The Journey Is The Destination* (see Eldon).
2. Winnicott viewed psychoanalysis itself as drawing on playing between the analysand and the analyst (50–51).

3. This differs from Caouette's approach, where he leaves *what* is being looked at when archival documents are shown open to interpretation, whether or not the child Jonathan is playing "himself" or someone else is an ambiguity that is central to Caouette's to the element of *Tarnation*'s narrative that deals with his experience of dissociative disorder. Although both Caouette and McDonald present narratives of their identity as artists, McDonald's is far more direct in the connection it draws between playing and the True Self.

4. See Poletti, "Intimate Economies" for a discussion of materiality as authenticating strategy in *Post Secret*; and Poletti, *Intimate Ephemera* for an analysis of materiality in autobiographical practice in zine culture.

5. Winnicott uses the term "good-enough" mother to distinguish between the real woman and the figure of the mother in his developmental theory, but also to stress that "good" mothering will be in response to the development of a specific infant, rather "good" being an objectively defined quality (Abram 221).

6. For the adult McDonald, the success of the video is evidence of the success of YouTube as a space of experimentation and play: "When I was a kid, I was just playing. I don't know how far in advance I was thinking, and of course, I didn't think anyone would see it anyway. It was purely for my own enjoyment. I think maybe by the time I was 20 years old, I said, 'This is something really cool.' Even then, I didn't know how I was going to use it because, certainly, there was no YouTube at the time. When YouTube started, I knew that this would be something that was perfect for that. I did an early version. I consider YouTube as a playground, it's a place to experiment" (Strecker).

7. "Sorry," the adult responds, distractedly, "I was just thinking out loud".

References

Abram, Jan. *The Language of Winnicott: A Dictionary of Winnicott's Use of Words*. 2nd ed. London: Karnac Books, 2007.

Douglas, Kate. *Contesting Childhoods: Autobiography, Trauma, and Memory*. New Brunswick, NJ: Rutgers University Press, 2010.

Eldon, Dan. *The Journey is the Destination: The Journals of Dan Eldon*, edited by Kathy Eldon. San Francisco: Chronicle Books, 1997.

Gilmore, Leigh. *The Limits of Autobiography: Trauma and Testimony*. Ithaca, NY: Cornell University Press, 2001.

Lazar, Shira. "Jeremiah McDonald Interview: Talking to the Creator of 'A Conversation With My 12 Year Old Self' (VIDEO)." The Huffington Post 9 July 2013, The Huffington Post.com Inc. <http://www.huffingtonpost.com/shira-lazar/jeremiah-mcdonald-interview_b_1656414.html>. Web 1 Jan. 2013

Lejeune, Philippe. "The Autobiographical Pact." In *On Autobiography*, edited by PaulJohn Eakin. Minneapolis, MN: University of Minnesota Press, 1989, 3–30 trans. Katherine Leary.

Jeremiah, McDonald (weepingprophet). "A Conversation With My 12 Year Old Self: The Prequel." 6 Dec. 2012. <http://www.youtube.com/watch?v=7IyJeasvs40>. Web 17 Jan. 2013

————. "A Conversation With My 12 Year Old Self: 20th Anniversary Edition." 5 July 2012. <http://www.youtube.com/watch?v=XFGAQrEUaeU>. Web 10 July 2012

McDonald, Jeremiah. "I Wanted to be an Animator, But Then I Got Lazy and Went into Filmmaking." Tell Me To Draw Something. n.p. 28 Dec. 2012. <http://tellmeto-drawsomething.tumblr.com/post/39053793368/i-wanted-to-be-an-animator-but-then-i-got-lazy>. Web 17 Jan. 2013

————. "Some Projects I'll be Working on in 2013." Tell Me To Draw Something. n.p. 15 Jan. 2013. <http://tellmetodrawsomething.tumblr.com/post/40597230054/-some-projects-ill-be-working-on-in-2013>. Web 17 Jan. 2013

Poletti, Anna. "Intimate Economies: PostSecret and the Affect of Confession." *Biography: An Interdisciplinary Quarterly, special issue Life Writing and Intimate Publics* 31.4 (2011): 25–36.

————. *Intimate Ephemera: Reading Young Lives in Australian Zine Culture*. Carlton: Melbourne University Publishing, 2008.

————. "Reading for Excess: Relational Autobiography, Affect and Popular Culture in Tarnation." *Life Writing* 9.2 (2012): 157–72.

Rak, Julie. *Negotiated Memory: Doukhobor Autobiographical Discourse*. Vancouver: University of British Columbia Press, 2004.

Smith, Sidonie, and Julia Watson. "The Rumpled Bed of Autobiography: Extravagant Lives, Extravagant Questions." *Biography: an Interdisciplinary Quarterly* 24.1 (2001): 1–14.

Strecker, Erin. "Jeremiah McDonald Q&A: Viral video star on interviewing his future self." Entertainment Weekly. 12 July 2012. Entertainment Weekly Inc. <http://pop-watch.ew.com/2012/07/10/jeremiah-mcdonald-qa-viral-video-star-on-interview-ing-his-future-self/>. Web 1 Jan. 2013

Winnicott Donald, W. *"Playing: A Theoretical Statement." In Playing and Reality*. New York: Routledge, 1989, 38–52.

Leena Kurvet-Käosaar

" 'WHO KNOWS, WILL I EVER SEE YOU AGAIN,' SAID THE ONE-EYED DUCK." REFLECTIONS ON A SOVIET CHILDHOOD IN LEELO TUNGAL'S LIFE WRITING

The article focuses on the representation of childhood trauma in Seltsimees laps (Comrade Child 2008) and Samet ja saepuru (Velvet and Sawdust 2009), a childhood autobiography of a well-known Estonian children's author Leelo Tungal. These works offer a multilayered insight into sociopolitical and historical climate of the Soviet 1950s in Estonia from a young child's perspective who, as a result of the Stalinist repressions, has to spend the prime years of her childhood without her mother. Tungal creates an idyllic childhood scene that is interlaced with the traumatic story of a young child having to face a confusing world wrought with tension and insecurity. This article provides an analysis of Tungal's intricate textual strategies for tackling the traumatic impact of her childhood experience. This experience is mediated in her life writings through a portrayal of emblematic aspects of the era and the creation, in Lauren Berlant's terms, of an intimate public centered on a horizon of expectations about happy childhood.

In the two-volume childhood autobiography of a popular Estonian children's author, Leelo Tungal, titled *Seltsimees laps* (Comrade Child 2008) and *Samet ja saepuru* (Velvet and Sawdust 2009), these words are "uttered" by a toy of the young protagonist during a game. The game is a journey where Leelo assembles a makeshift train of two abacuses and her pink hair-ribbon and loads her toys onto the train to be deported to Siberia. The words of the one-eyed duck echo those of the protagonist's grandmother who, when she was deported in March 1949, said to her grandchild who was then nearly two years old: "I am crying, you are laughing, who knows, will my eyes ever see you again" (55).[1] There is, however, another more gravely felt absence in Leelo Tungal's life that forms the core of her childhood autobiography: on April 12, 1951, Leelo Tungal's's mother, a former headmistress and teacher at a small country school in Ruila in North-Western Estonia, was arrested in her home in front of her three-year-old daughter and husband. In Tungal's memoir, the mother says to her daughter Leelo before she is taken away: "Be a good child, then *memme* [Mommy] will come back very soon! Perhaps tomorrow, perhaps the day after that ..." (Seltsimees 12). In an interview about her work, Leelo Tungal has explained that as her mother had committed no crime against the Soviet regime, she believed her arrest to be a misunderstanding and thought she would return home in a few days (Lotman 9).[2] In reality, after five months of imprisonment in Tallinn Patarei prison, Helmes was sent to the Gulag, to a forced labor camp in Inta, and not released until May 1955.[3] Leelo was left to the care of her father (*tata*) for four long years and her childhood autobiography is the account of a child trying to cope with and make sense of her experience, wrought with fear and uncertainty not only for the young girl but also for the grown-ups around her.

Throughout the post-Soviet period, starting with the regaining of independence in 1991, various life-writing practices have flourished in Estonia, among them childhood narratives that form an important thematic axis in Estonian post-Soviet life-writings, relating to certain commonly accepted configurations of meaning and affect. Although scholars of childhood life writing emphasize its relatively late emergence (Saunders 203; Coe xi) and slow process of gaining recognition (Coe 10), a noteworthy thematic emphasis on childhood can be found in a considerable number of well-known autobiographies. Frequently, the author looks back with nostalgia; this period of life is depicted as exceptionally idyllic and blissful (Saunders 203; Douglas 84−105). Such a perception of childhood, however, forms but one half of the binary that seems to make up the referential frame of childhood autobiography, with experiences recalled as "profoundly unhappy" (Saunders 203) forming the other half. As Kate Douglas has argued, "autobiographical writing concerned with childhood experiences" can be viewed as "the most notable and perhaps most infamous publishing trend in the 1990s", standing out, in particular for "the depiction of challenging, often traumatic childhoods − characterized by abuse, poverty, discrimination, and identity struggles" (1). In her consideration of life writing and Asian American childhood, Rocío G. Davis highlights the ways in which autobiographies allow us to examine how "cultural resources, conventions, and histories are deployed in the recreation of [...] cultural contexts in which lives are lived" (3). With a slightly different focus, Douglas, relying on the paradigm of cultural memory, looks at "the myriad of ways in which memories of childhood are mediated or shaped through social institutions and cultural practices" (23).

Childhood memoirs or life writings, where childhood emerges as an important phase of the author's life, have been part of Estonian life-writing tradition from its beginnings at the end of the 19th century. In post-Soviet life writing, including a substantial corpus of personal narratives that have been written in response to various public calls for submitting life narratives, childhood memories are frequently used to highlight the radical socio-historic ruptures in relation to the events of WWII, forced emigration to the West (exile autobiographies) and the Soviet occupation. Childhood, if it falls to the pre-war period, is represented in the nostalgic mood, highlighting an idyllic period not only or not primarily in the author's own life but also in the country's general well-being. Often these memoirs evoke an image of harmonious childhood that lays a foundation for a strong sense of national identity in adulthood, confirming the view of childhood as "the most intensively governed sector of personal existence" in different ways "linked in thought and practice to the destiny of the nation" (Rose 123). Socio-political changes are presented as taking their toll on the authors' families, yet they are rarely discussed in terms of subsequent parental failures or other serious deprivations and absences in the child's life that are connected to these circumstances.

However, some Estonian life-writings of childhood, in particular those by women, also reframe such premises by foregrounding a child protagonist caught within the familial repercussions caused by political and historical factors. In addition to Leelo Tungal's life writings, this is, for example, visible in the canonic autobiographical novel *Seitsmes rahukevad* (The Seventh Spring of Peace 1985) by well-known Estonian poet and novelist Viivi Luik, often read as a credo of the post-war generation, and in Eeva Park's controversial *Tolm ja tuul* (Dust and Wind 1992). Set in the 1950s, the novels of Luik and Park make visible the impact of dysfunctional family relations and conflicts between family members issuing from political tensions to the child protagonist who has to make sense on her own of the complex interrelationship of the familial and interpersonal and public and political tightropes of the era. The novels are written from the perspective of the adult narrator looking back on her childhood who perceives it as a phase toward growing into an awareness of an artist's vocation. The autobiographies of Luik and Park roughly follow the model of childhood autobiography proposed by Richard N. Coe who has defined childhood autobiography as

> narrat[ing] the development of a hero [. . .] from a point of nonawareness to a point of total awareness of himself as an individual, and particularly as a writer and as a poet, who will produce, as evidence of his mature poet-identity, the Childhood which he has written. (9)

The life writings of Leelo Tungal, however, convey the child subject's perception of the surrounding world without any direct reference to "a sense of what the subject was to become" (Saunders 203) in adulthood. Revisiting a complicated and hurtful period of the author's life, the texts allow for at least a tentative reading as a trauma narrative. At the same time, they also create a humorous, charming, and convincing lifeworld of a young girl that is not cancelled out, though it is disturbed by her mother's arrest and imprisonment.

In an interview after the publication of the first volume of her autobiography, Tungal comments on the interviewer's ironic connotations of "a happy childhood" for a child who for many years "has to grow up without her mother who has been taken away from her by the [Soviet] power" (Lotman 9):

> Yes, clearly the title is to an extent ironic. [...] Yet there's also a grain of truth in it, since children growing up even in the poorest of conditions can be happy if they feel loved. In addition to my father, I was surrounded by many good people [...] and I never had time to feel bored. Longing was a different matter. (Lotman 9)

The use of the phrase, "happy childhood" has yet another connotation, pointing to the operation of Soviet ideology that actively promoted the idea of "the idealized happy Soviet childhood as 'evidence' of the success of the Soviet system" (Knight 790) through propaganda both for and about children (Kelly 6). As *Seltsimees laps* and *Samet ja saepuru* make visible, despite the fact that her own childhood was shadowed by losses and deprivations caused by the regime, Leelo was an enthusiastic recipient of such propaganda.

On the one hand, the explanation Tungal provides about the existence of different modes and textual impulses in her childhood autobiography is convincing. On the other, it does not entirely cater for a certain ambiguity – the author creates an idyllic and nostalgic childhood scene, confirming the reader's horizon of expectations, but this is interlaced with the traumatic story of a young child missing her mother and having to face a confusing world wrought with tension and insecurity. The memoirs are further complicated by the incompatibility of the textual representation, an experience that stays within the heuristic and linguistic frame of reference of a three-year-old, and the sophisticated design of the volume from a cloth-clad cover to collages of illustrations, featuring artistic remodeling of Tungal's childhood drawings, family photographs, and visual images of the 1950s and 1960s.

To use the conceptual frame elaborated by Lauren Berlant in *The Female Complaint*, *Seltsimees laps* and *Samet ja saepuru* seem to enter into diverse processes of both negotiating for and resisting "an intimate public", a shared space of "recognition and reflection" (viii), embedded in conventionality as an important site of "negotiating belonging to a world" (3). Berlant's research focuses on the intimate public of "women's culture" in the United States, which she analyzes through a reading of "gender-marked texts of women's popular culture" (5). In my reading, the notion of the intimate public as a "culture of circulation" that is based on an affective belief in the possibility of expression of commonality in that culture will be used with regard to popular perceptions of childhood, featuring circuits of nurture, love, and close communal attachments that are as if every child's birthright regardless of his/her specific socio-historical contexts. By forming an intimate public that "foregrounds affective and emotional attachments located in the fantasies of the common, the everyday and a sense of ordinariness" (Berlant 10), it becomes possible for Tungal to touch upon childhood trauma caused by violent separation from her mother without drawing too much attention to it. A strong appeal for "an intimate public" effectively camouflages the author's other, semi-hidden agenda, trying to retrospectively make sense of the hurtful and traumatic side of the experience.

My research on different modes of dealing with the hurtfulness of women's experience of the repressions of the Soviet regime in the Baltic States (see, e.g., Kurvet-Käosaar "The Traumatic Impact", "Vulnerable Scriptings") has demonstrated that although the retrospectively recorded deportation narratives of Baltic women dating from early and mid-90s contain ample illustrations of experience that could be perceived of as traumatic, these narratives do not easily lend to an interpretation compatible with the general theoretical framework of trauma ("Vulnerable Scriptings" 93). An important aspect here is the relative unfamiliarity of the conceptual framework of trauma in both academic and popular discussions of the repressions of the Soviet regime as well as resistance to accepting its impact. Within the accepted representative codes for conveying the repression experience of this era, the emphasis is placed, on the one hand, on its inhuman and harsh nature and the many losses it has brought about and, on the other, on a sense of survival through even the most excruciating ordeals. Such normative frameworks are also present in Tungal's childhood autobiography, yet it also attempts to make visible the traumatic effect of the losses she had to suffer from that do not seamlessly fit into the picture of a "happy childhood" even if it presented with a degree of irony. In my analysis of *Seltsimees laps* and *Samet ja saepuru* I focus on different textual strategies the author employs for touching upon the possibly traumatic aspect of her childhood experience, most importantly, in Berlant's terms, via "cultiva[ting] fantasies of vague belonging as an alleviation of what is hard to manage in the lived real" (5).

For Berlant, the concept of the intimate publics effectively facilitates a critique of one aspect or sphere of American popular culture. Although Tungal's life writings belong to a different geopolitical and temporal context and concern different aspects of culture, critique of similar kind can be extended to *Seltsimees laps* and *Samet ja saepuru* as well, most importantly, for cultivating versions of common (idealized) perceptions about childhood that no actual experience can render completely invalid. In her life narrative published in *Eesti Rahva Eluloud*, Tungal describes herself as a "Sunday's child" (332) and the reception of her childhood autobiographies reinforces this self-perception: "Leelo is a capable and joyful child [...] she misses her *memme*, has nightmares of men in black but by nature, she really is a Sunday's child: perceptive, bold, resourceful and verbally talented" (Olesk 1590). I would argue that the young protagonist's at times dramatic reactions to her experience are not so much pushed to the background by the more joyful side of her childhood experience, presented to the reader humorously through the 'wisdom' of a three-year-old and the utilization of many commonplace themes and images about life in the Estonian Soviet Socialist Republic (ESSR) in the 1950s, instead, they are camouflaged so that they would not emerge as the primary aspect of the text. By subtly depicting the traumatic impact of the repressive nature of the Soviet regime on her otherwise happy childhood, Tungal does not place herself outside the normative framework of the Baltic memorial culture but problematizes it from within.

> Some children are good and exemplary from the start [...] If I were a good and exemplary child, my *Memme* would never have left me, this much is clear [...] Things that an exemplary child wouldn't even dream about always happen to me. When I help my mommy with the dishes, I am bound to drop the finest and most beautiful cup or saucer [...] If there's as much as one little puddle on the road, I step into it and when two men in long black coats and guns stand on the doorway, I stumble over the big boots of one of them [...] And *memme* gets tears in her eyes when she looks at me. (*Seltsimees* 7–8).

The above-quoted opening section of *Seltsimees laps* introduces to the reader the perspective of a three-year-old who is making an effort to interpret a situation that seems like a matter of small mischief, yet assumes ominous overtones. At first glance, the child seems to be reflecting on quite common parental expectations for good behavior. However, as she perceives it, it is because of her failure to behave that her mother abandons her. Such perspective is further enhanced by the account of the arrest that is focalized in the text through the child: the mother is taken away against her will by these "men in black coats" because Leelo, once more, doesn't seem to know how to properly behave in the situation and thus makes the men agitated and angry. The text offers here, and elsewhere, enough clues for an adult reader to understand what is happening – that Leelo's mother is arrested by the Soviet authorities. Yet the memoir pushes this knowledge to the background so that the perspective stays with the child, who interprets the event according to the norms of her world and with herself as its nexus. Throughout the episode of the arrest the focus is on the child's frightened contemplation of the mischief she has done earlier that day (scribbling on the door, letting the dogs run around in the house) that is for her the only way to make sense of the events. It is the incompatibility of the child trying to make sense of the experience and the framing of the narrative in sociopolitical realities of the era that sets the ambiguous mood of the text and allows for a reading of Tungal's childhood experience as traumatic. The impact of mother's arrest and other repressions that befall the family are also made visible through the long-term effects they have for the child, such as, for example, nightmares, irrational fears, and complete loss of appetite. Yet, none of these effects are foregrounded as such but blend into the narrative texture of the work as a whole.

The episode of the arrest, apart from detailing the little girl's separation from her mother, also includes a rather gruesome and dramatic scene where the girl becomes a victim of the NKVD official's psychological and physical aggression.[4] Dressed in long black leather coats and carrying guns, the two men confirm the typical image of Soviet security officials in Estonian life stories of the repressions of the Stalinist regime, standing in as a symbol of fear and violence. Yet their appearance is not what causes fear in the little protagonist, for her the men seem "like ordinary people with guns, like *tata's* hunter friends", it is their actions that lead her to conclude that these are really "the men in black" (11). When the officials come to arrest the mother, Leelo's presence distracts them, they want "the little bastard" (8) out of their way, and she is sent to the adjoining room to play. In order to calm herself and to show the men what she really is – a little songbird, which is term of endearment her parents use – she starts to sing, as it "was an activity that always improved the mood of grown-ups" (*Seltsimees* 10). Unfortunately, however, her singing had quite an opposite effect on the NKVD officials:

> Suddenly the door burst open [. . .] and the man in the black coat dashed towards me. He grabbed me by the shoulders and shook me so hard that tears burst both from my eyes and my nose. "You damn contra[revolutionary] brat! Shut up or we will take you with us as well! Damn offspring of the kulaks!" [. . .] I did not cry on purpose, my word of honor for that! I wanted to escape, from this bed, from this room, from this world where black men can appear any moment both in dreams and in reality, from this small shaken body [...] why cannot a person become just a voice and fly away? I woke in my bed, with a taste of strange medicine in my mouth. (10–11)

The traumatic impact of the act of violence by the NKVD official toward the child is visible on several levels in the narrative. The reader is prompted to deduce this from the description of the event: the little protagonist cannot recall what happened to her and when she comes around she learns that that she has wet her pants. More importantly, however, the impact is inferred from the changes in the narrative mood. In the extract cited above, the words "I didn't cry on purpose" (11) refer to the child's understanding of the event, in the section "I wanted to escape [. . .] from this small shaken body" (11) the register suddenly switches from the child's perspective to that of an adult narrator looking back at the event with pain and empathy. Tungal herself has commented on her awareness of this dual perspective: "When writing the story I felt again alive in me that small child who had been treated in such grossly unjust manner

[. . .] and I also needed to suppress the grown-up who would have wished to reach her protective hand over the protagonist and expose and stigmatize evil" (Lotman 8).

This incident is also related to the child's nightmares of "black men" who "often come to haunt" her in her dreams after she witnesses the arrest of her maternal grandmother. If previously, "climbing to bed between *memme* and *tata*" (*Seltsimees* 11) would save her from the nightmares, her mother's arrest means this method of coping with her fears disappears, and but the nightmares continue. When Leelo stays with her paternal grandparents, they do not close the drapes fully but leave a gap. As the little protagonist contemplates, this is because, unlike for her parents, she has not informed them about the potential dangers of such a gap: "black men, wolves and who knows what could peep in through such opening. For example, ghosts. Or the Devil himself – when he comes for those who have sworn during the day" (65). Here the typical world of a three-year-old inhabited by creatures from fairy-tales who would not seem dangerous to the grown-ups blends into a real threat of further repressions by the Soviet regime: "Didn't you used to stay up at night with your coat and boots on during the worst period of deportations," grandmother rhetorically asks her husband when he scolds the little girl for disturbing his sleep (66). However, the threat is presented though the eyes of the little girl, who imagines that "the black men are right here in this room" (66) ready to take her grandparents away. When grandmother switches on the light it becomes clear that what the little girl had taken for glistening teeth is merely Leelo's mother's necklace glittering in the dark. The humorous closure of the episode, describing the grandparents singing and dancing in their bedroom in their nightgowns in the middle of the night (in order to calm the little girl), skillfully redirects the reader's attention away from the nightmares as it also soothes the little protagonist's fears. In general, however, there is little that Leelo or the grown-ups surrounding her can do to help her to fight nightmares the impact of which she sums up in the following manner:

> Whenever there was a talk about war, *tata* always said that coming home from the war was like escaping a dreadful nightmare. For me, waking up in the morning was like coming home from the war. (*Samet* 46)

Here, Tungal not only emphasizes the harmful impact of the nightmares to the little girl but also sums up the effect of the events she had to experience as child on a more general level. Despite the loving care of her father and other family members, she had to wage her own war, every day achieving small victories, yet never able to completely leave its battlefields behind.

In time, the little girl picks up on the words that the grown-ups use to describe what has happened to her mother, though they form no meaningful pattern in her mind and so cannot help her gain an understanding of why her mother was taken away.

> Grown-ups are certainly smart and skillful. Sometimes they can speak in such a complicated manner that you can grasp nothing of what they say although everything is as if said in plain Estonian. Some of these words you can even memorize, for example "to arrest", "NKVD", and "amnesty", sound quite mighty, but their meaning still remains fuzzy. I like to say those words, sometimes whispering by myself, sometimes singing them out loud." (*Seltsimees* 14)

Tungal's reference to "keywords" of the Soviet regime not only points to the inability of the girl to understand their meaning: they can be equally hard to grasp for the grown-ups. Thus it is difficult also for Leelo's father to move past the basic fact that his wife was arrested and obtain further information about what she is being accused of, what her sentence might be, or whether there is a chance that an appeal for amnesty would be successful. Even more importantly, different bits and pieces of the discourse of Soviet ideology that come to the attention of the little protagonist not only cause confusion but also function as a means of empowerment in various ways. Jūra Avižienis, in a critical consideration of Lithuanian deportation stories, highlights the important role of language as "a system of thought, an organizing structure, the grammar a subject must internalize in order to function and fit in a society" plays in the process of "'flawed colonial mimesis' in which to be Sovietized is *emphatically* not to be Soviet" (Avižienis 187, reference to Bhabha 87).

When Leelo is trying out different ways of uttering the mysterious words, she discovers that NKVD can be sung quite successfully using the tune of a popular Estonian folk song and when she presents this "discovery" to her parents, "they laugh tears" (*Seltsimees* 14). Here the girl's adoption of the term temporarily empties it of its ominous connotations: being able to laugh at the central security establishment of the Soviet regime might be a small step toward surviving its consequences. On several other occasions, however, the girl does not so much distort or reverse the meanings of the words belonging to Soviet jargon but adopts their rhetoric (in particular via songs and poems) as a way of making sense of reality and as a means of empowerment. When her aunt brings them a radio, Leelo is carried away by its joyful optimism: "I was no longer interested in what *tata* and Aunt Anne did or spoke about: the world that the songs on the radio mediated was sunny and cheerful – no lawyers or investigators, Russian machine-guns or shortage of money" (*Seltsimees* 134). Even when she overhears a conversation about Stalinist repressions and a fear of how "lightly built Helmes" that is, her mother "would manage in the camp" (*Samet* 136), her attention is carried away by "the beautiful color plates [in a children's book] where a white ship sails on light blue waves of the Moscow river past the Moscow Kremlin" (136). Viivi Luik, the author of a canonical autobiographical novel about postwar childhood has related "the spirit of the fifties in the Soviet Union [. . .] its pathetic and deceitful optimism and cruel brightness [. . .] to the kind of child she once was" (10). The two girls are not too similar: Tungal's representation is younger, more strongly embedded in familial contexts and through this also more vulnerable. However, coming from very modest rural backgrounds, both are quite receptive to the Soviet propaganda hailing a bright and affluent future for everyone, including children.

The title phrase, "comrade child" is also related to an episode foregrounding the empowering effect of language. When catching a bus to the girl's paternal grandparents, the conductor selling them tickets addresses her in the following manner: "Comrade child, I assume is under five years of age?" (*Seltsimees* 30). The narrator here humorously reminds the adult reader of the specificities of the Soviet discourse, yet such address also has a remarkable empowering effect on the young protagonist that by far exceeds the absurdity of the situation: "That was something", she muses, "I didn't [. . .] pay any further attention to the conversation between *tata* and the conductor but repeated to myself: "Comrade child! Comrade child!" This meant that I would pass for a full grown-up! Not just a good child or a naughty child but comrade child!" (30).

However, these words, phrases, and concepts, while clearly signifying different aspects of the Soviet life, also fail to assist the adult reader in making complete sense of specific events and meanings in the text because they concentrate on the child's primary and episodically experienced sensory world. As the narrative of *Seltsimees Laps* and *Samet ja Saepuru* unwinds, the reader is invited to follow the uneven narration that waddles from one episode or event to another according to its significance from the child's perspective, pausing along the way to get lost in dreams, nightmares, daydreams, and flights of imagination that sometimes take over the adults' world:

> Suddenly I smelled *memme*'s fragrance; it floated above the bed and all over the bedroom, this fragrance that she wore during parties and birthdays [. . .] soft, a little bit flowery and strawberry-like [. . .] "*Tata, tata!*" I dashed to the other room. "*Memme* is coming home any minute, her smell is already here!" (*Seltsimees* 85)

This clue to the mother's possible return is difficult to interpret not only for the reader but also for the girl's father who inspects carefully every nook and cranny of their bedroom as if really expecting to find his wife in the corner of the room: "*Tata* bent and sniffed the air like a hunting dog" (85). The girl's flight of imagination blends in with the father's own confusion and worry about his wife's unknown fate, creating a horizon of hope. This episode also reveals that though the father manages the role of sole caretaker of his daughter in more or less satisfactory manner, he himself is worn down by the situation, by the prolonged absence of information about his wife, and by uncertainties about his own future. The narrative puts no blame on the father but neither does it idealize or make him heroic, but makes visible the deep losses the little girl suffers. However, if the father's hope fades away the moment he rationally makes sense of the situation, the girl's power of imagination provides her far greater assurance about her mother's ultimate return: "Strange that *tata* didn't feel that smell! [. . .] Once in bed I felt again a small cloud of fragrance above my head. *Memme* can't be far!" (85).

Although, after the mother's arrest, the child's primary needs are taken care of quite capably by her father and the other family members supporting him, an additional problem is the possibility that the little girl may be categorized, like her mother, as "the enemy of the people" and thus subject to penalization. At some point, Leelo's father is offered the position of school director, providing that he fulfilled the following conditions: join the Communist Party, divorce his wife (as she is a political prisoner, her agreement is not needed) and send Leelo, "the daughter of the enemy of the people and granddaughter of a kulak" to an orphanage (*Seltsimees* 44). As *Seltsimees laps* makes clear, it is absolutely out of the question for the father to pursue any of these options. However, his discussion with his sister about his possibilities for promotion serves to demonstrate how poor his chances are to improve his situation by any other means. Leelo, who is a thoughtful and smart child, perceives the insecurities around her quite well and processes them in her own and often humorous manner. For instance, when she overhears the conversation about the orphanage, she asks quite matter-of-factly if she would need to eat the skin of chicken in the soup there, a topical question for her as at that moment she is struggling to manage a bowl of chicken soup (*Seltsimees* 44). As later events make clear, her inability to eat the soup, or indeed most of the food that she is served, either by her father or her aunts, is the sign of an eating disorder she develops as a result of her mother's arrest.

Much of the narrative and thematic structuring of *Seltsimees laps* and *Samet ja saepuru* follows the child subject as she attempts to handle loss, uncertainty, and confusion. However, there is another strong thematic line that has the opposite effect. Despite everything that happens in her life, the little girl retains a strong sense of the material, and even more importantly, affective, circumstances of what her life as a child should be. In other words, although *Seltsimees laps* and its sequel are not narratives of happy childhood, the idea of a happy childhood operates in the texts as a central structuring feature and a major attraction for the reader who is never allowed to forget the common horizon of expectations regarding childhood, including circuits of nurture, love, and close communal attachments. It is the range of these underlying assumptions that form the affective and ethical foundation of the text, which is also attached to the construction of an intimate public. In Tungal's life writings, the traditional western perception of childhood that Barry Goldson posits as "an unproblematic period of innocence, fantastic freedom, imagination and seamless opportunity[...] limited responsibility and minimal obligations" and the child–adult relation as "an exclusively benign and consensual arrangement, guaranteeing and protecting the interests of the child", (2) is reframed in relation to other socio-historic and individual particularities of growing up that problematize and subvert this, though they also never render it completely invalid.

An initial set of assumptions about the essence of childhood is never entirely rejected or disproved but forms an affective common ground informing the expectations that the reader may have of the text. This makes visible two opposing characteristics of the child: on the one hand, her vulnerability and helplessness in the face of the events she is drawn into, on the other, her resilience to them that emerges via a focus on the small details and pleasures of a child's world, what Coe refers to as the "inventories of a small world" that make up the "supreme experience for the child" (225–226). This "small world", as Coe argues, "dominates absolutely, and the first intellectual preoccupation of the child is to establish its inventory" (239). In the case of Tungal's life writings, the absolute domination of such a world is debatable, as the child's (traumatic) experience of the repressions of the Stalinist regime forces her to face the world of grown-ups at a very early age. She does so partially by assimilating the competing events and discourses into her child's world (playing deportation with her toys or singing the word "NKVD") and through this the threatening and frightening impact is at least partially neutralized. Even more importantly, however, much of her child's world that is described in *Seltsimees laps* and *Samet ja saepuru*, in ways that evoke a strong sense of recognition in the reader, goes on despite the events. For example, only a few days after he mother's arrest when the little protagonist and her father are on their way to visit her paternal grandparents, she muses about life's pleasures:

> Grown-ups have no idea of many of life's pleasures. For instance, what fun it is to slide on frozen stretches on the village road and what an especially cool feeling it is when your foot happens to drop [...] into a fresh light brown puddle on the road! (*Seltsimees* 26)

In a similar manner, she contemplates the imaginary figures she sees on the wood-paneled ceiling of her bedroom; how her left and right foot that she has named Nogi and Kota serve as playmates for her; how she plays racing games with her father, enacting famous athletes; and how she desires an aviator cap that is currently the height of fashion.

Thus, Tungal's life writings enter into dual processes of camouflage. On the one hand, the child is trapped in the familial repercussions of political tensions in a period that seems to call into doubt any possibility for idealistic conceptions of happy childhood. On the other, these ideals are kept operative through convincing and emotionally representative moments of happiness, both in the actual lived experience of the child and in her daydreaming and flights of imagination. An example here is the opening section of *Samet ja saepuru*, which conveys a moment of pure joy and happiness that renders unimportant the factors that, in reality, would disturb its perfection:

> The sun smells of linden blossoms, chamomile and honey and I feel so good I almost cannot breathe [...] this wonderful feeling that the world is good and I am good and life is so wonderful, shines through me like sunrays. On such days there are no prisons, black men and sad thoughts [...] everything is all right and gets even better [...] as it always does in fairy tales. (5).

Seltsimees laps and *Samet ja saepuru* also invite particular kinds of reading through their intricate design and illustrations by Urmas Viik, a well-known Eastonian graphic artist. The illustrations make use of the author's family archive and other visual materials such as Soviet stamps, drawings from fashion magazines and images of the political leaders, including those of Stalin. However, as the design of the illustrations is elaborate and sophisticated, it offers the reader no direct visual references to the era and the people described in the text but primarily foregrounds the artist's interpretation of the source materials. The question of referentiality rises in particularly strong manner in relation to photographic material used. As Timothy Dow Adams has pointed out, "because photographs are in a sense physical traces of actual objects, they somehow seem more referential than words" (xv). However, recent scholarship on life writing and photography has demonstrated that photos can enter into intricate relationships with written life writing texts, inviting a variety of readings in terms of referentiality (see, for example, Adams; Rugg). Yet for an average reader of life writing, photographs do not necessarily problematize referentiality but rather confirm and consolidate it. The illustrations of *Seltsimees laps* and *Samet ja seapuru* contain no full photographs but only cut-out figures that are strongly stylized by tinting and blurring of the images and the text offers no explanation for the origin of the photos and other visual sources. By closely following the narrative threads and connecting them to the figures that have been extracted from photographs, the reader can assume that they depict Tungal and her family members. However, the reader is still left wondering about the extent to which the work invites or enables the restoration of referentiality. In an interview Tungal mentions using as source materials for her text documents from her family archive, including the correspondence between her mother and herself and the drawings that she sent her where gradually "girls with red flags and Christmas trees with pentagons" started to appear (Lotman 9). Tungal also appreciatively comments on the work of the illustrator who succeeded in creating a "half fairytale-like, half historical atmosphere" (Lotman 9) that characterizes both the era and Tungal's process of recollection of it.

An illustration on the last page of the first chapter, the first one of the book, shows a couple with the woman holding a baby in her arms. Even though figures that have been cut out from a photo are blurred, the couple's clothing and the woman's hairdo indicate the style of the 1950s. With the smiling faces of the parents turned toward the baby, the figures on the illustration form a happy and peaceful unity, an impression that is further enhanced by soft white dots that surround and cover them, creating a dreamlike atmosphere against yellowed beige background. On the upper right-hand side of the illustration are three Soviet stamps with the Soviet coat of arms composed of a sickle and hammer on a globe, framed by ears of wheat. The coat of arms has been scribbled over so the wreaths have changed into threatening faces with black bulgy eyes and rows of glistening white teeth. As the first chapter contains the description of the mother's arrest and the aggression of the NKVD official toward the little girl, it is not difficult for the reader to interpret the illustration as a reference to the violent and unjust rupture by the Soviet regime of a harmonious family idyll of an ordinary Estonian family. However, given the fairly strong emotional vigor of the chapter, an intensity not found anywhere else in the text, the illustration seems fairly mellow given the image of the happy idyll dominating, and as though suggesting a happy ending despite the troubling start.

The implications of the illustration are particularly interesting in relation to Tungal's actual text that focuses very intensely on missing her mother, great longing for her and hoping against hope for her return. The illustration serves to strengthen such hope and can be viewed as almost providing a clue to the reader about the mother's return at the end of the book. However, the mother does not return. In the episode that concludes the first volume, Leelo asks her father when her mother will return. "*Memme* comes after thirty years" the father replies as he has just learned that his wife has been sentenced to 25 years of hard labor and 5 years of deportation (*Seltsimees* 211). The second volume ends only with a slightly more hopeful note about the possibility of steady correspondence between the family members: Leelo and *tata* can write *memme* as often as they want but only in Russian and she can write two letters a year.

The next two illustrations also offer more clues about the consequences of the intrusion of the Soviet power into the author's family life: both are photos of a little girl and a man. In one of them, two dark figures are standing beside a Finnish sled, small and lost on the white page, a stylized and barely visible image of the Soviet pentagon arched above them. In the other, a father and daughter sit as if at the bottom of a flight of stairs, their eyes cast toward a number of images of women's and girl's fashion of the fifties laid out on the facing page. In a similar way to the very first illustration, a Soviet stamp with the coat or arms turned into a face looks over them. Although the father and young girl convey a sense of loss and of being lost, they also make visible (as do the corresponding chapters in the book) an intimate world shared between two people, drawn closer together by small funny incidents arising from having to manage a household on their own. If the text of *Seltsimees laps* and *Samet ja saepuru* conveys the past dominantly, though not exclusively via the consciousness of three-year-old, the illustrations are presented from the nostalgic perspective of a grown-up, almost literally "glossing over" memories to present a particular view of the past and of childhood. Therefore it can be said that the joint impact of Tungal's style of narration and focalization on the child and atmosphere created by the illustrations maintains a horizon of expectations about happy childhood that informs the creation of an intimate public guiding the reading of the text.

In her childhood autobiography that at first glance leaves the impression of a straightforward and transparent rendering of the first decade of the Soviet regime in Estonia, Tungal skillfully positions the figure of the child between the axes of the historical, the universal, and the personal. Revisiting the difficult 1950s, her life writing creates a rich and multifaceted insight into a period in rural Estonia, presenting the sociopolitical and historical climate of the era from a young child's perspective who, as a result of the Stalinist repressions, has to spend the prime years of her childhood without her mother. By making visible in detail the process of a child making sense of the complex world around her, wrought with political tension and insecurity, Tungal revisits the emblematic aspects of the era, providing enough explanations to make the period accessible also to the younger generations of readers. However, the child protagonist is not only a product (and victim) of her time but also an embodiment of universal beliefs about childhood as a strong horizon of expectations about happy childhood pervades the two volumes of Tungal's childhood autobiography. In Berlant's terms, this horizon creates an intimate public as "an affective confirmation of the idea of a shared confirming imaginary in advance of inhabiting a material world in which that feeling can actually be lived" (3). These implications of the text are enhanced by the illustrations by a well-known Estonian graphic artist Urmas Viik whose artistic interpretation of material from Tungal's family archive and other visual sources provides attractive insights into the era and heightens the text's positive affective affiliations. Hidden within the portrait of the era and elaboration of the horizon of expectations about happy childhood is yet another, most deeply personal textual layering: an account of the painful loss the child suffers at the hands of the regime. Although the impact of the experience is only implied, textual clues as well as author's comments on her life writing allow for an interpretation of that experience as traumatic. Writing a childhood autobiography that through the limited and (in its own way) diverse viewpoint of a young child helps the author to revisit this difficult period of her life and initiate a process of coping with the experience and healing from its lifelong impact.

Notes

1. All translations from Estonian are by the author. The article was written with the support of Estonian Science Foundation grants ETF 9035 and ETF 8875 and Target Financing project SF0030065s08.
2. In an interview Leelo Tungal has noted that though her story may seem atypical, when she was doing research for her autobiography, she learned that during the years 1950–1952 more than 600 school teachers were fired by the Soviet authorities all over Estonia and more than 150 of them were sent to prison camps like her mother (Lotman 9).
3. In addition to Leelo Tungal's own life writings, her family history can also be accessed through her mother Helmes's life story, submitted to the Estonian Literary Museum. Helmes also produced (and submitted to the Museum) an acccount of the life story of

her own mother Silima Mann. The life story of Helmes Tungal provides an account of what it means for a mother to be violently separated from her daughter: "Leelo was a lovely three-year-old girl when I was torn from her. This was the hardest and most painful event of my life. If one wishes to punish someone with utmost strictness, and in particular to cause a lot of pain to a mother, she should be separated from her child. [...] I felt that I was the victim of huge injustice" (32). Leelo Tungal did not know that her mother had sent her own life story and that of her grandmother to the Estonian Literary Museum, but by the time she submitted her own life story, and later wrote her autobiography, she must have been familiar with her mother's story. It is, however, difficult to estimate to what extent it influenced the focus of her life writings. Her life story published in *Eesti Rahva Elulood* (*Life Stories of the Estonian People*, 2003) stands out among others included in the volume for its primary focus on her childhood, in particular the years spent without her mother. In it, she mentions the weary years of longing for her mother's return and the pain her constant question "When will *memme* [Mommy] come back?" must have caused to her father who took care of her (334).

4. NKVD is the abbreviation of The People's Commissariat for Internal Affairs that was the public and secret police organization of the Soviet Union that executed the rule of power of the All Union Communist Party, including political repression, during the era of Joseph Stalin.

References

Adams, Timothy D. *Light Writing and Life Writing. Photography in Autobiography*. Chapel Hill: The University of North Carolina Press, 2000.

Avižienis, Jura. "Learning to Curse in Russian: Mimicry in Siberian Exile." *Baltic Postcolonialism*. Ed. Violeta Kelertas. Amsterdam: Rodopi, 2006. 186–202.

Berlant, Lauren. *The Female Complaint: The Unfinished Business of Sentimentality in American Culture*. Durham and London: Duke University Press, 2008.

Bhabha, Homi K. *The Location of Culture*. New York: Routledge, 1994.

Coe, Richard N. *When the Grass Was Taller: Autobiography and the Experience of Childhood*. New Haven: Yale University Press, 1984.

Davis, Rocío G. *Begin Here: Reading Asian North American Autobiographies of Childhood*. Honolulu: University of Hawaii Press, 2007.

Douglas, Kate. *Contesting Childhood. Autobiography, Trauma and Memory*. New Brunswick: Rutgers University Press, 2010.

Goldson, Barry. "'Childhood': An Introduction to Historical and Theoretical Analyses." *'Childhood' in 'Crisis'?* Ed. Phil Scraton. London: UCL Press, 1997. 1–27.

Kelly, Catriona. "A Joyful Soviet Childhood: Licensed Happiness for Little Ones." *Petrified Utopia: Happiness Soviet Style*. Ed. Marina Balina and Evgeny Dobrenko. London and New York: Anthem Press, 2009. 3–18.

Knight, Rebecca. "Representations of Soviet Childhood in Post-Soviet Texts by Liudmila Ulitsakaia and Nina Gabrelian." *The Modern Language Review* 104.3 (2009): 780–808.

Kurvet-Käosaar, Leena. "The Traumatic Impact of the Penal Frameworks of the Soviet Regime: Pathways of Female Remembering." *Teaching Empires: Gender and Transnational Citizenship in Europe*. Ed. Mary Clancy and Andrea Petö. Stockholm: Stockholm University Press, 2009. 69–80.

————. "Vulnerable Scriptings: Approaching Hurtfulness of the Repressions of the Stalinist Regime in the Life-writings of Baltic Women." *Gender and Trauma. Interdisciplinary Dialogues*. Ed. Fatima Festić. Newcastle upon Tyne: Cambridge Scholars Publishing, 2012. 89–114.

Lotman, Rebekka. "Läbi õuduste raamatu poole. Leelo Tungal, intervjuu." *Postimees AK*, 29.3 (2008): 8–9.

Luik, Viivi. *Inimese kapike*. Tallinn: Vagabund, 1998.

————. *Seitsmes rahukevad*. Tallinn: Eesti Raamat, 1985.

Olesk, Sirje. "Meie aja muinasjutt Stalinist ja tsirkusest." *Looming* 11 (2009): 1589–91.

Park, Eva. *Tolm ja tuul*. Tallinn: Eesti Raamat, 1992.

Rose, Nikolas. *Governing the Soul: the Shaping of the Private Self*. London: Free Association Books, 1999.

Rugg, Linda H. *Picturing Ourselves. Photography and Autography*. Chicago and London: University of Chicago Press, 1997.

Saunders, Valerie. "Childhood and Life Writing." *Encyclopedia of Life Writing*. Ed. Margaretta Jolly. London: Fitzroy Dearborn, 2001. 203–4.

Tungal, Helmes. "Elulugu." *Eesti rahva elulood. Sajandi sada elulugu kahes osas. I osa*. Ed. Rutt Hinrikus. Tallinn: Tänapäev, 2003. 28–35.

Tungal, Leelo. "Elulugu." *Eesti rahva elulood. Elu Eesti ENSV-s*. Ed. Rutt Hinrikus. Tallinn: Tänapäev, 2003. 246–332.

————. *Seltsimees laps ja suured inimesed. Veel üks jutustus õnnelikust lapsepõlvest*. Tallinn: Tänapäev, 2008.

————. *Samet ja saepuru ehk seltsimees laps ja kirjatähed*. Tallinn: Tänapäev, 2009.

Index

Note: Page numbers followed by 'n' refer to notes